Divorce with Decency

Divorce with Decency

The Complete How-To Handbook
and Survivor's Guide to the Legal,
Emotional, Economic, and Social Issues

Third Edition

Bradley A. Coates, Esq.

A Latitude 20 Book
University of Hawai'i Press
Honolulu

Library of Congress Cataloging-in-Publication Data

Coates, Bradley A.
    Divorce with decency : the complete how-to handbook and survivor's
guide to the legal, emotional, economic, and social issues / Bradley A.
Coates.—3rd ed.
        p.   cm.
    "A Latitude 20 Book."
    Includes bibliographical references.
    ISBN 978-0-8248-3310-7 (pbk. : alk. paper)
    1. Divorce—United States.   2. Divorce—Law and legislation—United
States.   3. Broken homes—United States.   I. Title.

HQ834.C62 2008
306.89~~0973~~—dc22
                                                        2008012816

β

COATES

Chapter illustrations by Charles Valoroso—Preface, Chapters 2, 3, 7, 8, and 9,
and John Pritchett—Chapters 1, 4, 5, and 6.

Designed by Nighthawk Design

Printed by Versa Press

To my late father, Mark Coates, and to my mom, Bette.
They taught me the meaning of family.

Contents

Preface

WHERE DO I BEGIN?

All the relationships, especially marriage relationships, must be based upon absolute openness and honesty.
　　—Dr. H. Norman Wright

Over twenty thousand divorces! As close as we can figure it, that's about how many divorce cases my law firm has handled during the last thirty gut-wrenching years. It's enough to make you sick or crazy or both!

I just knew I had to figure out some way to do it better, to handle things less acrimoniously, to perhaps turn things around and find a more positive focus. I had begun to question my own sanity. Was I starting to fit the frequent (and so often accurate) description of a "sleazy divorce lawyer"?

Throughout my career, my approach has been to try to handle my divorce practice in a radically different, more sensitive, and more positive way—one that endeavors to make the best of the bad situation that divorcing couples inevitably face. In the process I have successfully built the largest divorce and family law firm in Hawai'i. Coates & Frey, the nine-attorney firm that I founded, is generally recognized as processing more divorce cases through Hawai'i's family court system than any other.

My "raison de writing." Although I feel we do the best job we possibly can for our firm's clientele, it became apparent to me that the best way I could reach beyond my own paying clients to try to dispense whatever grains of wisdom I might have to share about my positive approach to the handling of the divorce experience was to write this book. Only in this way could I more widely disseminate information to readers interested in trying to explore a more enlightened approach to the entire divorce process. My intent was to package some of my entirely too extensive experiences into a book format that is available for around $20—thereby making it more accessible to people who are understandably put off by the $200+ hourly fees that I and other prominent divorce attorneys customarily charge in the privacy of our paneled offices.

Although my private practice is based in Hawai'i, I have deliberately broadened the scope of this book to include the basic principles of divorce law that apply in most jurisdictions. In this context, it helps that I am licensed in California and a couple of other jurisdictions as well as Hawai'i. My aim has been to write the definitive divorce text, providing the maximum possible amount of information about every aspect of the divorce process.

An all-encompassing divorce guide. I knew from the start that it would be a difficult and unwieldy task, but I felt strongly that I wanted to write a book that encompassed all the multifaceted emotional, psychological, and sociological aspects surrounding divorce—as well as its strictly legalistic issues. This conviction mirrors the way I have come to view my own role as a divorce lawyer. When I first started practicing, divorce law was basically a "meat ax down the middle" process characterized by a narrow, and narrow-minded, focus on the single issue of property division. I have now come to realize, however, that if you want to do a proper job of divorce lawyering you have to treat divorce as a multilevel, interdisciplinary behavioral science, essentially peeling away the multiple levels of complexity of the modern American family structure like the layers of an onion.

Not surprisingly, this book is by no means the first to be written by an attorney on the subject of divorce. Attorneys like to talk; they also like to write, and thousands of books and articles have been written about divorce over the years.

In conducting my research for this book, I have turned up numerous how-to books authored by attorneys and relating to the substantive legal and technical areas surrounding divorce actions. I have also read many treatises that consist primarily of a compilation of war stories recounting, often rather theatrically, actual cases, clients, and courtroom dramas that a given lawyer has handled during his or her career. Yet a third rapidly expanding volume of literature deals with a more sociologically oriented (and often touchy-feely) discussion of the psychological factors involved in divorce.

Some of the most useful new divorce guides focus on the art of successfully threading one's way through the thicket of emotional and personal issues surrounding a divorce by utilizing expertise from other disciplines, such as the mental health or negotiation fields. Many of these place a special emphasis on the rapidly growing area of divorce mediation.

I have yet to read any book, however, that combines all of these components into one single comprehensive, informative, and above all, readable work. Writing such a book was the goal I set for myself when I embarked upon authoring this summary of insights gleaned over my thirty-year career as a divorce lawyer. I hope you'll find this book to be useful, thought provoking, anecdotal, and—because divorce is often too tense for anyone's good—at least occasionally amusing.

A better and broader revised edition. I felt very gratified when immediately following the release of its initial first edition, this book went on to win the Hawai'i Book Publishers' Award of Merit for *Excellence in Guide and Reference Books.* I have also received many accolades from colleagues and professional peers saying that my book has turned into the single most valuable resource that they recommend to their clients. Several social agencies, academic institutions, and professional organizations have put it on their recommended reading list that they, in turn, distribute to students, clients, colleagues, etc. Perhaps the most rewarding responses of all, however, have come from individuals who were going through their own divorces and said it served as a great solace to them in the process. I can't tell you the number of readers who have told me (some actually with tears in their eyes) that they felt this book had been written "specifically for them." Many of these folks apparently felt like my book was speaking directly to them personally and describing precisely their exact individual situation.

I feel that part of this book's unique sense of personal relevancy is an outgrowth of its innovative indexing system. If you glossed over the index in the front, please go back and take a closer look at it. It is specifically designed to tailor the book's usage to be of immediate applicability to each individual reader's set of personal circumstances.

For example, if you are a thirty-three-year-old woman about to terminate her second marriage, with one teenage boy from a first marriage and an infant daughter from the second, you can find specialized chapters precisely addressing each of these situations and scenarios. There is one chapter on second marriages and another on stepfamilies. There is a chapter on how divorce will affect women differently from men, and younger women differently than older women. There is a chapter on how second marriages differ from first, and another on how subsequent remarriages will be different still. If your property settlement is going to focus primarily on the disposition of the marital home, or a spouse's pension plan, there are chapters designed to cover each of those scenarios. This makes it possible to hopscotch between the chapters and essentially customize the book to focus on any given reader's individual personal situation.

Following the incredibly enthusiastic response I received from my book's first edition, I suddenly found myself being pulled into what has now become a virtual second career as a lecturer, educator, public speaker, and commentator on many of the "spin-off issues" surrounding the divorce phenomenon and on its attendant effects and ramifications on society as a whole. Nowadays I frequently find myself giving speeches not only here in Hawai'i, but also on the U.S. mainland, and even internationally, on such diverse and esoteric topics as: "How the divorce epidemic will change the face of American society"; "The key causes of marital conflict and how to solve them"; "Hot tips on achieving sexual fulfillment"; "What the structure of the 'All American Family' will look like in the 21st century," etc.

Couples who are contemplating marriage will now frequently call me first for premarital counseling and advice. I do a lot of mediation sessions for "rocky couples" contemplating divorce in an effort to put their marriage back on track before divorce becomes a necessity. I was even asked by the American Association of Single People to serve as a Hawai'i spokesperson for their organization.

You get the basic idea . . . I now seem to be as much of a "talking head" as I am a lawyer. What has essentially occurred is that my areas of interest and expertise have been forced to go way beyond standard divorce lawyering and have instead broadened into far more wide-ranging areas. I have expanded my focus to include more general themes such as the preservation and repair of relationships, and the psychological and sociological effects of marital dissolutions on the divorcing spouses, and on their families, and on society in general as well as the best ways to mitigate those effects.

I have spent literally hundreds of hours conducting ever more research on all these interrelated topics, and this expanded third edition of *Divorce with Decency* contains many of the fruits of that laborious research. I then tried to integrate some of the more popular materials from my lecturing, teaching and other public appearances, and they too are contained in this "pumped up" third edition. Since I do so much marriage and relationship counseling nowadays, I wanted to insert the entirely new sections at the end of Chapter Two entitled: "Can Your Marriage Be Saved?" "Understanding the Basic Biological Differences between Men and Women" and "Key Tips on Preserving and Improving Your Marriage." Many of my psychologist friends, not to mention more than a few "conflicted and confused" clients, have told me that these are the best sections of the whole book. I have also included updated material on any and all important changes in/to the legal statutes, case law, precedents or principles that have occurred since the release of the two earlier editions.

Even those folks who have previously read the prior editions of *Divorce with Decency* will find a wealth of newer and more informative data, observation and analysis in this revised edition. All in all, this should make the third edition a vastly more informative and useful resource for my many thousands of loyal readers. I certainly hope you will agree.

Intruding on intimacies. One of the really wild parts about being a divorce lawyer is the way it enables, or even entitles, one to participate so extensively and intensively in the lives of other people in a fashion that would never be permissible in any other context. How many other professions are there in which during the first one-hour meeting with a new client you are actually expected, or even obligated, to ask them every close personal question imaginable?

Just envision meeting a total stranger at a cocktail party and asking, "How is your relationship with your husband?" "How much money do you make?" "How good is your sex life?" "Do you cheat on your spouse?" "How much do your own family and friends know about what you are telling me?" "Are there any skeletons in your closet that no one else knows about but that I expect you to confide in me?" All these, and many more, are the sorts of questions that you would never dream of asking someone in any other context. Yet, asking every imaginable, and sometimes unimaginable, personal question of people you've just met, clients, is part of any good divorce lawyer's job. People walk into my office daily and pay more than $200 an hour to discuss these intimate details of their lives with me, a total stranger.

While on the subject of other people's intimacies, I should point out that many of the examples I draw from in this book pertain to the personal experiences of my own firm's clients. I have therefore had to alter some of the individual case studies/stories in order to prevent their identification. (Honolulu has often been described as the world's largest small town!) Although I have taken some poetic license in order to protect client confidentiality, the essential point of each example or experience remains accurate.

Cautions, caveats, and disclaimers. Although I try to be a less legalistic and more empathetic attorney than most, I am still a lawyer. As such, I must issue the following mini "CYA" disclaimer: This book contains only general information, and readers should not take any actions based on the summary information contained herein. This book is not intended as a substitute for hiring your own attorney. Instead, appropriate experts should be consulted for each individual's own case and/or fact situation. Although I have used my best efforts in assembling material for this book, I cannot warrant that its information is complete or accurate. Neither I nor the publisher assume (and in fact specifically disclaim) any liability to any person for any loss or damage caused by any errors or omissions, which may be contained herein.

Bottom line. Don't make any legal or other decisions in your own life based upon this book. Use it as background only and instead hire your own counselor, lawyer, etc., to analyze your specific situation before you take any actions.

Divorce "lite"? As you read through this book, you will notice that it contains cartoons, quotations, and editorial comments that often tend to point up the more humorous aspects of the divorce process. My clients over the years have often remarked on the light touch I use in handling my cases. Some of them have undoubtedly even been offended by it. It's not that I don't empathize with each of the individual clients. Au contraire! I take my job and the subject of divorce very seriously, indeed.

Instead, my admittedly peculiar personal style reflects two of my firmly held beliefs. First, after three decades as a divorce lawyer, I would by now have become stark raving crazy if I had allowed each case to consume me personally. Second, and more important, I strongly believe that since divorce is now so common in our society, it is probably best if people can accept it as a frequent, and frequently unavoidable, fact of life and then just deal with it as best they can. Humor can be therapeutic under these circumstances.

If divorcing clients can understand that they are part of a massive and overarching sociological phenomenon, there is less of a tendency for each person to feel like a failure or to blame themselves for being unable to maintain their marriage. Personally,

I feel that maintaining a light and upbeat (maybe even offbeat) touch in divorce cases ultimately serves to improve the psychological health of my clients, not to mention my own. In fact, my law firm even carries this philosophy so far as to host an annual "Heal the Hearts" Valentine's Day Ball as a show of appreciation for our many former clients, and to give them a chance to mix, match, mingle and commiserate with one another.

So there you have it, my "raison de writing," so to speak. My goal has been to write the first book that I know of that deals comprehensively with not only the legal, but also the psychological, sociological, and economic aspects of divorce, yet is presented from the practical and utilitarian point of view of a divorce attorney.

I'll never forget the insightful comment made by a fellow family law attorney when he opined "Face it, we divorce lawyers are basically in the Misery Management Business." Since there is probably way too much truth in that statement, I feel it becomes incumbent on us divorce lawyers to "manage the misery" as efficiently and holistically as possible.

I also know from my entirely too extensive personal experience that when a marriage unravels, the one thing every divorcing person needs is a good friend. And that's really what this book is all about. I sincerely hope it can serve as your friend when you need one. Aloha.

Acknowledgments

Lots of folks deserve lots of credit for helping to midwife this book from its early days of conception and along the winding and torturous road to its actually being published. Foremost among them is my long-suffering lady love, Sachi Braden. Sachi and I are typical of many of the couples described in this book. We were both previously married, then divorced; we jointly reared her son/my stepson, and we lived together for several years before we both got over our own phobias about remarriage. Sachi finally became my beloved bride about midway through the process of finalizing the first edition of this book. She has allowed as how I was something less than a joy to live with during the months, and ultimately years, that I wound up working on this manuscript.

A lot of appreciation is also due my hard-working staff at both the old law offices of Bradley A. Coates and its successor firm, Coates & Frey. These folks kept the doors of the law office open and the cases moving through while the boss spent many afternoons in seclusion "composing." Foremost among these are the seven associate attorneys who work in the Coates & Frey law firm that I founded and who have been with me for many moons: Paul W. Soenksen, Jessi L. K. Hall, Karl E. Phillips, Richard E. Dunn, Jr., R. Barrie Michelsen, Christopher D. Thomas and John D. Hughes. I now serve as "Of Counsel" to the Law Offices of Coates & Frey and I am the first to admit that many of the attorneys on our staff are far brighter in any number of areas than am I as the "old dog" who started our firm. In addition, I don't think there is a single member of my firm's clerical or administrative staff who didn't wind up putting several hours in various stages of typing, proofing, editing or "polishing" this manuscript. My special thanks go to my unwaveringly supportive alter ego in the Coates & Frey law firm, my close personal friend and successor as Managing Attorney Greg Frey, to our incredibly efficient law office manager, Kathy Yamauchi, and to my super secretary, Jamie Komatsu, who did the lion's share of the manuscript preparation while simultaneously keeping both my personal and professional lives intact.

Numerous professional colleagues have assisted, guided, and influenced my surprisingly successful career in family law. Foremost among these is Michael Town, former chief judge of Honolulu's family court. Judge Town has been one of my true personal mentors in the family law field, and it was he who showed me that a sensitive approach to divorce lawyering could be excellent cross training for real life.

My single largest note of appreciation goes to my former associate Tom Farrell. Tom put in an insane number of thankless and uncompensated hours helping to edit my original manuscript in order to submit it to the University of Hawai'i Press.

Mahalo all!

CHAPTER 1
The Need for Divorce with Decency

Nothing anybody tells you about marriage helps.
—*Max Siegel*

The very manner in which a divorce case is handled as it progresses through the legal system will be a major factor in determining how the parties will feel about themselves and one another afterward. If the parties can successfully handle their dissolution in an above-board and mature fashion, the stage will be set for them to maintain better communication between themselves and their children in the years following the divorce. This, in turn, greatly increases the likelihood that the divorce experience can serve as a springboard to something more positive in terms of each of their individual personal growth patterns thereafter. The constructive input of a caring and creative divorce lawyer at this stage can be crucial.

Let's take a look at just how bad the alternative can get. I will never forget the call I received one afternoon from Distraught

Doris who had just come home, totally without warning, to a completely vacant house.

Distraught Doris and Horrible Harry. Doris' husband, Harry, had hired a moving company to remove all the furniture, had had a locksmith change all the locks on the doors, had hidden both cars, and had even pulled their yacht out of the water and stashed it in an undisclosed shipyard. Then this prince of a guy had left a heartless note pinned to the front door saying that he had already physically taken the two children, and planned to keep them, that he would not tell her where they had gone, and that she shouldn't bother going to the bank, since he had already drained all their joint financial accounts.

When this scenario becomes the opening gambit in a divorce case, it is almost impossible to put the parties back on track. By his actions on just this one afternoon, Horrible Harry had managed to ensure that hatred, mistrust, and emotional devastation would inevitably become the primary emotions that would characterize his and Doris' feelings toward each other for the rest of their lives.

Perhaps the most bothersome factor in this case was that when we finally got into court seeking temporary restraining and other orders (including, of course, the immediate return of the children and the money), Harry testified that he had taken the actions he did based on the *advice of his attorney.* I was appalled, but hardly surprised. It's absolutely incredible the amount of (in)human damage that insensitive lawyering can do.

If this book does nothing else, I'm hopeful that it will serve as a blueprint to assist parties who know little about the divorce process to take control of their own cases. This must include knowing the right questions to ask of the lawyers when initially retaining them and learning to explore some of the more positive paths along which a client can direct their attorney's (and their own) actions throughout the course of the case.

Positive divorce—it's not an oxymoron. If the parties themselves ever hope to use their divorce as an opportunity to maximize their own personal growth, then they must both learn to act like adults in arriving at fair and principled agreements regarding child custody, support, property settlement, and other issues. This is an objective that is frequently at the forefront of the initiating party's mind, but is not always easy for the more surprised or reluctant responding party. It is nevertheless one that I firmly believe should ultimately be a goal of both parties.

Negotiations and subsequent agreements should be grounded in fundamental fairness, with maximum attention shown to the interests of the children, rather than either party simply using the children or the property settlement as a club with which to inflict pain or seek revenge on their former spouse. Particularly in the arena of child custody and support, both parents need to step outside their own personal agendas and reaffirm a complete commitment to their children for the long haul.

The phenomenon of mass-scale divorce in American society has arrived with a bang, and I suspect it will stay for a while. Since divorce is going to have such a far-reaching impact on our society and on our families, it becomes imperative that we learn more about the functional, logistical, and psychological aspects of the divorce process itself. Only then can we try to maximize whatever good may come out of it, and minimize the pain and the suffering.

Divorce Hawaiian Style

'Uo 'ia i ka mānai ho 'okāhi.
Strung like flowers on the same lei.
—*Hawaiian proverb, said of a married couple*

Some of my more "decent" instincts regarding the handling of divorce cases may well be derived from the fact that I practice in the relatively mellow and progressive State of Hawai'i. Hawai'i has been in the forefront among the several states in seeking far-sighted and practical ways to deal with divorce.

Hawai'i was an early jurisdiction to adopt a "no-fault" divorce statute. Under this approach, a party seeking a divorce need only allege that the marriage is "irretrievably broken." There is no need to allege adultery, mental cruelty, or other spousal misconduct, and the issue of fault is virtually irrelevant regarding custody, alimony, property division, and other issues.

Hawai'i has also adopted a property division statute that requires "equitable distribution." Rather than relying on who has title to any given asset, or on an arbitrary split down the middle, Hawai'i's divorce courts divide and award marital property on the basis of what is fair and equitable.

Hawai'i has a tradition of *ho'oponopono*, or family-to-family mediation and healing, which is well suited to divorce and custody cases. Mediation has gained wide acceptance here as a cheaper and more mature way than the court route of resolving divorce disputes.

One other aspect of culture in Hawai'i makes a big difference for the children of divorce: the concept of *'ohana*. Most of America still operates on the nuclear family model, but the Hawaiian tradition is multigenerational families and even multifamily families. In ancient Hawai'i, children were sometimes given to a close friend or relative to raise—a process called *hānai*. These children were not abandoned by their birth parents, rather they shared families and effectively had two sets of parents. Maybe that's why shared custody and stepparenting seem to be better accepted here than in other states.

Hawai'i has been on the cutting edge in other ways. We were the first to establish a consolidated family court to deal with all family law issues. Hawai'i has also established a mandatory educational program for divorcing parents called "Kids First." And as many folks may recall, we were one of the first states to consider legalizing same-sex marriage. Can same-sex divorce be far behind?

CHAPTER 2
Some Basic Background

Marriage . . . a master, a mistress and two slaves, making in all, two.
    —Ambrose Bierce

Over the last couple of decades the phenomenon of divorce for many Americans has turned into something akin to a rite of passage. Various milestones in individuals' lives have always been around. The first tooth, first communion, first diploma, the first time you went "all the way," first job . . . you get the idea. For my father's generation, one of the biggies was going off to fight World War II. For my generation, it was the draft and Vietnam. These are milestones that irrevocably change the way a country and its individual citizens define themselves. Nowadays, for the lives of at least half of our populace, the Big D of divorce has become another such milestone—with people referring to their lives as either "BS" (Before the Split) or "AD" (After Divorce).

Divorce meets Broadway, Oscar, and Grammy. Divorce now permeates modern American society. Let's look at a few examples. Ronald Reagan was our first "divorced" president. Turn on the radio and you'll hear the country music classic "D-I-V-O-R-C-E." We're all familiar with the ubiquitous articles on failed relationships in every magazine from *Cosmopolitan* to *Reader's Digest*. Old pro-love ballads like "We Can Keep It Together" have been replaced by cynical lyrics like "Love Stinks."

We watch wrenching movies like *Starting Over, An Unmarried Woman, The Last Married Couple in America,* and *The War of the Roses.* Another popular entry in this subspecialty of marital moviemaking was *The First Wives' Club,* which seemed to have struck a particularly raw nerve among our nation's expanding sisterhood of divorcees.

As Abigail Tafford, the witty, insightful (and herself divorced) author of the classic best seller, *Crazy Time: Surviving Divorce,* writes: "The old myths and manners of marriage are gone. You start to wonder what's 'normal' these days. With life expectancy of about seventy-five years for both men and women, 'til death do us part' is a commitment more and more people find they can't and—more interesting—don't want to keep."

Divorce is now big business, and divorce-related cottage industries have sprung up all over the country: singles bars, personal trainers, mental health clinics, boutique health clubs, psychologists, diet centers, Club Meds, cosmetic surgeons, singles' websites, marriage counseling institutes, not to mention thousands of divorce lawyers—all intended to assist the divorcing parties through the various stages of their divorce rite of passage.

Where Has the All-American Family Gone?

A marriage without conflicts is almost as inconceivable as a nation without crises.
—*André Maurois*

In the past, when it first became thinkable, divorce was viewed as a prerogative to be dabbled in by the very rich, or a forced economic phenomenon of the very poor. The big change that seems to have occurred nowadays is that divorce has expanded to the mainstream middle class. Divorce has become totally normal and acceptable or even expected, and it now ranks right alongside birth, marriage, professional career, and death as almost a right of passage—one of the primary milestones of American culture. The redistribution of wealth and upheavals in the class system in America over the last forty years have given America's middle class the moral and economic seal of approval to divorce.

It can be compellingly argued that the increase in divorce represents the single most dramatic change in the American family experience during the past fifty years. Certainly, marital terminations were not uncommon in earlier centuries, but a key difference that must be recalled is that widowhood was generally the precipitating event rather than divorce or separation. The large rise in the sheer number of divorces, to over five hundred thousand per year during the 1970s, and then to over one million per year during the 1980s, indicates that divorce has now caught up with death as a causal change for marital status in American society.

Some dire divorce statistics. Hard as it may be to believe, divorce has actually been on a modest upward trend since as far back as 1850. But at the turn of the 20th century, the divorce rate for first marriages was still only 7 percent. During most of the 20th century, divorce rates increased steadily. They peaked for a brief period following World War II, dropped off some during the 1950s, then rose steadily in the 1960s and soared dramatically in the 1970s. In fact, breakups more than doubled between the 1960s and the late 1970s.

Divorce rates have leveled off some and have actually been declining a bit over the last couple of decades. But, we must be realistic about the fact that it is an awfully high plateau. It may also be that we are enjoying a brief period of seeming stability—due to the fact that so many first marriages have already ended in divorce—but that the cycle of divorces following second marriages hasn't yet fully exploded.

A recent divorce boom among senior citizens would seem to support this theory. According to U.S. Census figures, whereas many mid-lifers were enjoying a period of relative marital stability between 1990 and 2000, the population of divorced senior citizens rose 34 percent (to 2.2 million people) during this same time frame. Many experts predict that this surge may continue if (as several have speculated) baby boomers become more divorce-prone as they age.

How do marriage and divorce rates in the United States compare with those in the rest of the world? It is interesting to note that *Americans marry and divorce more often than almost anyone else in the world*. Other nations—notably Russia and Sweden with their inordinately high overall divorce rates of about 65 percent—have even higher divorce statistics than America does. But, we are just about tops when it comes to the serial cycle of multiple re-marriages and re-divorces. Americans marry literally twice as often as the French, 40 percent more than Germans, 30 percent more than Japanese, 25 percent more than Canadians, and 20 percent more than Mexicans. Ninety percent of Americans will say "I do" at some point in their lives.

Not surprisingly, Americans then turn around and divorce more frequently than almost anybody else. In the United States, the divorce rate per thousand residents runs at about 4.8. In Canada, it is 2.9, in France it is 1.9, in Germany it is 1.7, in Japan it is 1.4, while in Mexico it is 0.6.

Social anthropologist David Murray says Americans think of marriage as "an individual choice based on love," in contrast to more traditional societies that view it as a family decision based on economic and social considerations. Compare the United States with India, for example, where there is a long cultural history of matchmaking and where as many as 90 percent of weddings are still "arranged." Although we all know that half of American marriages end in divorce, we still don't give up. Instead, that can-do American spirit takes over and we give it another go. Nearly half of all U.S. weddings in the 1990s were remarriages for one or both partners, according to a report by the Population Reference Bureau.

The most recent numbers, though, appear to indicate that Americans seem to have tempered their marrying impulses a bit in the last few years. According to the publication *Euromonitor*, the U.S. marriage rate—the number of marriages for every thousand residents—fell steadily from 10.5 in 1980 to 9.0 in 1993. Similarly, the divorce rate—the number of divorces for every thousand residents—has fallen, from 5.2 in 1980 to 4.6 in 1993.

Evolutionary obstacles to monogamy. In her book *Anatomy of Love,* author Helen Fisher studied patterns of love, coupling, dissolution, and divorce in sixty-two cultures around the globe. She made the sobering discovery that adultery occurred in virtually all of these societies—even where it was punishable by death. She also found that in most of these cultures divorce rates peak around the fourth year of marriage. An interesting argument can in fact be made that nature apparently meant passions to sputter out in about four years. Dr. Fisher calls it as she sees it: "Primitive pairs stayed together just long enough to rear one child through infancy before moving on to another mate. Add another three years to rear a second child and you have the Seven Year Itch."

Perhaps we humans are swimming upstream against nature's design when we attempt to wrestle a human pattern of monogamy into place. Fewer than 5 percent of all mammals form monogamous lifelong pairs, which might seem to indicate that in the natural scheme of things, romantic love is not designed to be either eternal or exclusive.

Many anthropologists argue that the whole concept of romantic love is something of an unnatural invention of Western culture to begin with. From a biological and evolutionary standpoint, it's to a man's advantage to sow his seeds far and wide. Women in turn seek mates with the best genes and the most to invest in offspring. These built-in conflicts in each gender's preprogramming can put the sexes in conflict and undermine love. Anthropology offers further evidence. Nearly 1,000 of the 1,154 past or present human societies ever studied have permitted a man to have more than one wife.

There is no dispute among evolutionary psychologists over the basic source of this male open-mindedness. A woman, regardless of how many sex partners she has, can generally have only one offspring a year. For a man, each new mate offers a real chance for propagating his genes into the future. Perhaps it was not all that surprising when Charles Darwin tactfully noted that, in virtually all species, the female is "less eager than the male"; or when

Sigmund Freud flatly declared that "marriage is not an arrangement calculated to satisfy a man's sexuality."

Are we fighting our own anthropology? Evolutionary psychology can provide further insights as to just how inhospitable America's current social environment is to monogamy. An article titled "Our Cheating Hearts" in *Time* took a close look at some modern obstacles to monogamy. Among its findings: (1) Infidelity is far easier in a large, anonymous city than in a small hunter-gatherer village; (2) contraceptive technology certainly complicates marriage; (3) for many males, the prevalence of erotic and/or suggestive photography and pornography are alluring alternatives to dull, monogamous devotion; and (4) economic inequality between men and women can be monogamy's worst enemy—affluent men are inclined to leave their aging wives for younger (and often less affluent) women who are willing to become their replacements.

One of my favorite quotes about the pressures and perhaps unrealistic expectations placed on a modern American marriage comes from the always insightful *Time* magazine columnist Barbara Ehrenreich, who writes:

> Consider that marriage probably originated as a straightforward food-for-sex deal among foraging primates. Compatibility was not a big issue, nor of course was there any tension over who would control the remote. *Today, however, a spouse is expected to be not only a co-provider and mate, but a co-parent, financial partner, romantic love object, best friend, fitness adviser, home repair-person and scintillating companion through the wasteland of Sunday afternoons. This is, rationally speaking, more than any one spouse can provide.* Then came the modern urban-industrial era, with the unprecedented notion of the "companionate marriage." Abruptly, the two sexes—who had gone for millenniums without exchanging any more than the few grunts required for courtship—were expected to entertain each other with witty repartee over dinner. American love of marriage is so gripping and deep that we are almost incapable of the discreet, long-term, European-style affair. (Emphasis added.)

The simple fact is that Americans now live much longer, and go through more transitions, than did our predecessors. We move between jobs, cities, and midlife crises. If our mate fails to keep up intellectually, physically, or sexually during these transitions, we tend to opt for serial marriages or relationships—one for each new stage of our lives. As actress Ingrid Bergman once said: "Five husbands, each for ten years, that would be just about right."

The seven-year itch. Ms. Bergman may have exaggerated our staying power. Remember the fabled seven-year itch phenomenon? It has been statistically shown that marriages that end in divorce do indeed last an average of about seven years. In fact, according to a recent study published in *Family Process*, one half of all U.S. divorces occur in the first seven years of marriage. Even second marriages that self-destruct typically do so after about seven years. Interestingly, however, it is actually the third year of marriage which is the single riskiest insofar as the chance of divorce occurring during any one given year. And, while on the subject of statistical averages, I should point out one other little "food for thought" tidbit: the key average ages for divorces overall are the early to mid-thirties.

Risk factors. What are some of the risk factors? Youth seems to be one—dissolution rates are definitely higher for people who marry at younger ages. Also, people whose parents divorced while they were growing up are more likely to divorce themselves. Another risk factor is relatively low educational levels. People with higher education are more likely to marry and less likely to separate. Premarital births are also associated with a higher incidence of divorce. Finally, several studies have shown that a couple's marital satisfaction drops off by up to 70 percent in the first few years after the birth of the first child (although later, having child(ren) does make a couple less likely to divorce).

It is interesting to note that while the first four or five years of a marriage have always been among the riskiest, the other deadly year for marriages seems to be the first year after the last youngster leaves home. Another high-risk period is during the couple's twenties—at the height of their reproductive years.

Many argue nowadays that it makes more sense to simply live together than to get married. This is certainly the choice of the more than six million partners of opposite sexes who, according to the U.S. Census Bureau, live together today in America. The number of households with unmarried adults and no kids has doubled within the last twenty-five years.

Experts estimate that cohabitation now precedes at least half of all marriages. Up until the mid-'70s, this figure was only about 10 percent. Yet living together before marriage doesn't seem to make for better marriages and may, in fact, increase the chance of divorce.

A semblance of stability may be in sight. In spite of all these negatives, according to a recent report released by the Population Reference Bureau, the American family appears to be stabilizing a bit after more than three decades of turbulence. The divorce rate has leveled off and the rate of out-of-wedlock births is slowing. The primary reason behind all this somewhat surprising surge in stability appears to be the aging of the baby boom generation.

The baby boomers have now passed at least the first of those stages of life where the odds of getting divorced are greatest. Also, because young people today are waiting until they are somewhat older (and presumably more mature) before getting married, marriages may be more selective now than in the past, thereby making the risk of divorce lower. Whatever the reasons, the Population Reference Bureau reported that the divorce rate remained pretty stable throughout the 1990s.

Some Scary and Saddening Statistics

Whoever thinks marriage is a fifty-fifty proposition doesn't know the half of it.
    —*Anonymous*

Most of the following information is comprised of real data researched by real statisticians. Let me preface it, however, by offering some slightly less scientific personal observations I have made based on my own law firm's cases.

In only about 20 percent of our office's cases do the parties simultaneously conclude that they *both* want the divorce. In about 40 percent of our cases, I would characterize the second (or responding) party as being somewhat less than thrilled about the divorce, but at least willing to accept it (usually in order to keep the costs down, or to avoid the extra stress of a prolonged fight over the kids, etc.). The remaining 40 percent of our cases involve at least one party who really hates the other's guts and wants a prolonged fight to the death.

I have also noticed some definite trends in the *timing* of divorce filings. A seemingly disproportionate 25 percent of my firm's new cases start up in the month of January each year, and another 20 percent in September. The certainty that I have always felt in narrowing down the largest single surge in new divorce cases to the month of January was recently borne out in another study I read that actually identified January 7 as the single *day* with the most divorce filings of the year. Perhaps people really do make, and then follow through on, their New Year's Resolutions. That study went on to cite the primary reasons given for divorce in the cases they had tracked—starting with infidelity as the leading cause, followed by lack of sex and basic boredom.

The other 55 percent of divorce filings are scattered pretty evenly throughout the other ten months of the year. I have concluded that spouses contemplating divorce tend to hold off during the typical family holiday periods (i.e., Christmas and New Year's Day and the end of summer/Labor Day family vacations). Then, as soon as school starts back up for the fall or winter session, folks begin to resume their individual lives and schedules—one component of which can now more easily include a visit to the divorce attorney's office.

So there you have my personal, quasi-statistical observations. Now on to a quick summary of the more scientifically quantified data on marriage and divorce.

Who gets married nowadays? About two and one-half million couples get married each year in America. Nonetheless, there seems to be a widespread perception that marriage is on the decline, and, in fact, this is supported statistically. Fewer people are marrying, many simply choosing to live together. As of 2006, 88 percent of Americans had married at least once, but that's down from 94 percent as recently as 1988.

Overall, however, the actual total marriage rate is in fact statistically higher than it was a century ago. This, of course, is thanks

largely to the relatively new phenomenon of multiple serial marriages. Obviously, when you've got everybody marrying multiple
times, it tends to kick up the overall numbers.

The highest numbers of both weddings and divorces occur in
the western part of the country. These numbers are in turn lowest in the Northeast, with the Midwest and South somewhere in
the middle. An average snapshot of the U.S. population during
the early 1990s showed about 22 percent of the adult population
as single/never married, another 63 percent as currently married, 8 percent as divorced, and another 8 percent as widows or
widowers. There is a higher incidence of single or never-married
status among men, whereas more women fall into the widowed
or divorced category.

There is important statistical evidence that fewer folks are marrying at really young ages nowadays but instead are waiting longer to get married. The median age for first-time newlyweds is
now at 27 for men and 25 for women. This is the oldest age for
first marriages in U.S. history! By contrast, in 1955 the average
ages were the youngest ever—22.6 for men and 20.2 for women.
In the 30 to 34 age group, only 9.5 percent were single as recently
as 1993. Now that percentage is up to 30 percent.

In about two-thirds of all marriages, the husband is older than
the wife, though the reverse is true about one-fifth of the time.
Nearly half of all marriages nowadays are remarriages for one or
both parties. And an astounding 16 percent of the U.S. population
has been married *three* times.

Marriage is still very much a part of the American dream. After
all, the concept of romantic love has been a universal human trait
throughout the centuries. Romantic passion taps the same dopa-
mine system which is triggered by drug addiction and other
obsessive drives.

Up to about 75 percent of all American adults will marry at
some point in their lives. Similarly, over three-fourths of all American women still say that their concept of the perfect life is to
be married with children, though this percentage has declined
somewhat over the last couple of decades. A majority of even
the unmarried people surveyed still indicate that they think marriage would increase their personal level of happiness. It's also

true that folks who are currently married report slightly higher levels of happiness than do single people.

Being married vs. staying single. A recurring theme throughout this book is that marriage-wise, the times they truly are "a changing." In the 1950s, married couples made up 80 percent of the country's households. Today they account for just over 50 percent and, according to the Census Bureau, singles are poised to take the lead soon. So what gives? Divorce, which is how about half of all marriages end, unquestionably plays a big part. And people are marrying later—or just not marrying at all. Nearly a quarter of the population older than 35 is divorced or has never married. That's an increase of 16 percent in just the past decade.

Marriage still has plenty of plusses. Medical studies have consistently shown that married people live longer than singles and are generally healthier throughout those extra years. Married folks also have lower rates of cardiovascular disease, cancer, stress, respiratory disease, and mental illness. Married couples also stash more cash. Surveys indicate that only 27 percent of single folks feel financially secure. Married folks, on the other hand, have been shown to accumulate fully 93 percent more money and assets over a fifteen-year period than either single or divorced people.

One basic bottom line bonus of marriage is that it almost always results in a healthier overall lifestyle both financially and physically. Married folks are less likely to smoke or drink heavily and have lower rates of all types of mental illness, suicide, and depression. Simply put, having a spouse who scolds you about smoking or is around to monitor your mood swings is a definite help when it comes to preventing cancer and depression. And needless to say, if you aren't regularly diving back into the dating pool, you decidedly lessen your likelihood of contracting sexually transmitted diseases.

What about divorce rates? Statistically speaking, about one-half of all marriages in the United States now end in divorce. As indicated earlier, America's divorce rate really went wild in the seventies and eighties. Since 1970 the divorce rate has doubled, and now more than 1.2 million couples break up each year. Various estimates indicate that between fifty million and one hundred million people have now passed through the divorce process in America.

There have always been obvious high-risk candidates for early divorce (i.e., couples who married too young, those with financial problems that crippled the marriage, etc.). However, a recent survey of the American Academy of Matrimonial Lawyers indicated that divorce attorneys nationwide are handling an increasing number of divorces among people age sixty and over. This would appear to be a particularly frightening indicator—when even the supposedly stable element of our society starts "splitting the sheets."

One response to the horrendous divorce rate during the cynical period of the late 1970s was a predictable decline in the marriage rate. But we have all heard Dr. Johnson's sarcastic definition of marriage as representing the "triumph of hope over experience," and for at least a while there, hope appeared to have triumphed once again—when the marriage rate rose slightly in the late 1980s and early 1990s. Then, true to the cyclical nature of these things, it has begun to drop off again as we have entered the twenty-first century.

Can we quantify the post-divorce fall out? Post-divorce follow-up studies have shown how bad the nasty emotional flak can be for divorcing couples and their kids. At least one-half of all divorcing parents remain fanatically angry at one another more than a decade following their divorce.

Various studies report that in approximately half of all divorce cases *both* spouses indicated they had indeed "wanted" the divorce. It appears to be the women, however, who seem to be more inclined to actually act on their instincts. It is the woman who initiates the actual legal divorce proceedings in approximately two-thirds of all divorce cases filed nationwide.

The statistics on severe depression as an outgrowth of divorce are saddening though hardly surprising. Over one-third of the men and three-fifths of the women were mildly to moderately depressed following separation. Another 30 percent of both men and women were diagnosed as severely or acutely depressed after separation.

What about the impact on kids? Only about one-half of all American children now live in traditional nuclear families (i.e., with both biological parents still present). Another 15 percent or so live in blended families with stepparents and/or stepsiblings. Fully one-third of all American kids will spend part of their childhood in single-parent households. A substantial majority of all children of divorce feel rejected by at least one, or occasionally both, of their parents. Some of these kids report back that they feel they are "in the way" of their parents' concerns about getting on with their own new lives. More selfish, parent-oriented needs suddenly become the focus of primary attention. This represents a major change from the picture-perfect intact family of yesteryear, when parents worked selflessly to meet the needs of their children.

The stats on remarriage. The (re)marriage and (re)divorce cycle appears to be becoming continuous. The vast majority of people who divorce will remarry—often within the first three years. Men are more likely to remarry than women. According to the U.S. Census Bureau, there are more than three times as many formerly married or widowed females age forty-five or over as there are formerly married or widowed males over forty-five.

Can Your Marriage Be Saved?

Love will break your heart . . . but it's worth it.
—*Anonymous*

O.K., so the statistics may look a little disheartening. But before we launch headlong into a discussion of the divorce option, let's take a look at the possible (and perhaps preferred) approaches that may be available to keep a marriage intact. We can start by analyzing the basic nature of marital conflict.

Several of the key causes of marital conflicts are detailed in an excellent book entitled *Stress and Marriage* by Drs. Lyle Miller and Alma Smith. Perhaps the most basic problem lies in the waning of the "romantic illusions" that once enabled the participants to ignore faults they now find intolerable. Sometimes we marry our own romanticized creations but (surprise) are disappointed when dealing with a real person with real shortcomings.

Unrealistic expectations of our partners have their roots in a primary staple of the psychoanalytic trade called "transference."

We often choose mates who remind us of our parents and then transfer to our mates the feelings we felt toward our parents. Whether we want to or not, many of us end up with marital relationships that mirror our parents' marriages.

As rudimentary as it may sound, it really helps to really *know* the person you marry. Far too many folks enter a marriage based on an initial infatuation. Although I hate to downplay the importance of "raw romance," it's probably wiser to pair up in a pragmatic relationship that makes good logical and common sense (i.e., comparable family and social backgrounds, educations and values). Why do you think those insightful Asian cultures emphasized arranged marriages rather than leaving it up to the guesswork of the couples themselves?

Major differences between spouses can turn marital bliss into marital blisters. Women are generally more emotional and empathetic than men. Each gender has entirely different styles of communication: men tend to focus on facts, whereas women tend to focus on feelings. Marriages where there is power sharing, in which both partners are relatively independent, and in which both partners have well developed nonviolent conflict resolution skills tend to be the least stressful and most satisfying.

Now here's a Big Shocker. It turns out that men and women truly are hard-wired to be *very* different creatures indeed. So, if you are going to try to understand relationships, it is crucial to understand the basic differences between men and women in general—and especially their vastly different communication styles in particular. Let's start with a quick overview of two excellent books that explore these differences. The first is Dr. John Gray's *Men Are From Mars, Women Are From Venus*. I think by now virtually everybody on the planet has probably heard of John Gray—he's kind of the acknowledged expert on the differing communication styles between men and women. He's a fabulous speaker, and I've met with him in Hawai'i, so I've gotten to know his work fairly well over the years.

Dr. Gray's Mars/Venus book has probably generated the most notoriety, but let me also recommend one other fabulous book on this topic as well: this one is called *"Why Men Don't Listen and*

Women Can't Read Maps" by Drs. Barbara and Allan Pease. The Peases' book delves even more deeply into the scientific differences between men's and women's biochemical brain structures including an analysis of neurological research on the human brain and the evolutionary biology of each gender. It certainly helps if each sex understands one another better.

I'll discuss the Pease's findings a little later, but first let me discuss Dr. Gray's theories. He feels, and I agree, that perhaps the single biggest issue in blown marriages is lack of communication. Part of that issue, you've got to understand, is that women communicate entirely differently than guys do. Men and women's brains literally evolve differently, each focusing on different thought patterns and processes. Women's brains physiologically have larger repositories devoted to the speech and communication functions than do men's brains.

Guys communicate for a specific purpose, to solve a specific problem in an objective way, kind of a straight line "get from point A to point B" approach. Women kind of like the very *process* of communication itself. Women have an ability to encompass a lot more material than guys. Women need to have just a sheer quantity of time to talk things out, to talk around issues.

A guy's response may be, "She's off on a tangent and I don't see an instant solution anyway. So why the heck are we even talking about this . . . she's making more out of it than necessary." But sometimes a woman just has to be allowed to make as much out of it as she needs to. Her first need is for it to just be okay to be upset for awhile. She wants him to listen to her feelings without trying to "fix" her.

Women have an ongoing need to be reassured within a relationship. Women want to hear "I love you and I understand." A man wants to hear "that makes sense," indicating a linear thought process. Women tend to be more easily overwhelmed when under stress. A man's reaction to stress is to be even more rigid in his focus on going strictly from point A to point B. Men instinctively look for solutions.

Women, in particular, sort of feel that a man just really ought to instinctively *know* her needs. This is often especially true with regard to the sexual arena, but I am referring to all aspects of communication in general. He ought to somehow just know when she is in a bad mood; he ought to understand her; he ought to know that she needs reassuring. And, she doesn't really want to have to ask him for any of this.

Regarding communication, the male motto is "don't speak unless you have something to say." Guys feel like once we get to a complacent "status quo/maintenance" level in a relationship, then obviously it goes without saying that we're happy. I mean, nobody's complaining . . . so, by definition, our marriage must be a decent one.

As Dr. Gray points out, for women, communication is not just the need to make a point. She just wants to share and connect. For her, communication is not just sharing of information. It is sharing of herself . . . it is the very basis for intimacy.

Other psychologists take views that differ from those of John Gray, so let me briefly describe Dr. John Gottman and an institute called the Love Lab that he runs at the University of Washington. As we'll see, Dr. Gottman takes a very different approach than that of John Gray.

Based on his two decades of intensely hands on, very clinical and scientifically oriented research that focuses largely on human biology, Gottman claims to be able to predict divorce with 90 percent accuracy. He has essentially brought science to the aid of matrimony.

Dr. Gottman contends that the single biggest factor in marital success is a husband's willingness to accept the controlling influence of his wife. In a way, that may mean almost letting her dominate the relationship. Gottman feels that a husband's failure to let his wife control things within the marriage is the single biggest predictor of divorce.

Although Dr. Gottman's findings always generate groans from the guys when I mention them in my lectures, they actually make some sense to me because I know from my experience as a divorce lawyer that it is usually the wife who brings marital issues to the table for discussion. She is the one who generally sets the social and interpersonal agendas within the relationship.

The wife also more often suggests solutions for problems. And when things are really on the ropes, more than two-thirds of the time it will be the wife who will initiate the actual legal filing for divorce.

The impact of birth order as a behavior determinant. It will certainly help your relationship if you can understand your mate's most basic character traits, and one key among these is understanding how one's chronological birth order ranking amongst their siblings can influence the way their personality and behavior traits develop. Not that you can really change your mate's birth order or background, but at least you can be more empathetic and understanding.

Eldest children tend to be conservative, critical, conscientious, judgmental, competitive, aggressive, responsible, successful high achievers, organized, dominant, and controlling. They are also generally smarter—enjoying, on average, a three-point IQ advantage over their siblings. Middle children, on the other hand, tend to be loyal, retiring, compromising, indecisive, peacemaking, easy to get along with, and good negotiators. They develop useful skills for mediating between their other siblings. Youngest children tend to be fun loving, adventurous, reckless, impulsive, self-centered, loving and rebellious. Last borns are often the humorous, clown around "wild child" of the brood, able to get their way simply by being funny or outrageous. Ironically, however, they may actually be more dependent on authority.

Only children tend to behave exactly like what they are—a combination of eldest and youngest. Eldest children can also be a bit pushy (and I ought to know, I am one).

Now the key here is that *same-birth-order marriages* (i.e., an eldest son marrying an eldest daughter) *are usually more stressful* than mixed-birth-order marriages. Theoretically, it's not ideal to have two eldest child spouses constantly competing with one another to be the top dog in the marriage. Neither are two adventurous "class clown" youngest sibling spouses ideal when someone needs to display "take charge" maturity. Thus, relationships generally go better when an only or eldest child is coupled with a middle or a youngest child.

Understanding the Basic Biological Differences between Men and Women

Love at first sight . . . saves a lot of time.
          —*Anonymous*

One area that warrants some serious attention is an analysis of the basic core biological differences between men and women, especially as they impact each gender's thought processes and communication styles and their way of relating to one another. Obviously, if my readers can better understand these issues (and their opposite sex in general), it may give them a better shot at solving some of the many problems that inevitably arise in marriages and other relationships.

As I mentioned earlier, I have found an excellent resource book that is particularly illuminating on this cross-gender/interspousal communication issue. This amazingly insightful (and cleverly titled) book is called *"Why Men Don't Listen and Women Can't Read Maps"* by Drs. Barbara and Allan Pease. The Peases' book is more "science based" and focuses upon the neurology of the human brain and on evolutionary biology. Another scholar who has focused extensively on this subject is Doreen Kimura who has written expansively on the crucial differences between the male and female brains. I particularly commend her excellent treatise "How Different Are the Male and Female Brains?"

In the next few pages, I will attempt to summarize in an admittedly oversimplified and "generalized" fashion some of the findings regarding the key biological differences between the genders made by the Peases, Dr. Kimura, and other experts in the field. (Author's Note: Since I am a lawyer and certainly no scientist, my attempt to outline these findings will be rudimentary and imprecise at best and undoubtedly doesn't do justice to this complex subject. Thus, readers with an interest in this area are strongly advised to read the Peases' books especially, in their entirety. The Peases' research is simply fascinating and their books are fun and phenomenally insightful to read. Others may come to entirely different— and perhaps even contradictory—conclusions from the Peases' research and books than I did. So if this subject is anywhere near as fascinating to you as it is to me, then don't rely on my admittedly subjective interpretation; instead go right to the source and read the Peases' actual books themselves. They are by far the best and most enlightening books I have found on this fascinating topic.

As it turns out, there are quite a few major differences between the genders, so I have broken down this analysis into five basic sections. Sections I and II will cover the mental and "values" differences between the genders. Section III will cover their opposite communication styles. Sections IV and V will cover their physical and sexual differences. I have tried to chart it out in alternating "point/counterpoint" couplings. And, being the consummate gentleman that I am, I will start with ladies first.

I. Mental Differences

1) A woman's brain has more of a crucial connective nerve tissue called *corpus callosum* that increases the connections between her left and right brain hemispheres by at least 25 percent over males. Essentially, women's brains are configured to flow and interface faster, are better designed for multi-tasking, and can do several unrelated things at the same time. Women tend to think out loud, often in a multi-track, indirect, emotive fashion. They are great talkers. They need and love to talk. If a woman is talking to you a lot, she likes you. If she's not talking to you, you're in trouble. A man's smaller corpus callosum means that he is less able to perform multiple functions simultaneously. In particular, his emotion is less likely to operate simultaneously with other functions. Men maintain a more direct, single minded focus. Men speak less, often talking silently to themselves. 2) A woman's emotion centers are spread widely throughout both her brain hemispheres. A man's emotion is limited to only two areas located in his right hemisphere. 3) Women have specific areas for speech and language located on *both* sides of their brains. Men use primarily their left brain for language, speech and vocabulary. 4) Women have dominant verbal, organizational, multi-tasking and communication skills. Men have strong spatial ability (evolved from skills required for hunters chasing animals). 5) The left side of young girls' brains develops more rapidly. This means girls will start speaking earlier than boys. A three-year-old girl has twice

the vocabulary of a three-year-old boy and it is 100 percent comprehensible. Boys develop the right side of their brain faster than girls. This gives boys better spatial, logical and perceptual skills. They see in three dimensions and are better at video games . . . this despite their limited brain locations for speech. 6) Men have around four billion more brain cells than women, but women score 3 percent higher in general intelligence than men, despite having slightly smaller brains. 7) Girls do better and develop faster. In school, they succeed in language, English and the arts. Boys do better at math, science, building, puzzles, problem solving, reading maps and navigation (i.e., spatial tasks). Boys who are good at math outnumber girls by thirteen to one. 8) Women's handwriting is generally more legible than men's.

II. Different Values

1) Female awareness is focused on communication, cooperation, harmony, love, sharing and people's relationships to one another. Male awareness is concerned with getting results, achieving goals, status, and power, beating the competition and getting efficiently to the bottom line. 2) Women are more internal and define their own self-worth by the quality of their relationships, whereas men define themselves by their work, sports, careers and other external accomplishments. 3) Girls like people. Girls' brains are wired to respond to people and faces. Boys like things. Boys' brains respond to objects and their shapes. 4) Women value relationships and they talk when stressed. Men value work, hate to be wrong, and clam up when stressed. They also love to "hang with the boys," tend to hide their emotions and hate advice. 5) Women love shopping, are faithful, fall out of love and often can't (and don't want to) separate love from sex. Men hate shopping, are promiscuous, fall in love easily and do tend to separate sex from love. 6) Women need monogamy, use first names ("Mitzie Dearest") to increase closeness. Men avoid commitment, use nicknames ("Hey Butthead . . . yes, you Numbskull") to avoid intimacy. 7) Women like people and cooperate. Men like things and compete. 8) Seventy to eighty percent of women say the most important priority is their families. Seventy to eighty percent of men say that the most important part of their lives is their work.

9) Eighty percent of relationships are ended by women. Ninety percent of affairs are initiated by men.

III. Different Communication Styles

1) Women use a range of high- and low-pitched speaking sounds including five different tones of voice. Men speak in a more mono-tone voice using only three tones. 2) A woman can speak an average of 6,000 to 8,000 words a day. She uses an additional 2,000 to 3,000 vocal sounds to communicate, as well as 8,000 to 10,000 gestures, facial expressions, head movements, and other body language signals. This gives her a daily average of more than 20,000 communication "words" to relate her message. A man utters just 2,000 to 4,000 words, and 1,000 to 2,000 vocal sounds, and makes a mere 2,000 to 3,000 body language signals. His daily average adds up to around 7,000 communication "words"—just over a third the output of a woman. (Author's Note: I should point out that a more recent study by a University of Arizona researcher named Matthias Mehl attempted to re-address this "chat gap" between the genders. Mr. Mehl strongly disputes the findings by the Peases and other experts and instead contends that both men and women communicate an *equal* number of 16,000 "words" per day. The major difference according to Mr. Mehl is not the actual number of words spoken, but rather the dichotomy between men's style of "report-talk" vs. women's "rapport-talk." So, I will leave it to my readers to decide who they think talks more. Meanwhile, here is something additional—and perhaps more novel—to ponder: Is anybody out there studying how well we *listen*?) 3) Seventy-four percent of working women and 98 percent of non-working women identify the biggest failing of their husbands and boyfriends as a reluctance to talk, particularly at the end of the day. If men want to get along better with women, then they need to talk more. They also need to listen more empa-thetically. In a typical male-female conversation, 76 percent of interruptions are made by men. 4) Women talk more in generali-ties, talk "around" issues. Men's sentences are short, direct, more structured, solution oriented and to the point. They draw on a broader, more specific vocabulary and pepper their statements with facts. They use quantifiers such as "none, never, absolutely."

This kind of speech helps close business deals quickly and efficiently. 5) Women have a sixth sense and are more "touchy-feely," whereas men tend not to listen, miss the details, and are "insensitive." 6) Women are four to six times more likely to physically touch another woman in a social interaction than a man is likely to touch another man. Men avoid touch and retreat into their own world when under pressure. 7) Mothers or sisters often feel compelled to "speak up," responding on behalf of their quieter sons/brothers, since speech and language are not specific brain skills for males. 8) In surveys, a third of all women said their average phone calls lasted at least fifteen minutes, whereas half the men said their calls were less than five minutes. 9) For women, shopping and eating out is a form of intimacy just like talking. Meanwhile, men tend to avoid intimacy. They don't like too much eye contact and would rather channel surf the T.V. than seriously focus on any one thing. 10) When faced with a problem situation, 78 percent of girls tried to walk away or negotiate it, whereas 74 percent of boys used verbal or physical aggression.

IV. Physical Differences

1) A girl's body has a ratio of 26 percent fat and 20 percent protein. A boy's body has a ratio of 15 percent fat and 45 percent protein. 2) Female hormones fatten the body (and are also used to fatten livestock). Male hormones reduce fat and build muscle (and are unsuitable for animal fattening). 3) A woman's skin is ten times more sensitive to touch and pressure than a man's. Female skin is thinner than male skin and has an extra fat layer below it. Men have thicker skin than women, which explains why women get more wrinkles than men. 4) Women's excess fat is distributed on their thighs, rears and upper arms. Men accumulate excess fat in what is usually called a "potbelly."

V. Sexual Differences

1) A woman needs to have a man get in tune with his feelings before she's turned on to sex. A man needs to have sex before he can get in tune with his feelings. 2) Most women like at least twenty to twenty-five minutes of foreplay before they are really ready for

sex, whereas men only need about one to two minutes of foreplay. 3) Women are auditory and feeling. They want touch and romance and are stimulated through their ears (i.e., sweet words). Men are visual and want sex. They are stimulated through their eyes (i.e., erotic images). 4) Only 36 percent of women wanted sex with the lights on. Seventy-six percent of men wanted sex with the lights on. 5) When a man sees a woman naked, he becomes highly stimulated and aroused. When a woman sees a man naked, she will often blush or giggle. 6) A woman's brain is programmed to communicate with talk and her sensitivity to touch is ten times greater than a man's. If a woman wants to pleasure a man by touching him, she normally does it the way she would like to receive it. She scratches his head, caresses his face, rubs his back, and tenderly brushes his hair. Conversely (and obtusely), when a man decides to sensually touch a woman, he "makes the moves" he likes—i.e., he gropes her breasts and crotch. Women hate this, so touch her gently, guys. 7) Women's sex drive has often been compared to an oven—it heats slowly to its top temperature and takes a lot longer to cool down. Men's sex drive is like a gas burner—it ignites instantly, operates at full capacity within seconds, and can be turned off just as quickly. 8) A woman's sexual peak occurs between the ages of thirty-six and thirty-eight. A man's sex drive peaks at age nineteen. 9) Men generally have a higher sex drive than most women. Less than 3 percent of women are addicted to sex. Roughly 8 percent of men are addicted to sex. 10) Most women take about fifteen to thirty minutes to reach orgasm (if at all). Men take about three to six minutes to reach orgasm. (And since British researchers have now calculated that the average act of sexual intercourse lasts seven minutes and fifty-four seconds, that would appear to leave an awful lot of unsatisfied women.)

Key Tips on Preserving and Improving Your Marriage

To explain a romantic break-up, simply say, "It was all my fault."
    —*Anonymous*

Let me wrap up this chapter by giving my readers my own set of Marriage Preservation Pointers from the perspective of a divorce lawyer. This is sort of my own personal list derived from various sources and from my more than thirty years in the field of dealing with relationships. Several of the observations in this list are based on an excellent book entitled *The Perfect Marriage* by Hilary Rich and Dr. Helaina Kravtiz and/or from the sage advice of one of my favorite "relationships counselors," Dr. Diana Wiley.

1. *Strive for real physical and emotional intimacy.* Intimacy is the emotional, connective tissue in a relationship. In Latin, *Intima* = the innermost layer of an organ—the very wall of a blood vessel. I can't think of anything more core than that.

   Remember that, as Love Lab pioneer Dr. John Gottman states, 70 percent of both husbands and wives say it is the quality of the *friendship* they share with their spouses that is the determining factor in how satisfied they are with the sex, romance and passion in their marriages. Also remember that studies have shown that 60 percent of wives consider themselves to be "relationship-centered" vs. only 40 percent of husbands (who tend to be more work and achievement centered). But take heed, guys, and work to change that behavior, because studies have also shown that once the actual threat of losing their marriage occurs, it turns out that men generally need marriage much more than women do.

2. *Make the ordinary extraordinary.* Do at least one nice "special" thing a day for your spouse. Greet each other warmly. Stop whatever activity you are doing . . . often it's turning *off* the T.V. (not just hitting mute for a minute) and physically walking to the door to greet your spouse. When your spouse walks in the door, take his or her coat and ask if he or she would like something to drink. Take a few minutes to find out how your spouse's day was. Keep that T.V. off for a few minutes—it can be a real relationship killer.

3. *Keep the passion alive.* Create special "date time" together. Every once in awhile be sure to take out your photo albums and review them together. Build and imbue each other with a sense of marital history. Think of ways to surprise your mate. Stick a love note in your spouse's pocket, on his pillow, or in her lingerie drawer.

4. *Develop two-way communication skills.* Practice John Gray's reflective listening. After your spouse has told you something, rephrase and follow up on what he or she has said. This will make your spouse feel good by showing that you've actually heard what they are saying; that you are really listening.

   My marriage counselor friend Dr. Diana Wiley has a couple of favorite sayings that I think are insightful. She defines romance as paying "ingenious loving attention." She also contends that the two key qualities that make a man totally irresistible are "basic human kindness" and good "listening and communications skills." So, guys, when your gal rags about her day, don't just grunt. Instead, respond with something at least semi-empathetic like: "Wow, it sounds like the kids really gave you the run around today."

5. *Don't yield up your own life to your kids.* The single most important factor in having happy children is to be happy in your relationship with your spouse. If the two of you feel close to each other and are supportive of one another, then your children will feel secure. A marriage counselor friend of mine advises his clients that they should put their first dollar of disposable money into getting a baby sitter so they could have "date nights" out—doing this even before paying private school tuition.

6. *All marriages have conflicts.* It's not the absence of conflict, but learning how to resolve conflicts, that makes the difference between successful and unsuccessful relationships. And remember, some conflicts are resolvable just by identifying them.

   Here are my two simple but very effective *Tips on Resolving Conflicts.* (1) Discussing a problem right when it's happening guarantees a more heated argument . . . don't do it. Instead, schedule a specific discussion time for a bit later following a "cool down" period. (2) Don't get into heated arguments with your spouse (or anyone else for that matter) when talking over the telephone. Conflicts are much better resolved in person because it's generally much harder to say really nasty stuff face to face than it is over the phone.

And note that e-mail has become especially dangerous in this context. It's become way too easy to spew out short and snippy sentiments and then just hit "send."

In fact, my personal recommendation is that you try to go a step beyond just learning how to resolve conflicts effectively, and instead get out of the habit of arguing and fighting altogether. Now admittedly, there are two entirely different schools of thought on this. One is the 1960's "encounter group" style of thinking that it's "good to vent, to let it out, to get it out of your system." Sort of the "everybody needs a catharsis" approach. But, I go a step further and recommend trying to make it a point to *never fight*, period. Personally, I tend to feel that avoiding major outbursts altogether may be a far better approach.

I once attended a lecture given by a Chinese wahine professor who quoted a great old Chinese axiom: "Think three times before speaking." She then contrasted that with the seeming American habit of speaking three times before thinking.

So, if you want to "stay the course" and keep your marriage intact, you should always think in terms of resolving conflicts, not winning fights. Marital fights have no winners, only losers. Resolve conflicts rapidly when they happen. If you don't, unresolved conflicts from one stage of marital development will fester and impede growth in future stages. Remember, the longer a conflict goes unresolved, the more corrosive it becomes.

7. *Say I, not you.* Sentences starting with "you" are by definition accusatory. "You did this" starts things off negatively. But sentences starting with the word "I" have the opposite effect: "I feel this way . . . " These phrases help your partner sympathize with how you feel. Be a *good echo* of your mate's statements and feelings.

8. *Never say the word "divorce" just as a threat.* Don't even imply it unless you are serious about proceeding with it. Otherwise, it's one of the most destructive things you can do to your relationship. It weakens trust and creates fear about the future.

9. *Keep your problems to yourselves.* Asking advice from friends, family or neighbors about a recent argument with your spouse (although admittedly tempting) is actually a severe breach of trust. You will never repair a rough patch in your relationship by taking some sort of a Gallup Poll among your friends and neighbors as to whether it was you or your spouse who was right or wrong about a given issue/incident in your marriage. Never, ever, talk about negative aspects of your relationship with anyone except your spouse (and/or a professional counselor, perhaps). It's extremely destructive.

10. *Apologize and make up.* Just saying "I'm sorry" can change an angry argument into a constructive discussion. Couples who are the quickest to instinctively apologize and make up often have the strongest marriages. I sometimes analogize argumentative communication styles with the "unnecessary roughness" penalty in football. Once uttered, you can never really take those harsh words back, so be careful what you say in the first place. Remember that studies have shown that it takes about five positive interchanges to make up for one negative interchange, so be careful about those negatives or you're going to have to work awfully hard to make up for them.

11. *Be a romantic.* There is a worldwide romance shortage today. I read a recent Valentine's Day survey in which 49 percent of those surveyed thought romance was on the decline. Only 19 percent ranked themselves seven or higher on the romantic scale. We should all work to improve on those figures.

12. *Stay out of the Three P Soup . . . It's a recipe for disaster.* I once heard a great "Three P" analogy as to just how it is that otherwise normal communication can progressively deteriorate. You start off with a base of the *Personal*: "You're such a nag, there's no pleasing you." Follow that up with a dollop of the *Pervasive*: "You nag about *everything*." Add a pinch of the *Permanent*: "And you've *always* been that way." Then bring to a roiling boil with "I gave up on you a long time ago."

As I say, I suppose that my little Twelve Point Plan as listed above could be alternatively titled "A Divorce Lawyer's Guide to

Preserving Your Marriage." So as long as I am sounding schmaltzy anyway, let me conclude this section by providing a couple of final "cutesy" sounding, but perhaps prophetic, laundry lists of "relationship enhancement" pointers.

Here are seven somewhat silly, but certainly sweet and potentially significant *Tips on How to Have an Ideal Relationship*.

1. Take walks together (thirty minutes each day).
2. Give each other gifts often. A special book, a warm bath and massage, flowers, surprise experiences . . . try to offer up the sorts of special things your mate would enjoy and get excited about.
3. Write love notes. Hide them around the home, in clothing, pockets, in the underwear drawer and secret places.
4. Do not criticize, condemn or complain. To do so is a big no-no. Only praise and acknowledge the goodness in each other. There is no place for negativity in a loving and lasting relationship, ever! (Hopefully, your mate will do the right thing if you lead by example.)
5. Forgive and love. Release the past at every moment. Live in the present. Plan for the future.
6. Eliminate arguing totally. Anywhere, anytime. Especially in the morning, during meals, or while in bed.
7. Say "I love you" daily, many times. Especially when you wake up and before you go to sleep. Never, ever, take love for granted. Express it verbally as well as with action.

Need still more inspiration? The *Honolulu Advertiser* conducted an informal survey among its readers in 2007 as to "What makes a marriage last?" Here is a short list of their respondents' insights:

- Communicate and listen to each other.
- Mutual respect: Never put your spouse down in front of others.
- Similar lifestyle: If you eat together, share the same bed, go to sleep together and get up at the same time, you will have better communication.

- Faith: If you share the same faith, you will share the same life purpose.
- Having private time together on a regular basis.
- Don't offer too much advice unless it's requested.
- Never stop laughing

Lastly, here are Barbara and Allan Pease's "Surefire Romance Tips for Men" as listed in their excellent, eye-opening and "must read" book *Why Men Don't Listen and Women Can't Read Maps*.

1. *Set the environment.* The right lighting—dimly lit rooms make pupils dilate. A woman's superior hearing means that the right music is important. 2. *Feed her.* Taking a woman to dinner is a significant "intimate event" for her—even when she's not hungry. 3. *Light a fire.* Collecting wood and lighting a fire harken back subconsciously to cave man days when a woman wanted her man to be a hunter and a protector. 4. *Bring flowers.* That is to say, bring her fresh flowers. 5. *Go dancing.* Dancing has been described as "a vertical act of horizontal desire"—it allows close male/female body contact as a lead-up to courtship. 6. *Buy chocolates and champagne.* Champagne contains a chemical not found in other alcoholic beverages that increases testosterone levels. Chocolate contains phenyl ethylamine, which stimulates the love center in a woman's brain.

CHAPTER 3

The Dynamics of Divorce

More marriages might survive if the partners realized that sometimes the better comes after the worse.
  —*Doug Larson*

Let me begin this section on the causes of divorce by taking a quick look at Hawai'i, where I practice, to see if we can't divine some general insights. Hawai'i has a major problem with divorce. In fact, our beautiful islands are probably on the cutting edge of the overall nationwide problem.

Transients and hedonists. Why is the marital dissolution situation so severe in Hawai'i? For starters, we have an unusually high number of transient residents passing through our state. They, in turn, seem to feel much less restrained in their personal behavior by what would otherwise be the more self-regulating community watch (i.e., communally judgmental) approach that is often imposed by a permanently entrenched or status quo community.

If increased mobility is indeed a causal factor, the rest of the country will be heading down the same road as Hawai'i.

Many folks display a headlong hedonistic mentality when they come to Hawai'i. People come to our islands looking for fun in the sun. This tends to foster a disposable approach toward life in general. If it's no longer working, or no fun anymore, then toss it out! This can apply to your old surfboard, a disposable lighter, or your spouse.

A nation of spoiled yuppies. While these trends toward increased transience and self-centered hedonism may have hit the extreme stage in Hawai'i, they are typical of the nationwide drift. Several other states have equally high divorce rates, and a few are even worse. Often, the highest divorce statistics occur in exactly the kind of yuppie places that you would expect. Problem spots include California, Florida, parts of Colorado, and other life-is-a-playground resort-type areas. Statistically, Hawai'i's divorce rate is eleventh in the country, following California and a few other hotbeds.

Overall, the statistics are staggering. One often hears the catch phrase of "one divorce out of every two marriages." My guess is that in the long run we are probably heading toward a divorce rate that will be even slightly higher than that. (As discussed earlier, the divorce rate seems to have leveled off temporarily—but just wait until they come up with a vaccine against AIDS!)

The "uniforms theory." Here in Hawai'i we have a unique problem—what I call my "uniforms theory" of divorce. Anytime you've got a lifestyle with a high degree of mobility, constantly shifting work venues or schedules, or various other sorts of built-in fluctuations, there tends to be even more extreme stress put on relationships. So, in a place like Hawai'i, which has a high military population as well as a high percentage of its populace involved in the various facets of the tourist industry (i.e., flight attendants, hotel bellboys—basically anybody who wears a uniform to work), you can expect an increased problem.

By definition, whenever you have people constantly changing job descriptions (i.e., sailors heading out to sea for six months at a stretch, or the cop or fireman who gets transferred from day shift to night shift), the slippery and shifting logistics inherent in those kinds of situations begin to put more stress on the marriage. Sure enough, those are exactly the kinds of couples that are increasingly prone to divorce.

Causal Factors

The single greatest cause of divorce—marriage!
        —Anonymous

Whenever I lecture on divorce, I get asked the almost trick question, "What are the main causes of divorce?" My canned reply: "The same ones we see in the daytime TV soap operas . . . the big three are Sex, Money, and Family." Other key lightning rods are the allocation of household chores and responsibilities, alcohol or other substance abuse and, sadly enough, spouse abuse. Apparently, the soap operas are pretty accurate in highlighting these themes. No wonder millions of Americans watch them with such interest.

Let's take a closer look at the issue of interspousal communication (or the lack of it), since that too can be a major marriage buster. There is now strong evidence that the relationships most likely to end in divorce are not necessarily those in which the spouses fight too nastily or too often. Nor are those married couples who have their own in-house policy of trying to avoid conflict necessarily headed for trouble (something that previous research had suggested). Rather, the latest studies suggest that the marriages most likely to dissolve are those in which some or all of these four behaviors are chronic: criticism, contempt, defensiveness, or withdrawal.

"It's not the amount of empathy or understanding in a relationship that predicts who is going to make it and who is going to divorce," says Howard Markman, professor of psychology at the University of Denver. "It's the zingers or negative behaviors."

All marriages have conflicts, but that doesn't necessarily have to be a deal breaker. The key is the ability to resolve them. A marriage counselor friend of mine cites a popular quote that "the difference between a good marriage and a bad one is three to four things a day left *unsaid.*" She talks about smart spouses literally having "teeth marks" on their tongues from having bitten them to hold them, and she is quick to remind her clients that studies have shown that it requires five positive interchanges to make up for one negative one.

Wives call the emotional cadence. Many researchers agree that it is typically the wife who takes primary responsibility for the emotional status of the marriage. She is most often the one who takes the lead in setting up the couple's social and emotional agendas and, she is usually the one who brings up the thorny issues that need to be negotiated and resolved if the marriage is to succeed. She is also the one who persists until the discussion ends in either a satisfactory resolution or a screaming match.

It is when the wife gives up the role of emotional caretaker and withdraws (typically after years of destructive conflict) that many marriages hit rock bottom. "Once the woman gives up, that's when she's likely to file for divorce or have an affair," says Markman.

As I mentioned earlier, perhaps the most prominent advocate of this eye-opening assessment is Dr. John Gottman. He contends that a husband's failure to let his wife control things within the marriage is the single biggest predictor of divorce.

Husbands (and men in general) are much more uncomfortable with open conflict in personal relationships. Thus they are more likely to withdraw from a potential argument, either by placating their wives or by stonewalling—becoming silent and disengaged. Typical in this scenario is the husband who turns on the television or walks out of the room. Markman has found that consistent withdrawal or stonewalling by the husband is strongly predictive of divorce.

Two incomes, one of them the wife's. Two other key causal factors related to divorce are the evolving and emerging roles of women in our society, and the rise of the two-income family. Women are now out there full on in the work place. In fact, for the first time in history, one-third of working American women now routinely out-earn their husbands. These women have the added stresses and strains of their own business days, they also have a heightened emphasis on their own personal agendas, and they now have the ability to finance those agendas with their own earned income. This in turn can cause couples to splinter when the woman becomes understandably less willing to subordinate her own role and needs in order to "stand by her man" in the old traditional sense.

The key cause of divorce—marriage. When compiling a list of the key causal factors of divorce, it is probably a bit too facile to say, "Marriage is the foremost cause of divorce." One cannot underestimate, however, the difficulties inherent in embarking on any marriage. As George Bernard Shaw said in describing the inherently contradictory nature of the marriage ceremony: "When two people are under the influence of the most violent, most insane, most delusive, and most transient of passions, they are required to swear that they will remain in that excited, abnormal and exhausting condition continuously until death do them part."

Sociological Factors

Before marriage, a man will go home and lie awake all night thinking about something you said; after marriage, he'll go to sleep before you finish saying it.
   —*Helen Rowland*

Under the old-style value system of our grandparents' generation, the needs of the family took priority over the need of the individual. Today, exactly the reverse is true. The social pressure that would have been exerted on grandma and grandpa if they'd decided to split no longer exists. In fact, modern American society offers a multiplicity of options to cut and run when the going gets rough.

Great expectations. During the last couple of decades, a clutter of books, magazines, and self-help courses has emerged encouraging thousands to make their needs, desires, and preferences known to their spouses. Marriage enrichment programs instruct American couples how to better communicate with one another.

Clearly the expectations are higher today with regard to what constitutes a good or workable marriage. These expectations center not only on the quality of the actual time a husband and wife spend together, but also include the desire for a heightened level of meaningfulness in their communication during that time.

Remember also that the sheer quantity of time that spouses spend physically together has increased substantially given our longer life spans and the additional leisure time in modern society. Not only are today's husbands and wives expected to talk turkey to each other insofar as a sincere and serious level of communication is concerned, they are also engaging in numerous hours of formerly unheard of joint activities together. Traveling, shopping, working out, eating out, attending professional or cultural events, engaging in coed sports, etc., are all activities that are now frequently shared by husbands and wives.

As my favorite *Time* magazine columnist Barbara Ehrenreich points out, there is no other aspect of life in which we expect any one person to fill such a "huge multiplicity of needs . . . only in marriage do we demand the all-purpose, multi-talented, Renaissance person." She argues that "marriages lasted in the past because less was expected of them." Her half-joking, but half-serious, proposed solution is the availability of the "discreet, long term, European-style affair" or "separate marriages" for separate types of marital functions.

Kids = combustibility. Having kids puts extra stress on a marriage. A few of the obvious ones are additional scheduling and planning for more than two people; financial, time, and organizational pressures; and the potential for disputes over parenting styles and acceptable punishments—more authoritarian versus more embracing and coddling styles of parenting. All of these can increase the potential for a flare up. Stacy Rogers, a sociologist at Penn State, conducted studies that repeatedly found that childless couples were generally happier than those with children.

One of the less-obvious consequences is that once a couple has had children, the submissive spouse (often, but not always, the wife) can't continue to cater exclusively to the dominant spouse. Loyalties get divided between the marriage and the children, and so do the time commitments. The spouse who was accustomed to being catered too often gets uppity and irritable about the fact that they are no longer the boss.

Changing Family Structures

Divorce is the sacrament of adultery.
        —*French proverb*

As noted earlier, it is an almost trite saying that money, sex, and in-laws are the topics around which most marital disruptions center. Arguments about work and family issues, and about appropriate styles of disciplining children, are also significant factors. Conflicts emerge over feelings of unfairness about the division of tasks between spouses, i.e., housekeeping chores and childcare tasks versus who works outside the home for pay. Couples also disagree about how they want to spend their time together, and about just how much of their time they want to spend together versus independently.

Dual incomes = double the potential trouble. Nowadays couples get hit with both ends of this problem since during their dual-income (or is it "dueling incomes"?) yuppie years; while both are working, they have to keep a marriage together despite intense time pressures and an inability to enjoy much coinciding downtime or quality time together (i.e., *not enough time* together during the early years of the marriage—the amount of pure spousal time that young married couples spend alone together has dropped 26 percent since 1975). Later, thanks to longer life spans and elongated periods of retirement, they may have to learn how to spend more time together than might be their preference (i.e., *too much time* together during the later years).

Whatever happened to counseling or commitment? Surprisingly, entirely too few couples bother to talk to marriage counselors. Less than half indicate that they ever sought any help to deal with their marital problems and it's a pretty telling indicator that women are ten times more likely to seek counseling than men. Personally, I feel that the failure to undertake counseling represents a tragic missed opportunity, but some surveys seem to indicate that perhaps it wouldn't have made any difference. In post-divorce follow-up interviews, at least 70 percent of divorcing individuals later state they are doubtful that they could have worked things out. Over 80 percent go on to say that they still remain convinced that they made the right decision and would *not* go back.

Is society's glue dissolving? What is it about the modern-day American lifestyle that leaves so many feeling so strongly that divorce can represent a potentially positive element of contemporary living? As noted earlier, some of the most commonly cited reasons for divorce include drug or alcohol problems, infidelity, transience, and emotional problems. The argument can certainly be made that modern conditions have become particularly ripe for these types of problems . . . especially in the promiscuous, abusive, and morally ambiguous climate that has emerged in America during the last few decades.

The plethora of lifestyle options and interests that have emerged in our modern "connected culture" over the last twenty or so years have certainly contributed to the increasingly cloudy concept of modern morality (or should I say amorality . . . or even immorality?) along these lines. Experts estimate that at least 10 percent of all divorces in the United States are now in some way connected to computers and the Internet. People google, locate, and then re-contact long-lost loves. They get caught red-handed with totally traceable records of illicit and/or adulterous e-mails and/or cell phone calls. Not too surprisingly, wives really resent it when they walk in on their husband while he is surfing porn sites. And websites like marriedbutplaying.com and married-but-flirting.com certainly aren't geared toward helping to maintain marriages.

Conversely, the major factors in keeping marriages together (and which serve as societal barriers to divorce) include social pressure, hanging in there "for the children," strongly held religious beliefs, the severity of divorce laws, and mollifying parents or extended family. But over the last few decades, of course, we have witnessed the demise of many of these more rigidly conservative religious and family structures . . . and certainly the no-fault laws have made divorce easier.

People who ultimately decide to divorce often cite a basic sense of malaise or unhappiness, a desire to get away from a bad situation, improved alternatives for independent financial support, or becoming romantically involved with someone else as their motive. Whatever the reasons, the institution of marriage seems alarmingly fragile today. Even I, as a jaded old divorce attorney, was shocked to read that more than one-third of all currently married persons report that, just within the last year alone, they have seriously discussed the idea of separating from their spouse. (Again, wives are more likely to raise this issue than are husbands.)

Who cuts and runs? In general, women appear to be the instigators who most often want the divorce. Of all divorce complaint filings, 60 to 70 percent are initiated by wives. This is not to say that the men may not have caused the problem initially (they may have cheated or "quit communicating"), but it is the wives who take the bull by the horns and initiate legal action the vast majority of the time.

The level of commitment to marital stability is generally viewed as being somewhat less strong in younger people. And, not surprisingly, younger couples are far more likely to divorce than are older people. The fact that young couples are generally somewhat less mature and that their lives are less well established can make them sitting ducks for divorce. Younger people tend to feel that their social lives might be better if they were separated, but very few older people feel the same way. Older females, in particular, seem (legitimately) concerned that they will be worse off after divorce. Some folks—again most often the younger people—think that separation might improve their business or career opportunities.

Let's face it, today's generation of Americans is often pretty self-absorbed, and they now possess a multiplicity of "lifestyle options," many of which are seemingly simpler than toughing out the difficult periods inherent in any marriage.

The Women's Movement

The reason husband and wife do not understand each other is because they belong to different sexes.
—*Dorothy N. Dix*

Women have been flooding into the workplace ever since the 1970s. They have flourished in that arena and their economic power has grown steadily. Nowadays, women make up 47 percent of the work force and constitute 52 percent of the voting populace. Women are now awarded 57 percent of all bachelor's degrees.

This steady march of women into the modern workplace has been an exciting and generally very positive development, but it does seem to have caused some unavoidable disruption to the traditional family unit. If both parents are now working, they face a simple but overwhelming question: "Who is going to take care of the kids?"

As women's professional stature and economic power have grown, many have sought to escape marriages in which they have been dissatisfied, but upon which they had depended financially. An inevitable cycle of disruption has followed. As working mothers divorced, their already serious problems finding adequate childcare have worsened; the number of children living in poverty has increased because absent fathers are less likely to pay child support; and single-parent and stepfamilies have begun to evolve as being something of the norm.

I am woman . . . hear me roar. Many women, particularly the younger and better-educated, professionally minded "yuppettes," can quite legitimately view their newly found personal freedom as an auspicious development. Conversely, the sour-grape syndrome often abounds among the men. Many of my male clients, formerly rather complacent about their marriages, and hence astonished to find themselves in my office, are certainly quite vocal in accusing the women's movement of being a prime mover in causing the breakup of their marriages.

The women's rights movement has indeed fostered a more equal marital relationship in which the needs and wishes of both partners are jointly considered. Expectations concerning the quality of the marital relationship have been deepening ever since the 1920s. Husbands and wives are expected to communicate and "share" more with one another and to provide emotional support to a greater degree nowadays than ever before.

Relationships failing to live up to these higher standards may well be jettisoned. In fact, many experts feel that one significant reason there are apparently fewer unhappy marriages today is that many of the less-than-perfect marriages have already been ended by divorce.

Money . . . Dual-Income Families

Romance . . . without finance . . . ain't got no chance.
    —*Charlie Parker*

Couples frequently fight about money. One spouse is a saver, the other is a spender. One is a risk taker, a gambler, or an entrepreneur; the other is a conservative risk avoider. One party wants to join both their moneys together (often the man), while the other spouse (often the woman) wants to retain some money as separate. One worries about money and is always concerned with financial security. The other truly believes that money isn't everything. There is also a tendency by one or the other to use control of the money as a device to control the other person. All of these differences are intensified when each spouse has his or her own money to protect or is afforded the extra personal freedom and flexibility that comes with having one's own income.

Furthermore, the logistics involved in the pursuit of money itself add pressures to the relationship. Two-thirds of Americans with school-age children are now in the labor force and need to work out some sort of day care arrangements. About 60 percent of married men with kids have working wives.

Commuter marriages. Time magazine did a fascinating article entitled, "Till Work Do Us Part" on the relatively recent phenomenon of dual-career/dual-address married couples. This insightful and amazing article pointed out the fact that as of 2005, there were more than 3.5 million married American couples who had to live geographically apart due to their disparate job postings. These are not folks who have separated due to marital discord. Rather, they have intact marriages, but each spouse is simply following his/her own job. This kind of marriage now constitutes 2.9 percent of all American marriages. Furthermore, their numbers have increased 30 percent just since the year 2000. Perhaps this phenomenon isn't as surprising as it seems given today's preponderance of dual-career couples (now constituting 80 percent of the current American labor force) and the ever-accelerating nature of our highly mobile society.

Awareness of Abuse

It takes two to make a marriage a success and only one a failure.
—Lord Samuel

I would estimate that nearly one-third of my law firm's divorce caseload involves some form of either interspousal or intrafamily violence. This may even be on the low side, since my firm's clientele is somewhat upscale and thus is probably a bit less prone to outright physical violence. I have heard figures closer to one-half so far as the general populace is concerned.

One sad outgrowth of the period surrounding marital separations is the propensity for physical violence that accompanies it. Husbands and wives who have never in their lives hit one another can suddenly find themselves pounding away at each other in furious physical outbursts.

"Hurtful" statistics. The American Medical Association and the U.S. Surgeon General have declared that violent men now constitute a major threat to women's health in our country. The National League of Cities estimates that as many as half of all women will experience violence at some time during their marriage. The FBI reports that an estimated ten million American women are battered every year. That's one every fifteen seconds. Between 30 and 35 percent of all visits by females to emergency rooms are for injuries from domestic assaults. Forty-two percent of murdered women in the United States are killed by current or former partners.

Ironically, although men are unquestionably the culprits in most spousal violence, the statistics even out a bit when it comes to fatal cases. Half of all spousal murders are committed by wives—a figure that has remained surprisingly stable over time.

The really terrible part of the abuse and violence cycle in relationships is the incredible statistical likelihood that a child who witnesses abuse while growing up will tend to mimic that sort of abusive behavior in later life—including entering into abusive relationships of their own. In a home where one parent is violent toward the other, the children are 50 percent more likely to be abused themselves. The vicious cycle continues when 40 to 50 percent of those children who were exposed to family violence while growing up then turn around and incorporate abusive behavior into their own later relationships.

Sex

Sex drive: a physical craving that begins in adolescence and ends at marriage.
      —Robert Byrne

I am still somewhat amazed (even after listening to literally hundreds of clients describe it in excruciating detail) by the degree of sexual starvation that seems to characterize many marriages prior to a divorce. Some of these folks have been sleeping in separate bedrooms for decades. It is hardly surprising then that the California Children of Divorce Project discovered that more than one-third of both men and women rank sexual deprivation as the major cause of their breakup. A substantial percentage of the couples involved in that study had not had sexual intercourse (at least not with each other!) for three to five years.

The relative degree of importance that sex plays in any given marriage will obviously vary from couple to couple. But, maintaining at least some level of sexuality is probably a good idea for any couple. After all, sex is a function of communication, and sexual intimacy and communication are two key bonds that hold marriages together. So couples are probably well advised to keep their "sexuality quotient" as high as possible. Yet, an AMA study in 1999 found that 43 percent of women and 39 percent of men complained of dissatisfaction in the bedroom.

Since good sex is to some degree a skill that develops through experience (requiring good communication and a sincere desire to please your mate), both genders would be well advised to take it seriously. Men, in particular, should understand and remember the sexual studies I cited earlier which show that women generally take four to five times longer to reach arousal/orgasm than do men (i.e., an average of eighteen to twenty-five minutes for women versus four to five minutes for men). Be a little (or a lot) more tender, guys.

Women seeking a healthy sex life may want to remember that the best time to approach their man for sex may well be in the morning. A man's *testosterone is highest at sunrise*—up to twice as high as at any other time in the day. A man's testosterone is 30 percent lower in the evening.

Sex is definitely an important aspect of relationships for males. Marriage counselors routinely report that if they can successfully "fix" the sexual problems for their couples clients, they can often bring at least the husband back into the fold. Sex is probably also healthy for males from a purely physical standpoint. Studies have shown that men who have regular orgasms have up to 50 percent lower rates of prostate cancer. (How's that for a motivator?)

Meanwhile, women can ponder the immortal words of *Penthouse* magazine publisher Bob Guccione who (not totally surprisingly) contends: "for a man, sex is the single most important thing in the world." Surveys have shown that men dream about sex more often than do women and that men dream of multiple partners twice as often as women do. So gals, if you may have come to think that sex isn't all that important a factor in keeping your guy happy and your marriage intact . . . you may want to think again.

Cindy Meston and David Buss conducted a study published in the *Archives of Sexual Behavior* that concluded that there are 237 reasons that motivate people to have sex. Since we haven't got room to list all 237, let's scale these findings down to just the top ten reasons for both men and women ("Late Night" style, if you will).

We find that the Top Eight Reasons for having sex are virtually identical for both genders. These are: (1) I was attracted to the person. (2) It feels good. (3) I wanted to experience physical pleasure. (4) It's fun. (5) I wanted to show my affection to the person. (6) I was sexually aroused and wanted the release. (7) I was "horny." (8) I wanted to express my love for the person.

The order of priority of these Top Eight reasons were slightly different for men than for women, but the reasons themselves were virtually identical. The interesting (and telling) key differences came in items number 9 and 10, which for men were: (9) I wanted to achieve orgasm. (10) I wanted to please my partner. For women, on the other hand, they were: (9) I realized I was in love. (10) I was in the heat of the moment.

It's obviously a squishy, subjective, and imprecise exercise to attempt to establish any sort of a standardized baseline as to what constitutes a quote "normal level" of sexuality within a marriage. No marriage counselor or therapist could possibly tell you exactly how much sex you should be having, but most agree that you should be having at least some. Sex may be only one component of a good union, but most happy marriages usually include it. As one particularly eloquent client of mine put it pretty graphically, "If you're not f---ing, you're fighting."

According to a 2002 study by the National Opinion Research Center, married couples say they have sex about sixty-eight times a year, or slightly more than once a week. This "sex once or twice a week" (i.e., fifty to one hundred times a year) has thus become, almost by default, something of the benchmark standard for a healthy sex life for a married couple. At the other end of the spectrum, psychologists estimate that 15 to 20 percent of couples have sex no more than ten times a year, which is how the experts basically define a "sexless marriage."

As if these various yardsticks for what constitutes a "normal" level of sex frequency weren't confusing enough already, let's throw in one more. This one includes the rest of the world as well as the United States and also counts in single folks as well as marrieds. In a recent survey of twenty-eight nations worldwide, Japan ranked dead last in sexual activity, with the average Japanese having sex just thirty-six times per year. Conversely, we red-blooded Americans (God bless 'em) ranked number one in the world . . . coming in at 124 times a year.

Want still more stats on sex stuff to ponder? *Playboy* magazine conducted a nationwide survey of 900 randomly selected adult males and females between the ages of eighteen and sixty-four. Their findings, as published in a February 2008 article entitled "Sex in America," were that (1) only 26 percent of all respondents reported being "very satisfied" with their sex lives; (2) the average age at which folks lost their virginity was 17.7 years; (3) the average numbers of sex partners whom respondents had been with was 10.9; (4) on the issue of sexual frequency, 47 percent indicated they had sex one or more times a week; (5) 22 percent indicated they had been involved in, or would be willing to engage in, an adulterous affair; (6) Republicans are more sexually active than Democrats (for whatever that's worth!); and finally, (7) the sexiest area in the United States in terms of both activity and behavior is the Pacific region, whereas the Northeast came in dead last in sexuality.

Stories and studies abound about the notorious drop off in couples' sexuality quotients and frequency following the birth of their child(ren). (Some cynics would say that this follows the marriage itself.) Not only are the overloaded logistical scheduling and the lack of physical privacy and quality "downtime" together daunting for many new parent couples, but natural biological shifts occur. Studies have shown that a man's testosterone level actually drops after he has settled down to marriage, his wife's pregnancy and a pending family. Nature seems to have designed both men and women to become biologically prepared for parenthood. In one study, the very act of having men hold baby dolls lowered their testosterone. All of which may be great for a couple's parenting skills regarding their kids . . . but probably not great for their sex life (and, perhaps by extension, their marriage).

Affairs and their aftermath. Most married couples claim to believe in the value of monogamy, but a sizable number of married men and women stray from the fold. In many ways it seems as though America is obsessed with extramarital sex. Various estimates, including those of Masters and Johnson, suggest that anywhere from 26 percent to 66 percent of married American men, and 18 percent to 69 percent of married American women, have had extramarital affairs. The wide ranges in these figures alone would seem to indicate that lots of folks are at least thinking about it, though perhaps not admitting it.

Various other imprecise estimates abound: (1) The *Kinsey Report* estimated that 33 percent of divorces have an infidelity component. (2) Author Susan Barash in her book, *A Passion for More*, skews much higher when she estimates that 60 percent of all American women will have an affair during their marriage. (3) *Playboy* magazine attempts to break it down by year. They estimate the odds that a married woman will have an affair at one in eight before two years of marriage; one in five thereafter. Meanwhile, they rate the odds that a married man will have an affair before two years of marriage at one in seven; one in four between years two and ten; and one in three after ten or more years of marriage. (4) Dr. David Barash in his book, *The Myth of Monogamy*, estimates that 30 to 50 percent of married women and 50 to 80 percent of married men have had affairs. I suppose you can pick your own personal favorite as to the statistical probabilities . . . but, it sounds like a fairly serious issue to me.

Meanwhile, the gut feelings and suspicions of the cheated-on spouse often prove accurate. According to one group of researchers, 90 percent of the wives questioned who suspected their husbands of straying outside the marriage were correct in their assumptions, while 87 percent of the husbands who thought their wives had extramarital experiences were accurate.

There is no question in my mind that the greatest difference between men and women in the motivation for having affairs is this: men tend to seek mainly sexual variety and excitement; women, on the other hand, look primarily for emotional returns. Women embark upon extramarital affairs for numerous reasons, of course, but the vast majority of those wives who are unfaithful explain their motivation in terms of a search for heightened emotions and intimacy in the face of being emotionally dissatisfied with their husbands. Whereas a "fling" style affair undertaken by a husband may not necessarily threaten a marriage unduly, the more "seriously seeking meaning" style affair undertaken by a wife may indeed be a more serious and problematic issue for the marriage and a stronger predictor of divorce.

Affairs are not fair. There is an innate deceit involved in extramarital dalliances, and that deceit breeds numerous and often unanticipated complications. If a person's extramarital activities are discovered—which happens in a surprisingly large number of cases—there is a sizable risk that this will seriously undermine the trust and intimacy of his or her marriage.

Another big negative follows the discovery of an affair—it victimizes the uninvolved spouse. The cheated-on partner may be victimized in a number of other ways beyond simply having their feelings hurt and their trust eroded. For instance, they may have been exposed to sexually transmitted diseases, or have been victimized economically as well.

Nor do affairs come cheap. *Time* magazine recently tallied the average cost of a four-month extramarital affair (including getaways and gifts) at $20,639.00. Meanwhile, *Time* estimated the legal fees for the average divorce filing at $5,025.00, thereby (I presume) allowing their readers to make their own informed choices.

Many marriages were never entered into on a truly equal basis. Instead, there may be an unspoken framework wherein one partner is assumed to have the dominant and controlling role and the other is generally the supportive and submissive partner. This is often a basic theme that underlies the entire initial relationship. In the event these roles start switching around as time goes on, it is often by way of the formally submissive partner trying to break out of his or her prior role as the underling. This often occurs by way of deception on the part of the formerly submissive partner—often through the act of undertaking an affair. The dominant spouse, unable to accept this fact, enters a phase of denial.

Many psychologists feel that a prolonged extramarital affair is almost always an indicator of a conflicted marriage (although some experts will allow that an occasional one-night stand or short-term extramarital affair can sometimes be viewed as a harmless transgression).

Oftentimes, a decision by one spouse to divorce or separate comes as an outgrowth of a commitment already made to some other third party. This is usually an indication that one party left the marriage psychologically a long time ago.

Psychological Factors and Fallout

Success in life is more than finding the right person to marry. Being the right person is even more important.
 —*Elos Nelson*

The decision to divorce is perhaps the clearest indication imaginable of a clean break with the initiating party's past and the start of their emotional rebirth or rebuilding. Still, as author Abigail Tafford clearly demonstrated when she chose the title *Crazy Time: Surviving Divorce* for her landmark book on divorce, the experience brings

one right up to the edge of insanity. Divorce is an extremely dis-
orienting experience both logistically and financially. As several
of the other sections of this book clearly demonstrate, the couple
of years time frame surrounding divorce is a time characterized
by intense mood swings and seesawing emotions.

Common Phases of Divorce

Love has been described as a three-ring circus. First to come the engagement
ring, then the wedding ring, and after that the suffer ring.
    —*Bob Phillips*

After twenty-five years of divorce practice, I am convinced that
Ms. Tafford got it about right when she described the divorce
process in *Crazy Time: Surviving Divorce*:

> Most people go a little crazy. You are rarely prepared for the practical
> or emotional turmoil that lies ahead. You swing between euphoria,
> violent rage and depression. You may be promiscuous and drink too
> much; you may withdraw from people and not answer the phone.
> Health statistics tell that you are prone to getting sick and having
> car accidents. Reports of triangle assaults and murders of estranged
> spouses make regular newspaper headlines. In the dark hours of
> loneliness, you think about suicide. At some point, almost everyone
> coming out of a marriage mutters to what was once the other half:
> "I could kill you." This is crazy time. It starts when you separate
> and usually lasts about two years. It's a time when your emotions
> take on a life of their own and you swing back and forth between
> wild euphoria and violent anger, ambivalence and deep depression,
> extreme timidity and rash actions. You are not yourself. Who are you?
> At the time you don't want to know. You might go on a sex binge. . . .
> Or you lie very still in bed, your muscles tense, your breathing shal-
> low, your imaginings as dark and lonely as the night.

Predictable Emotional Way Stations

I've heard marriage defined as the best method for getting acquainted.
    —*Haywood Broun*

Many of my former clients would concur with the experts that
the initial period of depression and disorientation surrounding

a divorce can be expected to last about one to two years. This is then generally followed by what has been called the recovery period, a stage that usually lasts three to five years; it's essentially the time when you rebuild your life. This is a gradual process characterized by making new friends, perhaps physically relocating, redefining your relationships with your children, taking a fresh look at your job or career, etc. For many folks, a key part of the recovery period is falling in love again or getting involved in a new relationship. For others it is adding some new focus, outside interest, or alternate track to their lives from which they can derive a sense of satisfaction.

Periods of Promiscuity and Personal Sexual Revolutions

Sex: the thing that takes up the least amount of time and causes the most amount of trouble.
    —*John Barrymore*

I have noticed that many of my clients seem to go through a fairly intense period of sexual activity and experimentation in the period surrounding their divorce. They sleep with a number of different people, and for many of them (particularly those who got married relatively young) this is apparently the first occasion they have ever had the opportunity to engage in multiple sexual encounters.

As we noted earlier, although the precise statistics are cloudy (do you suppose anybody tells the truth in these surveys?), men do generally seem more prone to engage in extramarital affairs during their marriage. Another good example of this was highlighted in the California Children of Divorce Project study, which indicated that over 70 percent of the men interviewed had sexual affairs during their marriage as compared to less than 20 percent of the women. It's probably safe to infer from this that whereas the average male has probably had more sexual experiences than his wife by the time they split up, for many women (though by no means all), getting divorced often signals the commencement of a personal sexual revolution.

Over the years I've watched a number of recently separated players be thrown back into the smorgasbord of the sexual marketplace. It's not unlike watching a wholesale return to adolescence. For many of these folks, the recently singled period is characterized by fleeting and somewhat frantic sexual liaisons. Fortunately, this behavior usually subsides within a year or two following the separation.

For the majority of my clients, whatever period of post-divorce promiscuity they may undergo is usually fairly short term and often serves as a steppingstone to the return to more meaningful relationships. On the plus side, engaging in a new sexual relationship can help to bring back one's sense of self-confidence and overcome lingering fears of intimacy. Some of my clients have told me that their marriage made them feel powerless or inadequate, but that a subsequent love/sex relationship gave them an opportunity to learn more about the opposite sex—and about themselves.

When we ponder this issue of being in better touch with one's own sexuality, it is important to note that, biologically speaking, whereas almost all other species basically engage in sex for *procreation* only, humans may well be the only species (apparently with the possible exception of those perpetually giddy dolphins) who also have sex strictly for *recreation*. In fact, sexually speaking, we humans are a pretty highly evolved bunch. For example, scientists tell us that regular orgasms are essential for good health in males (reducing, as I mentioned earlier, the risk of prostate cancer by up to 50 percent!), and that the female clitoris is a particularly unique organ in that its *only* apparent function is for sexual pleasure. Studies have also shown that if couples remain sexual and make love with a fair amount of frequency, they have fewer arguments, better self-esteem and feel closer to each other. So for those folks who were stifled sexually during their marriage, perhaps a period of sexual awakening following their divorce is a positive development.

Separation: The Beginning of the End?

The only solid and lasting peace between a man and his wife is, doubtless, a separation.
   —*Lord Chesterfield*

The good news is that for those marriages that really aren't going to make it, the very act of initially separating will often provide some much-needed relief from the extreme level of stress that led to the breakup. In the California Children of Divorce Project's survey, over half of the adults responded that they felt a significant level of relief at the time of separation. Surprisingly, even some of the spouses who had initially opposed the breakup indicated that they too felt relieved.

The bad news for the separating parties is that things often get worse before they get better. I've even noticed that some of my divorcing clients are frequently functioning worse after the first year than they did during the first few months. My own observations on this issue are in line with the findings of the California Children of Divorce Project, which concluded that after separation most of the participants in the study underwent an extremely turbulent period that continued for a couple of years. In addition to documenting the fairly predictable elements of widespread anger and depression, the researchers in the California study also found substantial indications of guilt and low self-esteem on the part of the "deceivers" (i.e., those who initiated the breakup by commencing extramarital activities). Meanwhile, the "deniers" (i.e., those who opposed the divorce) seemed to suffer still worse psychic harm—even extending to high incidences of violence.

Separation . . . are we ready for this? Most of my clients (even the ones who initiate the divorce) aren't really ready, either psychologically or emotionally, to break up when they first separate. This lack of psychological preparedness seems to be the cause of many of the major emotional problems that show up during the separation. Studies support this view. In one study, only about 30 to 40 percent of the husbands and wives reported having truly been prepared for the divorce—this despite the fact that approximately half of these folks had already undergone at least one trial separation before their final breakup.

Perhaps the old quip that one of the first signs of impending divorce is pretending to fall asleep before your spouse comes to bed has some truth to it. Many people seem to prefer to ignore the impending separation and instead sleepwalk (so to speak) right up to the precipice of their impending divorce.

Divorcing Couples

Often the difference between a successful marriage and a mediocre one consists of leaving about three or four things a day unsaid.
   —*Harlan Miller*

Try as I may to be a "sensitive guy," I fully recognize the fact that I am an attorney and not a psychologist. Successful divorce lawyering requires an in-depth understanding of human behavior, however, so I began early in my career to read every psychological study of the divorce process I could get my hands on. Over the years I have tried to synthesize and distill out some of the key observations and analyses of the psychology of divorce. I will attempt to summarize them here.

Some of the most astute insights have been propounded by America's prominent marriage and family counseling professionals. Preeminent among them are Dr. Judith Wallerstein and Dr. Constance Ahrons.

Divorce's good news/bad news dichotomy. Based on the innumerable studies I have read, there appear to be two rather dramatically different schools of thought as to just how hard a psychological and emotional hit the respective parties, and their kids and family, take in a divorce. The more upbeat and positive divorce-can-be-a-plus view, as espoused by Mel Krantzler in his 1970s best seller *Creative Divorce*, is that the divorce process represents an incredible opportunity for personal growth. Krantzler's basic focus is on how much each of the spouses can grow, mature, find increased self-awareness, and perhaps even "find themselves" through a divorce.

A corollary to this upbeat analysis, best expressed by Constance Ahrons in her book *The Good Divorce*, is that the kids (as well as their divorcing parents) can use the experience of their parents' divorce as a springboard from which to leap into some exciting, new, and diverse approaches to living. The idea here is that for the children of divorce, the experiential base (and hence the opportunity for their own personal growth) essentially multiplies as an outgrowth of the fact that they will now have contact with broader extended families. These will in turn be comprised of many more numerous, varied, and unique parental and other role models to draw upon (i.e., new and different stepparents, step grandparents, half siblings, etc., from whom to learn and to grow).

A far less upbeat assessment was made by Judith Wallerstein in her book *Second Chances*. Dr. Wallerstein ran a series of follow-up studies on the divorcing parties and their children at intervals of ten, fifteen, and twenty years after the divorce had occurred. Somewhat reluctantly, she came to the startling conclusion that divorce did indeed continue to have a major, and oftentimes very negative, carryover effect upon virtually everyone who was touched by it. Furthermore, she found that this downbeat effect continued for many years longer than anyone who had previously espoused the more upbeat, "divorce-can-be-good-for-you" school of thought had been willing to admit.

The statistical data seems to be somewhat split between these two schools of thought. Apparently, just over one-half of the divorcing parties indicate that they are happier with their lives after the divorce than they were during the marriage. However, about one-third to one-quarter of divorced folks report back that the sense of overall anger and depression that they felt as an outgrowth of the divorce is still consuming them years later. This problem seems to be slightly worse for women than for men—and worse still the older the party is.

Let's face it, in the vast majority of all divorce cases, *only one* party really emerges more happy and self-satisfied in the years immediately following the divorce. The other is generally not a happy camper, at least not initially. Only in a relatively small number of the cases (perhaps only 10 or 15 percent) do *both* parties manage to emerge from the divorce having pieced together more satisfactory and fulfilling lives than they had before. This tends to support Dr. Wallerstein's findings that oftentimes the emotional hit of a divorce is a lot harder on at least one of the parties than had previously been believed.

The Uncoupling Process

The most difficult year of marriage is the one you're in.
    —Franklin P. Jones

There are a couple of different aspects involved in almost every divorce. Initially there is an overwhelming desire to break free from a marriage that has developed in at least one person's mind into a stifling, suffocating, and generally impossible situation. A second incentive that sometimes emerges a little further along down the line is a strong desire to change the very way one lives their life—to get started on recreating or redefining an entirely new personal identity or existence.

The first two or three years after divorce are generally the most stressful, but they can also be stimulating and full of growth. I have heard it said that getting divorced is almost the exact opposite mirror image of falling in love. It tends to bring out the most intense human emotions—ranging from anger to passion and love to hate. With all these emotions literally shifting actively back and forth, there can be a fair amount of opportunity that does indeed open up to change one's life.

Just whose brilliant idea was this divorce anyway? The issue of who initiates the breakup will often provide important clues to future psychological trouble in the period just after the breakup. The one who starts the divorce (often referred to as the "divorce initiator") will have been better prepared and may fare O.K. On the other hand, the spouse who gets left behind (often referred to as the "divorce resister") is usually taken by surprise. This is often followed by a lingering disbelief that it's not really going to happen. The divorce resister will be more prone to denial and hence more vulnerable to being "outfoxed" in the settlement process, or to violence or other forms of disturbed behavior.

It appears that the divorcing parties themselves feel varying degrees of either relief and liberation, or conversely, distress. This is more or less in proportion to their respective roles either in having initiated the separation or having been the one who feels dumped.

The divorce initiators seem to consciously, or at least subconsciously, welcome the arrival of the actual physical separation. Their initial reaction seems to be one of relief that the chains of marital misery and dishonesty have finally been broken. One key difference is in the timing itself. Divorce initiators often have been struggling with the notion of divorce for a long time before they finally get up the courage or energy to actually do something about it. For them, their greatest period of stress may have already passed during this interval. In a University of Colorado study of one hundred and fifty-three recently separated adults who were asking for divorce, the highest incidence of stress-related symptoms (weight change, upset stomach, nerves, headaches) had occurred during the six months before the separation.

Different ages = different emotions. People in their thirties seem to be in a crucial pivotal period insofar as just how hard they are likely to be affected by the divorce process. Women who are well into their thirties or older seem to take a dramatically harder hit from divorce than do younger women. These women have generally been married longer and have invested much more of themselves into their marriages and families. They also have older children to whom they have given their all, and it is generally much more difficult for them to focus on a new format for their life that does not center almost entirely around their marital identity.

Ironically, when divorce comes for a man in his late thirties or older it presents an entirely different picture. These men are often well established professionally and financially, and they often also benefit from the fact that their children are already a bit older—since this tends to be a plus for improving their visitation, communication, and continuity with their kids even in a noncustodial context.

Many clients have confided in me that the breakup of their marriage caused them to question their entire personal value system. They go on to point out that the level of anger inherent in a divorce is compounded by the nature of the legal process itself. It is certainly unfortunate that our country's legal system in general seems to encourage aggressive and adversarial behavior. And especially in the context of divorce court, many clients simply cannot resist the temptation to use the legal system as a vehicle for venting hostile emotions.

Do divorce courts double the damage? To compound matters, the timelines implemented in most family court systems is such that most couples are put on a fast track toward legally completing their divorce action within the first year or two following their initial breakup. Unfortunately, this is the precise time frame during which they are passing through the most angry and intense psychological period surrounding their breakup. The anxiety and trauma of litigation inevitably increase the anger level.

I wish I had a dollar for every client who has come up to me at the end of his or her divorce and said: "I thought things were just about as bad as they could get with my spouse when we *first* separated. Little did I know how much I would *really* hate him/her after that we have dragged each other through months/years of this divorce court mess." I could have retired years ago.

The Women

Bride, a woman with a fine prospect of happiness behind her.
   —*Ambrose Bierce*

Since about two-thirds of the time it is the woman who initiates the divorce, many a shrewd divorce lawyer will deliberately solicit female clients, knowing full well that they will be the ones most likely to need an attorney to get the ball rolling. Many men are apparently surprisingly happy to limp along in a bad (but at least stable) relationship. So long as a guy has his La-Z-Boy lounger, his remote control, perhaps an occasional mistress, and is getting fed three square meals a day, he is basically content. Perhaps guys just have different (lower?) standards as to just how "good" a marriage is really expected to be. Women on the other hand seem to instinctively and definitively know when their needs (the primary one being *communication*) are simply not being met. It is thus not surprising that the ladies are the ones most likely to finally act upon that instinct by initiating the actual filing for divorce.

Ironically, however, when it is the man who initiates the divorce, the wife is often more willing to go along and simply cooperate in allowing the divorce to happen. Perhaps this is because a wife in these kinds of marriages may already be conditioned to being somewhat more submissive. Conversely, when it is the woman who files for divorce, she more frequently faces very strenuous opposition to/through the entire divorce process from her husband, who still cannot resist trying to dominate the situation.

Older Women

I married beneath me. All women do.
    —*Lady Astor*

Age tends to be a crucial factor for a divorcing woman. In one of Dr. Wallerstein's studies, she came to the rather sobering finding that every woman in the study who was forty or older at the time of her marital separation remained unmarried fully ten years later. Conversely, half of their former husbands had remarried within that same ten-year period.

Tough times for older women. Many of my older female clients complain that it can be brutally difficult for them to reenter the job market in any kind of meaningful way. If they do find work, the fact that they often can get only lower-echelon jobs understandably depresses and discourages them. All of this has the cumulative effect of further reducing their self-esteem. As if this weren't bad enough, whereas their ex-husbands have the luxury of dropping down ten, fifteen, or even twenty years insofar as their dating prospects are concerned, the "talent pool" of eligible mates for women in their forties or fifties becomes notoriously shallow. According to the Census Bureau, a single woman at 40 had a 40.8 percent chance of eventually marrying.

The impact of education/career. Many experts have studied the impact of the educational status on a woman's marriage. It turns out that the divorce rate has gone down for college-educated women in the last two decades, while it has gone up for those without college. It appears that women with education and earnings have more ability to leave a bad marriage, but they also have more ability to alter the terms of an existing marriage so as to make it more durable.

As per a recent study done by Nancy Burstein, career women are now more likely than stay-at-home-moms to have marriages that endure. "The more recent and more convincing studies tend to show that women's employment and earning increase marital stability," says Ms. Burstein. Her statement would seem to contradict the arguments often cited by "family values" conservatives about the negative impact of working wives on marriage. These social conservatives are, in turn, quick to point out their own slant on statistics which show that the higher the income for working women, the higher the divorce rate.

One plus . . . older women are more resilient. Women in general often have a hypersensitivity to their own and other's feelings which is noticeably absent in many men. These are probably hardwired female traits which help guarantee the survival of their young during the long parental emergency known as child rearing. Women's more diffused attention, multi-tasking skills and focus on the abstract are all qualities which often help them adjust better and, in fact, actually soar to new heights in later life.

Indeed, there is a lot of evidence that indicates that right around age fifty is when many women can begin to take off big time. Numerous studies have shown that women in their fifties frequently show greater gains in inner harmony, life status and overall well-being than at any other time in their lives. Professional working women in particular often have great spurts in their careers during their fifties. I should note that many of these studies pertain to women in general and do not focus on the subset of divorced women, for whom things may not be quite so rosey. But overall, life may seem to go better for women as they age than it does for many men.

One of the most daunting aspects for women when they hit their sixties is the likely transition to having to live on their own. While most older males have spouses (either original or replacement) to lean on when their health fails, most elderly females do not. Women live an average of 5.3 years longer than men. (The good news for us guys is that this gap is down from about eight years just a few years ago—so we're gaining on them, fellahs.)

American women live to an average age of eighty, whereas men live on average to about 74.7 years. Actuaries use this statistical fact to justify the fact that women pay less for life insurance and more for annuities. More than nine million elderly Americans live alone; 78 percent of them are women.

Believe it or not, the average age for widowhood is seemingly way too young . . . fifty-six years old. And given the fact that the ordinary woman who reaches age sixty-five can fully expect to make it to eighty-five, that's a long time to live alone.

Younger Women

Wife: a former sweetheart.
—*H. L. Mencken*

The degree to which the divorce experience turns out to be a positive versus a negative one for a woman hinges largely upon her age at the time it occurs. I have noticed that among my clients, it is often the younger women (who divorce while still in their twenties or early thirties) who seem to be able to bounce back the most readily. In fact, these women often seem to experience a substantial amount of personal growth through the divorce process—not to mention a significant level of social and financial enhancement.

Young women on their way up. In many cases these younger women were the ones who initiated the divorce in the first place. Perhaps they matured faster than the guy they married who was with them in high school and have gone beyond his stage of development. Whereas their young husband may not yet have found satisfactory or lucrative employment, or may not be mature enough to handle the demands of fatherhood, these young women are still attractive, energetic, and upwardly mobile. They are capable of making substantial changes in their lives, including shifting to new careers, furthering their education, and ascending to lofty social circles. They are also more capable of making intelligent decisions for their second marriages than they generally were for their first (which may have come impulsively as the result of an elopement with a high school sweetheart or in response to an unplanned pregnancy).

These women often feel far less depressed about leaving the marriage than they did being in it. They may feel relieved to get out of their youthfully indiscreet first marriage, especially since they can feel confident that many of the best years of their lives still lie ahead of them. They are still young and attractive and are often successful at meeting eligible men to date or remarry. They may be particularly attractive to older, well-established men looking for a youthful second wife.

Frankly, it would be difficult to overstate the importance of each gender's most basic (base?) instincts when analyzing what the primary sources of attraction, at least *initially*, are between men and women. Although it is probably too politically incorrect to admit it in "official" studies, a majority of men have consistently responded to confidential surveys by conceding that the first thing which initially attracts him to a woman is her beauty and physical appearance. Female breasts in particular are apparently a specific primary draw. Men prefer women with large breasts and low waist-to-hip ratios, both of which are seen as indicators of fertility. This is presumably good news for younger women. (Conversely, women are apparently biologically driven to gravitate toward men with muscular shoulders, a broad chest, a full beard and deeper voices . . . all of which they see as signs of high testosterone and virility.)

Meanwhile, a smaller, but still substantial, plurality of women when queried "off the record" will admit that a primary (if not *the* primary) thing that may attract them to a man (again, at least *initially*) is the aura of wealth, power and success. This is presumably good news for older, more-established men.

Undoubtedly, many members of both genders do function on loftier levels and seek more serious and substantial qualities in their mates. Thus, it obviously represents a gross (literally) over-generalization to say that "men want beauty, and women want bucks" and I certainly don't want to be cast as a chauvinist pig here, but I am simply reporting to my readers what respondents to these confidential surveys themselves report.

In any event, when they do remarry, these young women often have a much better idea as to what they are looking for—and it often represents a vast improvement over their first choice. No more is there a desperate marriage to their first high school boyfriend; rather, there is an upwardly mobile marriage to one of their superiors at work, or to a successful professional in some field related to their new employment. Statistics indicate that the vast majority of these young women remarry—most often within the first five years or so following their divorce.

Lately, I have observed a growing trend in which women in the late thirties to early forties age group seem to be leaving their husbands in droves. These women seem to instinctively sense that their youth is somehow fading and to be viewing this as their last chance to "change the course" of their lives as they transition from being desirable young ladies toward becoming middle-age matrons. If the first tick of their biological clock occurred for these women during their primary childbearing years in their twenties and early thirties, then it appears that a second tick nowadays seems to occur around age forty. Perhaps these young ladies are pursuing one last hope or dream of obtaining the better life they somehow vaguely felt they deserved. The midlife crisis used to be the prerogative of men, but for the modern working woman, the approach of age 40 seems to have turned the midlife crisis into a woman's issue as well.

My own observations concerning this discombobulating scenario in which midlife crises seem to hit women as they head into their forties (thereby often upending their marriages) have been borne out by recent studies which found that both men and women in their forties are generally more likely to struggle with depression. Two prominent economists, Andrew Oswald and David Blanchflower, conducted an extensive international study of two million people from eighty nations. They concluded that middle age (i.e., midlife per se) is such a low point for well-being that it's in fact at the very bottom of a U-shaped curve where greater happiness exists among both the younger and the older ends of the spectrum. Mr. Oswald theorizes that the forties is the time when people tend to become depressed as they reluctantly realize that the path of their life's actual achievements hasn't measured up to their youthful aspirations/expectations (i.e., shouldn't I have a better life, better husband, better wife . . . by now?). For both genders, the probability of depression peaks around age 44 . . . right about when I notice so many of my young and vaguely dissatisfied female clients wanting to bail out of their marriages—what a coincidence! Rather than getting divorced, however, perhaps a more realistic approach would be to follow Mr. Oswald's advice when he says, "If you are finding life tough in your forties, maybe it's useful to know that this is completely normal."

One bit of good news for divorcing women of any age pertains to a potentially fulfilling maternal role as a divorced mom. My experience has been that the relationship between a custodial mother and her kids may grow to be even closer following the divorce than it was in the original intact family.

The Men

Husbands never become good, they merely become proficient.
       —H. L. Mencken

As we have seen, men don't generally initiate more than about one-third of all divorce cases. Men seem instinctively less inclined to rock the boat. They may screw up, screw around, or whatever, but they tend to try and keep their marital structure intact along the way. It is no coincidence, therefore, that when it is the man who initiates the divorce, his "raison de divorce" often has to do with his already having another woman waiting in the wings. In fact, this particular other woman will usually already have been prequalified as a serious subsequent relationship, i.e., the next wife. If she were anything less, the guy would likely have just stayed married and fooled around.

Older Men

Many a man has fallen in love with a girl in a light so dim he would not have chosen a suit by it.
       —Charles Bukowski

For successful older men, or for those who are the initiators of the divorce action, divorce often seems to be easily handled and even welcome. This may stem from the fact that power (whether measured in dollars or brawn) is an aphrodisiac in all societies. According to evolutionary psychologists, women instinctively seek the protection, resources, and genes of successful men. Subconsciously at least, men seek success in order to attract women.

The cost of alimony was a running joke for comedian Johnny Carson, who by age sixty-eight had married four times (each wife being at least six years younger than her predecessor). Texas oil baron J. Howard Marshall acquired new wives at thirty-year intervals, marrying his first in 1931, his second in 1961, and ex-Playboy playmate Anna Nicole Smith in 1995. Aristotle Onassis was sixty-two when he married his second wife, thirty-nine-year-old Jacqueline Kennedy. Billionaire J. Paul Getty was married and divorced five times. Said he, "A lasting relationship with a woman is only possible if you are a business failure."

On the economic front overall, the news may not be too bad for older men who divorce. Studies have consistently shown that a man's standard of living rises approximately 40 percent following divorce, whereas a woman's may drop off by up to 70 percent.

Older, poorer, dumped guys have less fun. A less auspicious scenario is in store for older men who are somewhat less successful or who are the dumpees in situations where their wives have left them. For some men, their personal and social success is often defined by their marriage. This may seem somewhat ironic in view of survey results which indicate that only about 39 percent of husbands interviewed considered themselves "relationship centered," rather than work centered, compared with 59 percent of the wives. A traditional husband often got away with paying less attention to the actual quality of his relationship because he believed he could still rely on his wife to keep the home front together regardless of whether the marriage itself was picture perfect. This is an increasingly dangerous assumption nowadays.

Low self-esteem is common among men whose mates leave them. Men are much more fragile than women when it comes to coping with these role changes. A man can lose his pride. Once that happens, he may begin to experience performance anxiety. When a man's self-image suffers, sexual dysfunction is always a possibility.

By way of an overview, let's take a quick look at the basic trajectory that men's lives take as they grow up and grow old. Young men from their teens to their forties are hard wired to be somewhat single-minded *competitors*. From cave man days onward, guys were designed to be physical, to literally be warriors, and not to waste a lot of downtime on introspection or emotion. This gets reinforced all along the way as young men compete at everything from making sports teams to climbing the corporate ladder. So, what most men want to do as they hit middle age is to stay put where they are, to stick to their old habits and keep what they've got. They don't really want to make what author Gail Sheehy has so presciently referred to as "a Passage" to something new and different.

Thus, men at middle life probably face the roughest patch of all in mapping their new adult lives across time. Generally, it is a much harder passage for men than for women. The psychic compensation is also greater for women because they started with so much less. Men already had the good jobs and the greater authority in the family. To make a passage to what Ms. Sheehy calls the Age of Mastery often means, for men, giving up being the master.

Especially nowadays, and for the first time since World War II, men in their late forties and early fifties are suffering a steep decline in wages. Today men in their fifties in corporate life are in a precarious position. They are a high-ticket item in a era of downsizing. Ever since the mid-1980s, layers of middle management have been stripped away in company after company. In fact, current studies clearly indicate that nowadays once a man hits age forty—not even fifty—getting a job in the business world becomes immeasurably more difficult.

It doesn't take all that enormous an extrapolation of these trends to realize that men in middle or late-middle life today may become increasingly dependent on their wives for financial help. Consider the fact that as men continue to drop out of the work force at ever earlier ages (fewer than 40 percent of all American men age fifty and over are still salaried job holders nowadays), women are meanwhile toiling longer and later. By the mid 1990s, almost half of all American women age fifty-five to sixty-four were still in the work force, compared to 41 percent fifteen years before.

As they take up the slack in household income, women are also exerting greater control over the purse strings. Amazingly, by the mid-1990s almost a third of those American women who worked full-time earned more than their working spouses, according to the Bureau of Labor Statistics . . . and one would have to be awfully naïve to think that fact alone doesn't change the very nature of modern interspousal relations.

In my lectures, I often talk about the phenomenon of the quote *"Save-Your-Life Wife."* It turns out that men, almost invariably, need a partner. When it comes to romance, men tend to be first in and last out. Men generally fall in love more quickly, more easily and more viscerally (i.e., often based upon raw physical attraction). Ironically, men may be more romantic (at least initially) than women—they just want to fall in love and be in love. Women on the other hand have a lengthier and far more specific set of criteria that they want to see met.

Married men from the ages of forty-five to sixty-four are twice as likely to live ten years longer than their unmarried counterparts. Unmarried men in this age group are also twice as susceptible to depression and even suicide. Fully 94% of men surveyed said they would be happier married than single.

The happiest men (and presumably the ones most likely to be most attractive to their mates) are those who move from devoting most of their energy to competing and sexual conquest to devoting more of their energy to finding emotional intimacy and trust, and companionship and community with others. I see this as the essential task for men in middle life: to move from competing to connecting.

Moving from competing to connecting. Gail Sheehy has analyzed this phenomenon in her iconic *Passages* book. She found that the good news is that once men over fifty have made this admittedly difficult transition, they seem to be pretty happy campers. They indicate that they feel closer than ever before to their wives. Nearly all have developed passions or hobbies that happily occupy and challenge them outside their workday routines. Almost half of all men in their mid-fifties describe themselves as being "pleased" or "delighted" with the state of their lives as a whole. This was not true in their mid-forties, when almost half went through a depressive or "midlife crisis" period. As their power orientation subsides in their fifties, the happiest men grow noticeably more expressive and sensuous, more gregarious and likable. They've cultivated their feminine sides and are more intuitive, too!

The point of this brief outline of the "life course trajectory" of the modern male is to remind my guy readers of the qualities that may make life easier for both themselves and their mates as they age as gracefully as possible. These pointers are equally applicable whether they are trying to hang onto an existing relationship or hoping to make themselves more attractive for a new one.

Kiss daddy good-bye. Let's take a sobering look at the agonizing phenomenon of a father having to deal with the pain of having his children ripped away from him. Dr. Wade Horn of the National Fatherhood Initiative publishes the following somewhat shocking statistics in his booklet *Father Facts.* The United States is now the world's leader in fatherless families. We took over first place from Sweden in 1986. Some 40 percent of America's children do not live with their biological fathers. It is estimated that 55 percent to 60 percent of all children born in the 1990s will spend part of their childhood living apart from their fathers. Some 40 percent of those children who live with their mothers have not seen their fathers in at least a year. One-fifth of divorced mothers have responded to surveys by blithely stating that they see no value in a father's contact with his children. Of that number, many try to outright sabotage the father's attempts to see his children. Only one in six children of divorced or separated parents sees the father at least once a week. Ten years after divorce, only one in ten children has weekly contact with the father.

Fatherless families. The long-term societal costs of these fatherless families may prove to be horrific. Of the juveniles in state reform institutions, 70 percent grew up in single-parent or no-parent situations. Fatherless children are twice as likely to drop out of school than are their peers who live with both parents. Studies have shown fatherless children to be at a dramatically greater risk of suicide, mental illness, drug and alcohol abuse, poor academic performance, pregnancy, and criminality.

Younger Men

Bachelor: a thing of beauty and a boy forever.
　　—*Helen Rowland*

I've represented lots of young guys over the years who got divorced in their twenties or early thirties. My experience with them indicates that these fellows seem to have a much rougher go of things than do divorcing women of their comparable age group. In the majority of cases these men were on the receiving end of a divorce action initiated by their wives. Oftentimes, these guys were continuing merrily along during the first few years following their marriage to drink, party, and carouse with their youthful, exuberant, male-bonded buddies. This behavior seemed to them to be a perfectly normal carryover from high school or college, but was beginning to be viewed as childish by their more rapidly maturing young wives. Several of these guys didn't seem quite ready for fatherhood in their early twenties, and this undoubtedly contributed to some of their problems if they had kids early on.

Ironically, once these playful and undisciplined young bucks get divorced, the real world hits them hard and fast. They find themselves saddled with child-support responsibilities (often when they are still at their low earning stage and unable to afford much). Furthermore, their now noncustodial kids are often still toddlers whom they may visit only infrequently. (The temptation seems to be stronger on the part of a custodial mom to limit the dad's visitation with an infant or a very young child than she would if the child were in its teens.)

Forced male maturity through divorce? Young men in this situation are often left in a fairly miserable state. They are often shocked to find out, too late, that their now ex-wives have suddenly begun to place more of a premium on maturity and social and economic stability in their mates. These young women are no longer enamored with their husbands' aging "party animal" behavior, and may have left in search of a more established and dependable career man. Meanwhile, the poor jilted young husband has had a tough time getting established financially and still hasn't put together a stable career. According to a study by the Pew Charitable Trust, the median inflation-adjusted income for a man in his thirties in 2004 was 12 percent *lower* than it was in 1974. Statistically speaking, a young fellow at this stage may well get remarried within the first couple of years following his first divorce, but only to find that somewhere between 70 to 80 percent of these second marriages follow right along in the failed tracks of the first.

The divorced younger man may simply have a harder time putting together the viable life-support system needed to keep a wife and stable family intact. He still doesn't own his own home and hasn't got a good job. Worse still, he may be having a difficult time establishing workable visitation and communication with his kids. If, as is often the case, his kids were extremely young when the divorce occurred, there may never have been a sufficient opportunity to put together the kind of strong relationship between child and father that would otherwise have already developed had the divorce taken place later.

Young dads missing young kids. If the divorce occurred when the child was old enough to have developed a close and verbally communicative relationship with the dad prior to the parents separating (i.e., any age beyond about six to eight), the likelihood is increased that a strong father-child relationship can be maintained. If not, then these young men may well suffer the twin trauma of being divorced from their kids as well as their spouses.

The structure of the child visitation framework is more difficult and unsatisfactory for young guys in this situation since the really positive part of a young father's continuing pride in being a dad may never have quite gotten off the ground. Again, perhaps this was due to the young age of the children at the time of divorce, or maybe it was deliberately forced onto the back burner by the exiting wife who may have intended the divorce to be a complete break (perhaps based on the unfortunate, but not uncommon, theory that since the kids are still young they probably won't remember much anyway). Instead, the dad is left feeling like an automatic cash machine spitting out child-support payments for out-of-sight and out-of-mind, absentee kids. This, in turn, becomes a factor that puts still more pressure (economic and otherwise) on trying to maintain a successful second marriage. All in all, a pretty bleak picture emerges for this cross section of young divorcing males.

Unhappy campers. The preceding section obviously consists of some overbroad and imprecise generalizations—but suffice it to say, these young divorced guys who have been reluctantly wrenched away from their wives and kids are among the least happy campers of all my clients.

One plus, however, is that for young men emerging from a recent divorce, one of the trickier tasks they finally get to (are forced to?) master is "advanced" parenting skills. Many young men tell me that they belatedly discover the more maternal or female side of themselves while caring solo for their children during custodial or visitation periods.

The Economics of Divorce

By all means marry. If you get a good wife, you will become very happy. If you get a bad one, you will become a philosopher—and that is good for any man.
     —*Socrates*

Divorce makes everybody poorer—at least initially. The California Children of Divorce Project found that three-fifths of the men and three-quarters of the women underwent significant declines in their standards of living commencing abruptly after separation. The major difference is that men rebound faster. Numerous recent studies show that the adverse long-term economic ramifications of divorce are much worse for women than for men.

Women suffer significant economic losses following divorce. Surveys show that women's family incomes drop by an average of about 20 percent in the first year after dissolution. This compares particularly unfavorably to the average first-year losses of less than 10 percent for men (which are in turn often followed by rapid rebounds). These losses are even greater in comparison to intact couples who gain about 17 percent during that same time frame.

Largely due to successful remarriages, some women appear to regain their prior economic status within five years. Women in low-income households actually improve their economic status on average following a divorce, but those in previously high-income households suffer losses of up to 50 percent or more. Meanwhile, the man has oftentimes increased his standard of living by a substantial margin.

Even those women who are entitled to receive money following their divorce have a hard time collecting it. Of those women who get divorced and are entitled to child-support payments, only about three-fourths actually receive them. Even then, only half receive full payment. Women below the poverty level are even less likely to receive payment. Nationwide statistics from the late 1980s indicate that average child-support payments received in a year ranged from about $2,000 to $3,000 (depending upon the number of children). This amount had not changed much between 1978 and 1987. It should be noted, however, that child-support levels have increased substantially since the early 1990s.

Neither can most women look to spousal support to save the day. Only about 15 percent of divorced women nationwide are awarded alimony (in Hawai'i it's less than 10 percent). Worse still, only about 5 percent are actually receiving their full court-ordered payments.

How about a little economic fairness for women? There is a significant movement afoot nowadays to try to equalize the economic disparity that occurs following divorce wherein women almost inevitably seem to take a much bigger hit economically speaking than do men. Many sociologists have now come to feel that the whole idea of no-fault divorce is a real mistake for society and are now rethinking the whole philosophical underpinnings of the no-fault concept. The concern is that it encourages divorce and severely disadvantages women.

There is, in fact, a sizable movement afoot to take a gender-fairness approach to analyzing the alimony and property issues in divorce cases. Something of this sort has already occurred in the child-support area. Judges and legislators have finally gotten sick of seeing husbands failing to pay court-ordered child support and have tightened up the amounts of the collections and the enforcement procedures.

It has been particularly difficult for me on a personal level to watch some of my favorite female clients begin to literally circle the financial drain during the years following their divorces. About all that any divorce lawyer can realistically do for their increasingly impoverished female clients at this post-divorce juncture is to go back into court for support increases—not exactly a satisfactory solution.

CHAPTER 4
Kids in Crisis

The most important thing a father can do for his children is to love their mother.

—*The Reverend Theodore Hesburgh*

The number of children involved in divorce has tripled in three decades. More than a million children are now affected by a divorce each year. Twenty-eight percent of kids under eighteen now live with only one parent—this compared to only 12 percent as recently as 1970. Recent estimates suggest that over half of all children being born today can expect to experience some aspect of marital disruption, either because their parents will divorce—or will never marry.

Compare this with prior generations. In 1900, about 22 percent of all children would experience the death of a parent during their childhood, but only about 5 percent would have their parents divorce. By the 1950s, however, only about 8 to 9 percent of the children born during that decade would lose their parents to death—whereas over 10 percent would see their parents divorce. Historically, children have always experienced the disruption of their parents' marriages, but now the form of that disruption has changed. Unfortunately, whereas the premature death of a parent can present some potential for positive and accelerated growth for a child (an adolescent boy taking over as the "man of the house" for his deceased father, for example), there is little evidence that this accelerated maturation is anywhere near as likely to occur for the children of divorce.

For kids, divorce isn't cool. As I have frequently reminded my clients, they must realize that the entire experience of divorce is a vastly different deal for their kids than it is for them. Frankly, I can't blame clients for thinking that since they feel the divorce is basically good, encourages growth, or is liberating for them, therefore it should somehow magically extend to including positive elements for their kids as well. Unfortunately, it does not follow that an adult who feels liberated after a divorce will necessarily become a better parent.

The sad irony is that the more happy and self-involved recently divorced parents become with their own life, the less likely they are to be fully available to their children. Furthermore, whereas divorcing adults are usually at least somewhat aware of the problems within their relationship (and thus are rarely completely surprised by a forthcoming divorce), the kids often have no clue. For them, the element of surprise is total and dismaying.

Kids can often be quite happy and oblivious to their parents' problems, even while mom and dad are in the midst of their deepest marital misery. Thus, it was not really surprising when Judith Wallerstein found that only one in ten children in her study experienced any sense of relief upon their parents' divorce. Instead, the primary response of children to divorce is fear. They become extremely fearful of being left on their own and feel very vulnerable. It is almost as though they have an instinctive sense that somehow their familial life-support system is being cut out from underneath them.

Hey wait, that's my life you're ruining. Regardless of their age, almost any child is bound to feel an intense sense of rejection when their parents divorce. Whereas adults may see it as one parent simply needing to leave the other and move on, the children interpret the act as including them (i.e., "She left Dad, she must not care much about me either. In fact, she may someday leave me, too."). Kids get angry at their parents for breaking what Dr. Wallerstein describes as an unwritten rule of parenthood—"parents are supposed to make sacrifices for children, not the other way around." Suddenly, no one gives priority to their needs, desires, and doubts. Children of divorce feel intense loneliness, extreme conflicts in their loyalty between parents, and also a severe sense of guilt. I had one client whose little girl quite literally thought the divorce was all her fault and said, "Daddy wouldn't have left us if I had just cleaned up my room like he told me to do."

Children also tend to be rather obstinate in their refusal to accept the finality of the divorce. Particularly if the actual divorce has been preceded by numerous separations, each of which seemed cataclysmic at the time, but ultimately turned out not to be final, it is not surprising that a child will tend to view divorce as somehow being a *reversible* process.

In fact, many children of divorcing families apparently do not believe that the divorce is really happening until a year or so later. Then, even after it becomes final, many children still refuse to accept the divorce and are instead hoping and fantasizing that their parents will reconcile. I have seen this behavior continue even as long as five to ten years after the divorce.

Unlike their parents, kids do not view divorce as an event accompanied by any positive aspects whatsoever. They feel unfairly robbed of their own kid-focused childhood. Divorce is the price they pay for their parents' failures. Ultimately, divorce may indeed be a positive opportunity for children, since there is considerable evidence that a conflict-ridden marriage is by no means in the best interest of the children. But kids certainly do not see it that way at the outset.

All along the way, growing up tends to be tougher on children of divorce. Their own evolving young lives tend to get overshadowed by the enormity of their parents' divorces. All the kid wants is for his dad to be at his Saturday ball game cheering for him. Unfortunately, dad is now spending Saturdays looking for a new apartment. Furthermore, these kids often get deprived of a wide range of economic, logistical, financial, and psychological supports that they could otherwise have expected as entitlements if their folks had stayed together.

The kids' conclusions. One discernible phenomenon that seems to result is that children of divorce embrace a morality that is more conservative than that of their parents. They want to achieve what their parents did not—a good, long-term, committed marriage. They want romance, fidelity, and permanency in their own relationships. They are somewhat more careful, perhaps inclined to live together before getting married and not to marry too young. Kids who are products of divorced families become extremely concerned about their own ability to preserve lasting relationships as they grow older. On the one hand, they seem to hunger for some kind of stable relationship, but based upon their own frame of reference, they are scared stiff about ever being able to achieve it. A divorce tends to fundamentally change the nature of the relationship between children and their parents. I frequently witness role reversals in my clients' kids where the children will begin to compensate by assuming responsibilities far in excess of what is normal for their ages.

The Children of Divorce

Americans, indeed, often seem to be so overwhelmed by their children that they'll do anything for them except stay married to the co-producer.
  —*Katharine Whitehorn*

Children of divorce often literally feel that one or both parents acted badly. They can remain critical of their parents for years thereafter and continue to blame them for having betrayed the marriage. Generally speaking, these children tend to feel less of a sense of entitlement than do other kids. They know from harsh experience that their individual needs may well be considered a lower family priority. Gone are the days when they could expect mom to be their personal chauffeur to every game. Instead these kids are forced to accept and understand conditions set down by a hurried and harried single parent: they have to share with their siblings, their restructured family's resources are limited, and they must shoulder responsibilities that would normally be beyond their years.

Adults seem to have come to treat divorce as one of life's inalienable rights. Many are quick to jettison a marriage or relationship if it fails to meet their needs or expectations—and rarely feel compelled to blame themselves in the process. Children, however, tend to place a fair amount of blame on their parents for having failed at one of the primary responsibilities in life. The kids feel they have been put on hold while the adults selfishly focus on their own individual lives rather than on the family unit.

Deflecting the damage. In the course of my practice, I obviously come into contact with huge numbers of kids whose parents are divorcing. Based on my experience, I can submit the following capsulized observations: (1) Most kids seem to absolutely detest the entire divorce process and are particularly upset at where it leaves them in its wake. (2) Although there are undoubtedly some children who feel relieved to have their parents separate rather than continue to scream and shout around the house, the old myth that kids are better off with one parent who "really cares," versus staying in a tension-fraught household after a marriage has gone bad, seems to be increasingly discredited. On the contrary, surprising numbers of kids report back that, from their perspectives, they would have preferred that their parents had simply stayed together and continued arguing and fighting rather than having separated in order to "spare them" from witnessing further supposed stress. (3) Certainly there are at least some kids who do experience substantial amounts of personal growth following their parents' divorce. This seems to be due primarily to the multiplicity of diverse and often positive new inputs they receive from a newly extended family and all the extra sources of stimulation and role modeling that it brings with it. (This is the more positive theory advanced by Dr. Constance Ahrons—and many of us in the divorce profession would love to be able to believe it.) (4) Unfortunately, the cold, hard statistics seem to indicate that at least half the kids in a divorce context suffer serious depression, lack of self-confidence, a dramatic decline in their academic performance, and a higher tendency toward rebellious or delinquent behavior than do their peers from intact families. (5) One somewhat ironic but presumably positive outgrowth of all this seems to be that Gen-Xers of both genders appear to have come away having a real commitment to marriage because so many of them watched their parents divorce.

In fact, the argument can be made that divorce is a far more destructive and emotionally ruinous phenomenon for the children than it is for their parents. After all, at least one of the parents is usually somewhat happy about the divorce since, by definition, it served a function that at least one of them felt was necessary. But there are virtually no positive benefits flowing to the children from a divorce.

Let's face it, divorce almost inevitably results in a reduced level of parenting focus or capability. Divorcing parents tend to spend less time physically with their kids and are less attentive to their needs. In fact, statistics consistently demonstrate that kids from divorced families have higher school absentee rates and lower academic scores. Studies have also shown that children who grow up in hostile home environments are more likely to begin having sex earlier and more frequently and to display more problem behaviors across the board.

There seems to be no question that most kids feel they have gotten a really raw deal when their parents divorce. They sense that they are going to get far less attention to their needs just at the time when they feel their maturation process ought to be taking center stage in the family theater. Instead, they are frequently called upon to assume a far greater amount of responsibility around the house and within the new (but not necessarily improved) family structure. Their parents are so consumed by their own desires or problems that the needs of the children take a back seat. Meanwhile, the family finances often take a horrendous downward spiral, and the kids tend to get less all the way around. They get less of their parents' attention and time availability, and also less in the way of financial and emotional support.

Let me conclude by shining a slightly brighter ray of light on the process. Research shows that it's not the occurrence of the divorce per se that affects children, but the quality of their lives after the divorce. This, in turn, depends upon the parents' adjustment to the breakup and upon the degree to which the child manages to maintain a good and ongoing relationship with *both* parents. So the moral of the story is that when parents focus on a rapid, intelligent, and positive resumption of their own lives and their communication with one another, they can vastly lessen the negative impact of their divorce upon their children.

Boys

The only time a woman really succeeds in changing a man is when he is a baby.
—*Natalie Wood*

Boys seem to have a more difficult time handling and recovering from a divorce than do girls. This seems to be especially true during the initial period right after their parents separate. Boys tend to be unhappy and somewhat lonely during the years immediately following their parents' divorce. Also, during these years, they seem to have fewer lasting relationships with young girls. Their socialization process seems to get shelved or a bit sidetracked.

Preschool-age boys in particular have to deal with another spin on the divorce situation, stemming from the fact that they are quite understandably in love with their mothers and often tend to feel rivalry with their fathers. This of course is a totally normal psychological phenomenon for young boys at this developmental stage—but imagine how badly it gets compounded by a divorce.

It's not easy being a boy. Many of my clients tell me that boys who are in the six- to eight-year-old range at the time when their parents divorce have an especially tough time adjusting. A disproportionately high number of these young boys seem to have trouble concentrating in school. They seem to withdraw from their peers, get into fights, and just generally start to lose ground rapidly, both socially and academically, during the post-divorce period.

Psychologists suspect that much of this behavior is related to the boy's anxiety at being left in the custody of his mother, just at the stage when he is or should be developing a strong identification with his father and consolidating his own masculinity. In fact, psychologists make the general point that many young boys in this situation are likely to blame their mothers when things go wrong. Some of these boys will exhibit fairly aggressive behavior and may refuse to do household chores or schoolwork.

Young boys seem to be having a pretty tough time of it in general these days and a divorce occurring right in the middle of their maturation process probably doesn't help. A number of recent findings are red flags that tend to foster the collective "boys are in trouble" alarmist concerns. No one seems to deny that girls are academically superior as a group. More boys than girls are in special education classes. Boys don't read as well as girls. Additionally, far more boys than girls are prescribed mood-managing drugs. More boys than girls drop out of high school.

Other indices abound which seem to show that boys are stumbling ever further behind their female counterparts. A smaller number of boys than girls take the SAT. Fewer boys than girls apply to college. Thus, fewer boys than girls are earning college degrees nowadays.

Monitors of the "boy crisis" contend that they are not just slipping through the cracks only in the area of academics. In many ways, it appears that families, schools and popular culture are all failing our boys, leaving them restless bundles of angst-filled malcontents in the classroom and video-game junkies at home. Two extreme examples seem to convey this point: It is not girls who are shooting up classrooms—it is boys. And sadly, boys are at least five times as likely as girls to die by suicide.

One way our society might try to pull its young boys out of this seemingly downward spiral would be to take a strong interest in them *before* they get into trouble. Boys seem to experience a strong and growing need for their fathers during adolescence, and for the sons of divorcing parents this need seems particularly intense. Perhaps the most powerful need for any adolescent male at this time is for a strong relationship with his dad, which can give him confidence to loosen the Oedipal ties with his mom.

As young men, these sons of divorce seem to be awkward with women and tend to shy away from dating. In fact, they are somewhat more reserved psychologically speaking and tend to hold back from relationships in general. Many of these young men seem worried that they won't find true love. Some seem to be disproportionately likely to commit too rapidly to the first serious relationship they stumble across—preferably one that gives high priority to issues such as trust and fidelity.

Girls

Before I got married I had six theories about bringing up children; now I have six children, and no theories.
    —*John Wilmot, Earl of Rochester*

Girls seem to fare much better psychologically during the period immediately following their parents' divorce than do boys. In fact, much of the research about the effects of divorce on children points out the relatively good recovery of girls as compared with the more troubled experiences faced by the boys. Boys generally appear to suffer more from divorce, especially initially, although the risk factors and negative impacts seem to equalize more over the long term. In general, daughters appear to better adjust socially, academically, and emotionally following divorce than do their brothers.

This is not to say that girls don't encounter some serious problems of their own. One peculiar but predictable twist in the relationship between single mothers and their daughters can occur when the daughter begins to feel a sense of responsibility for looking after her mom. At this juncture, a young girl will often develop advanced homemaking skills and take on other "super-womanly" responsibilities far beyond her years. Later, however, this can become problematic, since the already difficult period when a young girl must finally leave home can become even more wrenching if an extreme degree of closeness has developed between the mother and the daughter.

Can girls cope? Daughters of divorce, particularly in a situation where they watch their faithful, devoted homemaker mother face the ultimate rejection of divorce by their father, can develop some very dramatic reactions. These can range across the board from total rebellion and self-destruction, to immersion in sex, drugs, and rock 'n' roll—all in an effort to "not be like mom" and hence run the risk of facing her same fate. Alternatively, another manifestation can be an almost phobic desire for commitment, which can, in turn, result in an early or rushed marriage in an effort to avoid ever having to face being alone.

Not surprisingly, daughters whose fathers have left their mothers are often plagued by an intense fear of being rejected themselves. They can develop a severe terror of being alone or without a man. They can use whatever means they have at their disposal to try to increase the likelihood that guys will love rather than leave them.

One of the seemingly most effective methods girls have at their disposal (insofar as insuring their continued attractiveness to men) is to become extremely promiscuous in their sexual activities—often at a very early age. These girls may mistakenly separate out their desire to have "a relationship" (i.e., *any* relationship) from any expectation of real love. This phenomenon can be compounded if the divorce occurs while the young girl is undergoing her own adolescence and trying to sort out her own rapidly burgeoning sexuality.

Many young women from divorced families seem to live with an inordinately high level of anxiety about impending betrayal in their own romantic relationships. This can take the form of fear of getting initially involved, a fear of commitment, or even of extreme jealousy.

Girls who fear betrayal may find adaptive ways to cope. Some take multiple lovers simultaneously as insurance. Others seek out older men who are ostensibly less likely to betray a younger woman. (Another aspect of this particular motivation to get involved with an older man may be the young woman's psychological search for a parent figure.)

Young girls, while perhaps appearing initially to handle divorce better than boys, seem to have a later resurgence of psychological problems. These may well be related to the effect of the divorce on their development. The signs can manifest themselves fairly traumatically when the young girl hits her late teens or early twenties and finds herself facing a phobia about commitment. Some overcommit too quickly, perhaps turning into "loose women" with lax sexual standards. Others clam up and cannot commit at all.

Different Ages = Different Impacts

Never lend your car to anyone to whom you have given birth.
　　—*Erma Bombeck*

A child's initial response to a parent's divorce will hinge largely upon such factors as the child's age, gender, and general stage of development at the time the divorce occurs.

Infants and Toddlers

In general my children refused to eat anything they hadn't seen on TV.
　　—*Erma Bombeck*

Infants, toddlers, and preschoolers tend to be extremely dependent upon their parents for their actual daily physical care, maintenance, and feeding. Not surprisingly, this group feels the most threatened and fearful of total abandonment when their parents first separate. They may cry when left alone, have difficulty sleeping through the night, become inexplicably irritable or even physically aggressive. They are quite literally terrified. Every effort needs to be made at this stage to reassure children that their physical and personal safety and care will remain intact. It is paramount that kids at this stage be reassured concerning their own physical security . . . knowing where they will live, who will feed, clothe and care for them, etc.

Abandonment angst. For very young children, the biggest fear is one of total abandonment. They have watched one parent leave, and it is an entirely logical and legitimate concern to their way of thinking that if one parent can leave, then why not the other?

These younger kids are fearful of being deserted by both parents (i.e., of being physically left or abandoned). They may cry inexplicably and become truly terrified when left alone for even the briefest periods. Once they are over this initial hump, however, most of these kids come to realize that they will continue to be fed, housed, and cared for after all. In fact, these younger kids may actually recover somewhat more easily from their parents' divorce, at least psychologically speaking, than do their older siblings.

Grade School and Early Childhood

Children today are tyrants. They contradict their parents, gobble their food, and tyrannize their teachers.
          —Socrates

Kids who are in elementary school (ranging approximately from kindergarten to grade four) tend to have a more intuitively mental and quizzical response to their parents' separation (though undoubtedly much of this is subconscious). Their brains have become developed enough that they worry more about cause and effect. These kids may feel either extremely rejected or guilty, thinking that perhaps they were the ones who made mom or dad leave home. This is also the stage when kids tend to fantasize excessively about the family being rejoined someday.

Kids choosing sides. As children approach the end of elementary school (about ages nine or ten), they become more externally and visibly angry about the divorce (as compared to the more *in*ternalized sense of anger experienced by kids aged five through eight). They can become extremely, and vocally, angry. This unleashed anger is often directed particularly at the parent whom they blame for having caused the divorce. Kids at this stage are particularly susceptible to aligning themselves with one parent against the other. They are willing, and even anxious, to take sides in the divorce. After all, they are themselves at a stage when the linear or logic side of their mental development is just germinating. Thus they tend to see things in rather black-and-white terms. Not surprisingly, the performance of kids at this stage (in the contexts of both school work and relations with their peers) can sometimes drop precipitously during a divorce.

These kids have the clearest memory of the family during its fully functional days. Hence, they are the ones who feel the greatest sense of loss and trauma at seeing it shattered. They often also take the brunt of having to shoulder extra household chores and other physical and emotional responsibilities around the house. (Not the least of these is trying to stay supportive of their remaining parent.) Children in this age group seem to be the most willing to place blame when their family faces a divorce—since they have a much clearer sense of what they are about to lose.

Kids from the ages of about nine or ten, and continuing into their early teens, seem to be the most prone to taking sides in their parents' divorce. They can become outraged in their condemnation of the parent whom they view as having initiated the divorce. They may have zero tolerance of that parent's new relationship(s) and be more than willing to serve as spies in obtaining information about one parent's activities on behalf of the other. Neither are they shy about scolding the one parent who, in their view, jeopardized the continuity of their childhood. This is not necessarily a short-lived phenomenon. I have seen kids carry these sorts of grudges against their parents for literally years.

I once watched a jilted wife and her children become allies in an ongoing battle against the departing husband that continued for several years. A tragic aspect of these situations is the way a child may be thoroughly brainwashed and used as an instrument of revenge by a disgruntled parent. One of the saddest things we divorce lawyers see is such attempts to punish the ex via the children.

Mini adults. Children of nine, ten or eleven who might normally warrant a few more years of babysitters and supervision are often placed on a fast track to ostensible maturity. They are frequently left alone at home without adult supervision, watching TV, playing video games, and microwaving frozen food. Meanwhile, mom struggles to get her life back on track, to reenter the job market after a ten-year or so hiatus, and to handle her own very difficult time and organizational demands. Amazingly enough, many of the kids seem to be able to pull it off. One hears of the role reversal, where the child becomes the parent—trying to stay supportive of their mom or pop, who remains emotionally vulnerable.

When I watch such superkids emerge following their parents' divorce, I am amazed and impressed by their seeming ability to handle all this. But I can't help but wonder what price is being paid in terms of their sacrifice of their own development along a normal childhood track.

Adolescence

Adolescence is perhaps nature's way of preparing parents to welcome the empty nest.
    —*Karen Savage and Patrick Adams*

Adolescence is generally recognized as being the single most difficult child-developmental stage for parents to handle. This is equally true whether a divorce is occurring, or if the family is intact and darn near picture perfect. The adolescent is in transition between childhood and adulthood. This period is characterized by an alternating tearing down, and then rebuilding, of the child's own equilibrium. Thus, a child progresses toward adulthood in something of a back-and-fill fashion.

This transition does not move in a straight line, nor does it always move forward. Instead, it progresses three steps forward and then takes two steps back. This is what makes the adolescent so puzzling to the adult. In essence, the adolescent is not one person, but two.

Adolescent angst. Successfully guiding a child through adolescence is probably one of the trickiest jobs a parent can have, even in the best of times. Children during this stage are continually seesawing back and forth between trying to "find themselves" (to develop their own egos and personas), while at the same time being plagued by self-doubt as they question themselves and their surroundings.

During the early adolescent phase (between years thirteen to approximately sixteen), the child is anxiously trying to establish an identity in the context of his or her family structure and rapidly blossoming teenage peer group. Adolescent girls, in particular, seem to have an especially difficult time handling all the changes that seem to be coming at them so fast—not to mention the kicker that occurs when all this combines with a rapid physical and sexual development.

Kids going through adolescence seem to subconsciously understand that they have to make a break from their family and other traditional support systems in order to emerge with their own sense of themselves. This helps to explain their tendency toward rebelliousness at this stage. Yet, at the same time, they are also having difficulty coping with their own sense of confusion and insecurity. A divorce that occurs just when the parties' children are undergoing their topsy-turvy adolescent stage is probably the most difficult to handle for both the parents and the kids. If one of the kids is a teenage girl, then it may well be the toughest scenario of all.

I always find it somewhat surprising and ironic (especially given the average adolescent's "stay cool, rebellious, and blasé-at-all-costs" mentality) that of all the periods when a strong and reliable family structure is important to kids, adolescence may be the most crucial. This is the stage when kids are intent on testing the limits of what is right or wrong, their own sexuality, and their urge to experiment.

Teens on a tightrope. Peer pressures are also pushed to the max during this period. Kids want, and need, to rebel at this juncture, but they also simultaneously need the safe haven of a family to fall back on and to help define the limits of their own evolving behavior. Think of a kid on a tightrope or trapeze, but with a sizable and secure familial safety net to fall back on.

When analyzed in this manner, it really isn't all that surprising that adolescence is perhaps the most difficult period of all for the kids of divorce. This is especially so for those who have the misfortune to be entering the throes of their own adolescence just as their parents are entering the throes of their divorce. It is during the adolescent and young adulthood periods that one's relationship with the opposite sex becomes the central focus of development. The unfortunate factor that plagues the kids of divorce during this period is that this is exactly the wrong time for them to be lacking an appropriate role model. These kids need personal examples of enduring, successful, positive, and caring relationships between men and women at this stage. It is a hell of a time to instead be watching their parents' marriage blow up.

Who am I? The developmental task of the adolescent is to form a new selfhood, a new ego identity separate from his or her parents. The teenager is trying to answer the question, "Who am I?"

During early adolescence (ages thirteen to sixteen), teens seek the answer to this question within the realm of their families. They often go about it in a rather rebellious way. Toward the end of adolescence (about ages sixteen to twenty), kids seek to answer this question vis-à-vis the larger arena of their society. The fact that adolescents are already living on something of a perpetual seesaw is what makes them so vulnerable to the stress of a family breakup. Again, it is the adolescent girls in particular who often have the most severe problems dealing with these changes.

Rebel, Rebel! One characteristic hallmark of adolescent behavior is rebellion against parents. Although this is a difficult period for parents to endure, there seems to be no question, developmentally speaking, that this is a stage that kids need to undergo. Unfortunately, the act of rebellion against parents in a firmly established nuclear family (wherein a child can intermittently rebel for a bit, but then fall back to the safety of the family unit) turns into a dramatically different process in a single-parent household. In a divorcing family, the child's reaction may be to manifest his or her rebellion differently, or even to hold back on the normal rebelliousness process altogether. Either way, it is more difficult for the child to move through the two tentative steps forward, followed by one quick step back, "safety net" style of rebellion that I described earlier and that typifies a normal, healthy adolescence.

Adolescent children are by definition going through a stage in which they feel more sexually rebellious and aggressive. This is the crux of the adolescent period, and it is characterized by a period of extensive experimentation with new stimuli across the board. Acceptance by peers is everything.

Conversely, this is precisely the period when strong parental support and supervision are all the more crucial. Parents need to set and enforce basic values and rules during this period. These in turn serve as the springboard off which adolescent teens bounce, and then turn back, all in an effort to further find themselves. Even in the best of times, this is a tricky and precarious period, developmentally speaking. A divorce coming at this juncture can threaten the entire process, which essentially centers on breaking free of the parents and family, while at the same time feeling firmly grounded and secure within the family.

Parents as human safety nets. It is especially important for adolescents to have a well-organized and functioning household and a clearly defined sense of rules during this period. Can any parent fail to notice the acute importance of a teenager having his or her own room as a sanctuary? An organized and consistent home front serves as the safety net for the adolescent to fall back into between his or her periodic forays in search of self.

This need for a structured home life is extremely important for both sexes, but it seems to be even more acute for adolescent girls than it is for adolescent boys. Adolescent girls (particularly around the ages of thirteen to fifteen) seem to have a particularly intense need for closeness and direction from their natural fathers.

So we can see that adolescence is perhaps the most complex and painful stage of all for a kid in a divorcing family. In a single-parent relationship there is less opportunity to detach in the more gradual fashion associated with normal adolescence, since that parent-and-child relationship is likely to be both more central and more encompassing than is a dual-parent relationship in an intact family.

Certainly it cannot be easy to be the son of a woman who is alone. The rising sexuality of an adolescent boy is very frightening to him, and he wants to get away from his mother. Without his father present, he feels unprotected from his own impulses and fantasies.

Dr. Wallerstein found in her study that fully one-third of both boys and girls went to live with their fathers at some point during their adolescence. Of these, half stayed about one year. They grew disenchanted with what they found and realized, after a short time, that they had been "following a fantasy." Her observation was that this is a widespread phenomenon during adolescence—kids moving back and forth between two homes several times during high school, essentially customizing their custody with or without their parents' approval.

So here we have this snapshot picture of the typical adolescent: confused and confusing; sometimes delightful, but more often rebellious; and, to top it all off, a burgeoning full-tilt sexual being. A divorce during the adolescent stage is the hardest for both parents and children to handle.

Post-Adolescence

The trouble with the 1980s as compared to the 1970s is that teenagers no longer rebel and leave home.
—*Marion Smith*

The entry into post-adolescent young adulthood occurs roughly between the ages of eighteen and twenty-three. It is a difficult time for all young people—divorce or no divorce. To really become an adult, one must have established some sense of a separate identity during adolescence.

In the context of divorce, the adolescent period may be tougher for girls (the daughters of divorce), but the problems faced by boys during the post-adolescent period, when the time comes for them to leave home, are generally trickier and more complicated than those experienced by girls. First, boys and their mothers do not generally exhibit quite the same degree of close mutual emotional dependency found between mothers and daughters. Instead, according to Dr. Wallerstein, mothers and sons are intertwined in a powerful "psychological foxtrot" in which they are alternately drawn close together and then pushed apart.

Mama's boys. Sometimes divorced women will turn to their sons to take the ex-husband's place—treating them as heads of household. At the opposite extreme, many boys feel pushed away. Sometimes boys feel rejected for their maleness, as if they remind their mothers of their fathers.

The interaction between mother and son often reaches a climactic stage just at the time of adolescent separation, when the boy is ready to leave home. Boys feel a strong moral obligation to their mothers, yet they also instinctively perceive that it is psychologically dangerous for them to become too close to their mothers. They fear being a mama's boy. Because they are not protected by a father under the same roof, they may come to resent being disciplined or emasculated by a woman.

Many people are surprised at just how difficult divorce can be even for post-adolescent kids in their late teens and early twenties. The impact can manifest itself in weird ways. An otherwise outstanding young man may have an inexplicably unfounded fear of rejection or low self-esteem. A twenty-year-old girl may be totally unable to feel secure in planning for her future.

One of the primary causes of this malaise seems to stem from the fact that these young adults have lost contact with their fathers at just the developmental stage when they may have needed them most. They may have needed dad to serve as a role model or mentor in helping them take charge of some of the practical sides of their lives.

Many psychological studies indicate that girls have an especially strong need for support and reinforcement from their fathers during their early adolescence—around ages thirteen to sixteen. The need for boys to feel close to a father figure seems to come more strongly into play in their later teens. For both boys and girls, however, the increasing need for involvement with their fathers seems to rise dramatically during the adolescent and post-adolescent periods.

"Manly" models. Boys need male role models from whom they derive traditionally male management and organizational skills and the sense of teamwork and male bonding. All these are often derived from team sports or from the boardroom culture of business and from male mentors: coaches, bosses, and fathers.

As kids from divorced families approach entrance to college, they encounter the serious problems of having their psychological and financial support cut out from underneath them. Although most child-support agreements contemplate various approaches to maintaining support through age twenty-three for any child who remains a full-time student, there does seem to be something of a psychological barrier about an age eighteen cutoff date in the minds of noncustodial fathers.

Arbitrary emancipation at eighteen. All of a sudden the child hits the age of majority, and noncustodial parents may arbitrarily decide that childhood is officially over. The divorced, and often noncustodial, dad then either reduces his financial support or terminates it altogether. Often, even the parent's personal support stops abruptly at that point as well.

This situation is quite unlike intact nuclear families, where kids generally get a good deal more slack, with both parents remaining supportive for several more years. Not nearly enough divorce decrees include sufficient provisions for college education. The problem here is that particularly given its astronomical cost nowadays, college somehow seems to many noncustodial parents to be a logical time to cut off their parental responsibilities.

Relatively few college-age kids from divorced families receive anywhere near the level of financial assistance for their postsecondary (and especially postgraduate) education that they would have otherwise received had their families stayed together. Instead, noncustodial dads often seem to take this opportunity to make their removal from the parenting picture complete.

Custody and Visitation Arrangements

In loco parentis—Latin for "children can drive their parents crazy."
        —Anonymous

It is now generally acknowledged that fathers play a far more vital role in the lives and development of their children than was previously recognized. For decades, however, child-custody arrangements were centered around the mother-child bonding configuration. Fathers were often relegated to the status of noncustodial periodic visitors. A rather clear realization is now emerging that even noncustodial fathers play an absolutely crucial role in their child's development, particularly during the late childhood and adolescent years.

Father knows best (circa 1850). Up until the middle of the nineteenth century, child-rearing manuals in America were generally addressed to fathers, not mothers, since dads were largely viewed as the family's linchpin. But, as industrialization began to separate home and work, fathers could not be in both places at once. Family life of the nineteenth century was defined by what historians call the "feminization of the domestic sphere." This was accompanied by the relatively new trend of marginalizing the father as a parent. By the mid-1800s, child-rearing manuals, increasingly addressed to mothers, deplored the father's absence from the home. In 1900, one worried observer described the suburban husband and father as "almost entirely a Sunday institution."

Fatherless children. What alarms modern social scientists is that in the latter part of the 20th century the father was sidelined in a new, more disturbing way. Today he's often just plain absent. Rising divorce rates and out-of-wedlock births meant that more than 40 percent of all children born between 1970 and 1984 were likely to spend much of their childhood living in single-parent homes. In 1990, 25 percent were living with only their mothers. This compares with 5 percent in 1960. Says David Blankenhorn, the founder of the Institute for American Values in New York City: "This trend of fatherlessness is the most socially consequential family trend of our generation."

Anthropologists have actually tried to figure out why even some primates are better fathers than their human kin. A June 2007 *Time* magazine article pointed out a classic example: Titi monkey babies spend 90 percent of the daylight hours in their father's arms. Meanwhile, fathers in intact human families spend a lot less time focused on their kids than they think: in the United States, fathers currently average just under an hour a day. The good news, if you can call it that, is that this represents 153 percent improvement from 1965 when it was only about twenty minutes.

Worldwide, 10 percent to 40 percent of children grow up in households with no father at all. More disturbing is the statistic that in the United States alone, more than half of divorced fathers lose contact with their kids within a few years. Even uglier still, by the end of ten years, as many as two-thirds of fathers have drifted out of their children's lives completely.

The need for dads and discipline. Researchers argue that fathers should be more than just substitute mothers. They point out that men's parenting styles are quite different than women's, and in ways that matter enormously. They say a mother's love is unconditional, whereas a father's is more qualified, more tied to performance. Mothers worry about their infant's survival, fathers go a step further and worry about future success. Social scientists stress the fact that fathers produce not just children, but "socially viable" children. Fathers, more than mothers, appear to be haunted by the fear that their children may turn out to be failures—perhaps because a father understands that his child's character is, in some sense, a measure of his own character as well.

According to this school of thought, when it comes to discipline it is the combination of mother and father that yields justice tempered by mercy. Whereas mothers tend to discipline children on a moment-by-moment basis, fathers discipline more by set rules. Kids learn from their moms how to be in touch with their emotional sides. From their dads, they learn how to live as members of society. Thus, one major shift we are now witnessing in parenting styles and custody structuring is the dramatically increased participation of fathers who want to stay an active parent to their children.

Dads play a crucial role in shaping and influencing their children's sense of themselves, of their own sexuality, and of their future career and personal goals. This holds true both for daughters as well as sons. Furthermore, this is a role that the kids themselves are often quite anxious to have their fathers fill. Even in situations where the dad is not around to perform these functions on a regular basis (i.e., present only intermittently or perhaps not at all), the desire for parental guidance in these areas is so strong that the kids will fictionalize or fantasize a role for their fathers.

The bottom line is that the modern trend is to structure custody and visitation arrangements in such a way as to maintain maximum contact with both parents. The section of this book on child custody will discuss the specific legal doctrines such as joint custody that have emerged to meet this concern. That portion will also outline the mechanics of specific visitation schedules. My intent in this section, however, is to focus on the actual impact of the visitation arrangements on the kids themselves.

The vagaries of visitation. Many people do not realize just how difficult it is to put a really workable visitation format into place. First, there are obvious problematic issues involved in maintaining a good visitation schedule, such as overcoming geographical separation, or arranging the physical logistics, or dealing with financial expenses. Then there is the nature of the individual visits themselves, and just how complicated and strained they can be.

Drive-by visits on mom's turf can be extremely frustrating. So can a forced march of the children over to spend an excruciating weekend with dad and his new wicked-stepmother wife. (Meanwhile, this new wife is herself jealous of the time, attention, and money out of the family budget that are going to the kids of the prior marriage.)

Even those visits that do get implemented are then often followed, in turn, by a wrenching separation. I have had many clients tell me that it is so painful to depart from these short-burst visits that they would almost rather not exercise their visitation rights at all.

My personal experience has been that most moms seem to be pretty good about at least tolerating dad's visits, and quite a few of the more enlightened ones see the positive benefits of same and are downright supportive. I do, of course, run across the occasional ex-wife who now has custody and who will seemingly do anything in her power to prevent visitation from occurring, but I always try to discourage this type of behavior. (Author's Note: I am phrasing these examples in terms of mom having custody and dad having the visitation because that is still the situation in a majority of the cases. Dads can get custody too, of course—and more and more often they do. According to the Bureau of Labor Statistics 2007 report on the current status of single-parent households, 77 percent are headed by moms and 23 percent by dads. But regardless of whoever takes primary physical custody, they should try to remain supportive of extensive visitation periods.)

Unfortunately, my own relatively positive experiences with (and recommendations to) my firm's clients seem to be out of sync with the various studies indicating that in an incredibly high number of cases nationwide (perhaps as many as 40 percent) the dads virtually never visit their kids following the divorce. If these statistics are anywhere near accurate, I shudder to think of the huge sense of loss that those kids must feel.

The key to a successful visitation framework seems to be to allow the father and child a sufficient amount of quality time together so that they are able to rekindle a naturally close and intimate personal feeling. Only in this way can the child become comfortable enough to really feel a sense of the father's love and caring.

As noted earlier, this is particularly important for the linkage between teenage and adolescent boys and their natural fathers. Perhaps one of the best formats to ensure this kind of closeness is for fathers and sons to spend large chunks of time away together doing "real men's" activities such as camping, sports, or nature activities. These types of times spent together appear to be more valuable than how frequently the dad visits—especially if the frequent visits are short or shallow.

Are kids the key to a good marriage? As we conclude this chapter on the Children of Divorce, it may be interesting to review the findings of a Pew Research Center study which found that having children has dropped to one of the *least-cited* factors in a successful marriage. When today's Americans were given a list of nine features to consider as part of a successful marriage, only 41 percent said children were "very important," compared with 65 percent in 1990. The Pew report calls this drop of 24 percentage points "perhaps the single most striking finding of the survey."

This nonprofit Pew Research Center also found that on the list of nine key contributing factors to success in marriage, children were surpassed by faithfulness, a happy sexual relationship, household chore-sharing, economic factors (such as adequate income and good housing), common religious beliefs, and shared tastes and interests. The bottom line, at least according to Pew, would seem to be that kids are no longer viewed as being the top factor in ensuring a good marriage.

Another fascinating finding that comes at this issue from a completely different angle was a recent study of people's estate-planning practices conducted by Thomas Dunn and John Phillips for *Economic Letters*. They made the seemingly astonishing, but perhaps telling, discovery that 10 percent of all parents ultimately wind up disinheriting at least one of their children.

CHAPTER 5
Into the Courtroom

Lawsuit: A machine which you go into as a pig and come out as a sausage.
—*Ambrose Bierce*

There are two dramatically different types of divorce cases that can be processed through the family courts. Simply put, your divorce can be either contested or uncontested. This is an absolutely crucial difference for clients to understand.

Keeping divorces uncontested. If you are able to achieve an uncontested divorce, you reap the following benefits: (1) you save lots of money; (2) you avoid lots of stress; (3) you get your divorce completed within two to three months; and (4) you salvage some sort of decent relationship with your former spouse. This last issue is especially important when ongoing relations with the kids are concerned. In general, reaching an uncontested divorce settlement vastly minimizes the emotional and financial costs of the entire situation. This is certainly the goal to shoot for.

Hot Tips on How to Process Your Divorce Economically and Efficiently

Divorce. A resumption of diplomatic relations and rectification of boundaries.
—*Ambrose Bierce*

The approach we utilize in my firm is to try to keep cases on the uncontested track whenever we possibly can since that's what saves our clients their money. But this means that *everything* has to be uncontested. It means that we've got to be able to get both parties to voluntarily sign an agreement dissolving the marriage. This document must include a complete settlement of all the property and other issues in the divorce.

The settlement agreement. Once an uncontested property settlement agreement (i.e., divorce decree) is signed by both husband and wife, it is then submitted to the court as an essentially done deal. The parties are not asking the judge to decide anything/ everything regarding their lives or their divorce. Instead, they are simply asking the judge to approve the agreement as is. This is a much quicker, less adversarial, and more manageable procedure than a contested divorce.

Keeping the costs down. Uncontested divorces generally cost somewhere in the range of $1,000 to $1,500 in legal fees and can be concluded within a few months. I must stress the fact, however, that every single item of the divorce settlement must be mutually agreed upon.

If there is any disagreement and the other party is unwilling to sign, for whatever reason (whether good or bad, sensible or ridiculous, it doesn't matter), then you do not have an uncontested divorce. The disagreement can be over something as major as a million-dollar disparity in property valuations, or something as simple as who gets the family dog or the china, but if it prevents getting a signed agreement it will preclude an uncontested divorce.

People acting petty. Divorcing couples can be incredibly petty in bringing their areas of disagreement down to truly asinine levels. And believe me, an intransigent spouse can wind up costing you beaucoup bucks in divorce court. In my thirty years of divorce lawyering, I have seen folks become so "pissed off" at one another during divorce proceedings that they, somewhat understandably, begin to suffer from a serious case of what we in Hawai'i refer to as ADD . . . Aloha Deficit Disorder.

I once had to actually go out to a divorcing couple's house to physically divide up their houseplants—all at more than $200 per hour. The simple bottom line is that unless both parties voluntarily sign off on the same agreement, then they do not have an uncontested divorce. The roadblock can be over property, or money, or it may be emotional (i.e., one party isn't psychologically ready for the divorce or simply does not want to let go of the other person). Whatever the reason, either party's refusal to sign equals a contested divorce. This is true even in cases where there aren't any kids or assets to fight over.

Logjam = contest. If this logjam situation occurs, you are then off and running on the contested divorce track. Contested cases can take years and literally thousands of dollars in attorneys' fees to complete, and often turn into an absolute stomach churner for everyone involved. I suspect that everybody in America has had some experience with this sort of divorce, whether through watching *The War of the Roses* or *Kramer vs. Kramer*, or having served as an emotional life-support system for Aunt Mitzie or a sounding board for Uncle Ken during their divorces. These kinds of cases are absolutely grueling for all concerned.

So if you find yourself or your friends getting divorced, remember that the key is to try to get an agreement to keep it on the uncontested track if you possibly can. Unfortunately, spouses are rarely in total agreement about very much during the time period surrounding their divorce—if they were, they probably wouldn't be getting divorced in the first place.

Divorce lawyers should make every effort to encourage clients to settle uncontested and out of court. But unfortunately it doesn't always work out that way. When a case doesn't settle, we lawyers (and our clients) have to be fully prepared to go the contested litigation route. This is simply the nature of our legal system's adversarial structure. It is unfortunate and certainly has a tendency to fray everyone's nerves. Of course, it also has the perverse side effect of making far more money for the lawyers.

Attorney Selection

People are getting smarter nowadays; they are letting lawyers, instead of their conscience, be their guide.
    —*Will Rogers*

How do you go about making sure you direct your divorce down a productive settlement-oriented track, rather than letting yourself be led around by the nose by whatever attorney you happen to wind up hiring? For starters, you should interview several attorneys and ask them exactly how they plan to run the case. More important, you should insist on controlling the overall direction of the case yourself—don't let the attorney just take hold of your life and run amok with it.

Make your lawyer follow your directions. Stay an active participant, find out what your attorney's strategy is, look for settlement junctures, maximize the opportunities to physically meet directly with your spouse to discuss settlement (even though it's not always exactly fun seeing them). Above all, try to steer your case (and your lawyer) toward the uncontested track (i.e., costing only a few hundred bucks and requiring only a few months to complete), rather than letting it go contested, taking forever and costing a fortune. To a large degree this is your choice.

Considerations for female clients. Yet another sexist injustice seems to be at work against women in many divorce cases. A recent survey of New York divorce attorneys indicated that handling cases for women is often more expensive because of the time it takes to learn about the assets and incomes of husbands, who traditionally have controlled the family finances. Ninety-three percent of the New York attorneys surveyed agreed that more discovery time is needed when representing women.

Your turn to question the lawyer. Your relationship with your attorney can turn out to be both lengthy and intense. You'll want to be sure you get the right fit. Here are some key questions for you as the client to ask your prospective lawyer:

- What is your overall plan for the case? Are you a settlement-oriented attorney, or are we going straight to trial? Should we posture my case for trial as a strategic ploy and then talk settlement?
- What is your legal background? What law school did you attend? How many years have you spent as a practicing attorney? What percentage of your practice is matrimonial work? How many cases have you actually tried?
- How do your office procedures work? Who will I be working with on your staff? Who do I deal with in your billing department? What are your billing procedures? What will I be charged for phone calls, faxes, photocopies? What are your office hours? When can I reach you by phone? Who on your staff (i.e., associate attorneys, paralegals, etc.) will be assisting on my case? Can I meet them now?
- What is your best estimate for the eventual outcome of my case? How much will it cost? What problems do you foresee arising in my case? How long will it take? What will be the result(s) on the specific legal issues in question?

Lawyers are notoriously reluctant to be pinned down on answers to these kinds of questions, but if you can get any sort of commitments regarding projected outcomes, you can be sure that the attorney's feet will be held to the fire in trying to make the initial projection match the resultant outcome.

Facts about legal fees. The retainer agreement that you initially sign with your attorney will be the key document that governs your financial relationship with that lawyer. The retainer itself is the initial payment you make to retain the attorney's services. You must make sure that the fee agreement is in writing and provides for a refund of any retainer fees that are not ultimately used up.

Divorce attorneys generally charge by the hour. Current rates usually range upward from $200 per hour. Some top-of-the-line big-city attorneys charge double, or even triple, that amount.

Most attorneys charge for telephone time and also for any work they do on your case behind the scenes, in their offices as well as in court. Attorneys have been known to self-generate billable events. You can try to keep a lid on this by requesting that you be notified in advance of any major work that the attorney intends to perform on your case. You don't want to give your attorney *carte blanche* to file whatever motions or miscellaneous discovery they happen to feel like filing. What lawyers call the "discovery process" can be especially time consuming and costly (and is often overdone). Ask that these major work-product junctures in the case be cleared with you first so that you can veto any discovery or motion filings, etc., that you may feel are unnecessary.

Hot tips to minimize legal fees. Nobody likes paying attorneys' fees. Here are a few ways to keep them down:

- Make sure your lawyer sends you a detailed written billing statement each month (even if your retainer is not yet used up). Keep track of all time you spend with your attorney (both in person and on the phone). Crosscheck your own records against the attorney's bill.
- Ascertain whether minimum time increment charges will apply and if so how much (some attorneys charge for actual time spent, while others apply a ten- or fifteen-minute minimum charge). Also, find out who else will be working on your case in addition to the primary lawyer you are retaining (i.e., other associate attorneys and/or paralegals). Find out what their hourly charges are.
- Organize as many of your own materials yourself as you possibly can. I've had many clients show up in my office carrying shopping bags full of their important, but totally disorganized, personal papers. It's a waste of your attorney's time (and your money) to have him or her organize and collate your documents. Do it yourself. Save the attorney's time, and your legal fees, for actual court appearances (where an attorney truly is indispensable!).

- Most jurisdictions have court rules that authorize the tendering of "Offers of Settlement" in litigation. These essentially mean that if one side makes an Offer of Settlement at any point prior to the actual trial of a litigation case, but the opposing side initially rejects that offer, and if the originally offering party then gets a result at trial that is as good or better than the original offer (i.e., which the opposing side had earlier rejected), then the party who wrongly rejected the earlier offer can be required to pay all the attorneys' fees for *both* parties from the time the offer was made onward.

  In my personal and professional opinion, many divorce attorneys fail (for a variety of reasons) to make timely or sufficient use of this important legal tool. If your case does wind up in litigation, you should make sure that the lawyer you select is inclined to make fair and intelligent offers for feasible settlements as early in the case as is practical for your situation. You certainly want your attorney to be skilled, proficient and proactive about structuring and tendering such Offers of Settlement.

You should also remember that it is by no means mandatory that both sides, or even either side, have a lawyer in divorce cases. A recent study of domestic relations cases in sixteen courts found that in 53 percent of the divorce cases only one litigant had an attorney, and in 18 percent of the cases neither party had an attorney. Thus, both parties were represented in only 29 percent of these divorce cases.

Most courts have fairly well-developed systems for helping *pro se* parties (i.e., those who are representing themselves) process their own divorces. In some progressive states, such as Arizona, this is becoming more the rule than the exception.

Avoiding Attila the Hun. As the client, you have to be smart enough to find someone who will look for approaches that can make your divorce settle fast and cheap. If you are impressed by the style of a lawyer who comes out of his office sounding like Attila the Hun (Viking horn helmet optional!) and telling you how he plans to "win big" in a combative trial, then you may already be off on the wrong foot. After all, any lawyer who starts things off by talking about trial may be unlikely to spend much time trying to negotiate an out-of-court settlement. Unless your case really does require "trial by combat," then you've got to be careful about backing into it by accident.

Dividing by two. Conscientious lawyers will generally pursue a settlement-minded approach. I often joke: "Just how smart does a divorce lawyer really have to be to be able to divide by two?" After all, this really is the crux of most property settlements. Most of us who are experienced divorce lawyers have been appearing regularly for years before the various family court judges. We've learned what they are going to decide on almost any given issue. There are literally thousands of divorces moving through the courts nowadays, and the judges have been forced to come up with some pretty standardized resolutions for various issues.

For a good lawyer who is experienced in this field, there often should not be all that much question about what the end result is going to be. So if your lawyer can accurately predict that result at the outset, you can then head straight toward that resolution early on by putting that settlement proposal on the table right at the very beginning of the case. By utilizing this sort of "principled approach" to making the fairest possible opening settlement offer early on in the case, you can hopefully avoid running up the high attorney's fees that otherwise inevitably accompany the normal channels of litigation.

Churners can be costly. Beware: there are many lawyers who tend to "churn" cases in order to deliberately exacerbate and prolong them. Conversely, there are some lawyers (probably fewer, however) who look for the quickest, cheapest, and friendliest way possible to resolve the situation. Your job as a smart client is to learn to tell the difference.

Oddly enough, the churners have a built-in rationalization for their seemingly perverse approach to overworking and overbilling their cases. Many will claim that it is an outgrowth of the attorney's code of ethics that requires them as advocates to "zealously represent" their clients in an adversarial fashion. They may be less quick to point out the fact that churned cases generate vastly higher fees for the lawyers.

Mediation and Alternative Dispute Resolution (ADR)

Paper napkins never return from a laundry, nor love from a trip to the law courts.
    —John Barrymore

There is a significant trend in legal circles nowadays toward a process called Alternative Dispute Resolution (ADR). This rapidly growing approach includes mediation, arbitration, private judging, etc.—virtually any neutral system for moving cases toward settlement, short of conventional litigation. Many of my more-enlightened clients are choosing this tactic in preference to costly trials.

Taking the high road of divorce mediation. Alternative Dispute Resolution has become an increasingly popular way of end running the traditional legal system and its mysterious, convoluted, and costly procedures. Clients who want to pursue ADR as an approach to resolving their divorce must find an attorney with whom they feel comfortable and who will follow a mutually agreed ADR strategy in handling their case. Mediation is probably the most popular of the ADR options for the divorce context. It should be utilized near the beginning of the case if possible.

Mediation takes a much more streamlined approach to quickly bringing the parties in the dispute physically together and starting them talking. They sit down in the same room with the mediator and/or other advisors and work on trying to settle their own case. It may sound overly simplistic, but once people actually try it, mediation generates an amazingly successful set of statistics. Mediation has proven particularly worthwhile in the divorce context. My personal experience has been that about 85 percent of all divorce cases can be settled in a properly handled mediation context.

The mechanics of mediation. Mediation is a cooperative problem-solving process in which a neutral professional assists family members in clearly defining the issues that are in dispute during a marital separation or dissolution, and in reaching agreements that are in everyone's best interest. The mediator does not take sides or make decisions for others, but instead helps participants resolve misunderstandings and communicate more clearly with one another.

Mediation is essentially a process in which the spouses themselves settle the issues in their own divorce, acting with the help of a trained mediator. Any and all issues involved in a divorce case can be the subject of mediation. Even if the process doesn't successfully resolve all issues, at least partial agreements can be reached that help narrow the issues.

Mediation works best when both spouses have accepted and agreed that the divorce itself should occur (even if they don't yet concur on its terms). Likewise, both parties should have a handle on their overall financial situation and be fully informed of each other's assets and debts, since mediation relies on full disclosure and is not an investigative or discovery tool. Lastly, both parties must still be able to communicate openly and should be on a relatively equal footing with one another in order to take full advantage of the give-and-take flexibility that is inherent in mediation.

The benefits of mediation. When couples participate in divorce mediation, they:

- Maintain control over their own decision-making process. Any agreement reached in mediation is negotiated and agreed to by the couple themselves and is not imposed by a judge or any outside authority.
- Learn improved communication skills, including the ability to negotiate further disagreements amicably.
- Minimize the harmful effects of divorce on children. When the parents themselves select custody and visitation arrangements, it is easier to keep children out of the middle of conflicts.
- Generally save both time and money. Legal and counseling fees and court costs are minimized by avoiding protracted legal battles.
- Decrease the anxiety, pressure, stress, and anger placed on all involved parties.
- Emphasize a win/win rather than win/lose approach to conflict resolution.

Mediation minefields. There are some situations in which mediation is not recommended. If there is a substantial power imbalance between spouses (where one is a totally dominant control freak, for example, and the other is characteristically submissive), then the playing field will probably not be level enough for mediation to be workable. Likewise, if one side (often the husband) knows absolutely everything about the parties' assets and finances, while the other knows virtually nothing, then mediation is probably not appropriate.

If the parties are still so angry at one another that arguments and profanity rather than intelligent (or at least cordial) conversation ensues whenever they try to talk, then mediation probably isn't the answer. Finally, if spouse abuse or domestic violence has been a factor in the relationship, then mediation is generally not appropriate.

My pro-mediation sermon. I myself have been a trained mediator for well over twenty years. I have personally mediated literally hundreds of divorce cases during that period. In my opinion, a conscientious and responsible divorce lawyer should make extensive use of mediation and other Alternative Dispute Resolution techniques. In fact, my personal view is that it is almost unconscionable for any attorney to fail to advise their clients that they have a right to try mediation. Ultimately, it is up to you as the client to make sure your lawyer takes a responsible approach to the handling of your divorce case. There are several new and more user-friendly resources available in the legal marketplace nowadays. It's up to the consumer of legal services to demand that they be used.

One final concluding note for this chapter: I am certainly not naive enough to think that every case can be settled. There will always be some cases in which the parties are so intractable, or the issues so complex, that they simply have to go to trial. That is probably when you really do need the big-gun trial lawyer.

It is by no means my intent to oversimplify this process by suggesting mediated or even uncontested results in every case. But I honestly feel that these approaches are not tried often enough, nor early enough, in most cases. The bottom line is that you as the client have to make sure that you explore all the options when you go through a divorce case. Then find the one that works best for you.

CHAPTER 6
The Legal Issues

Marriage is really tough because you have to deal with feelings and lawyers.
—*Richard Pryor*

Nowadays divorce is no-fault. Hawai'i, where I practice, is a no-fault divorce state, as are almost all other states in the country. This means that you no longer have to make the kinds of sensational "fault-based" accusations against your spouse (such as mental cruelty, desertion, alcoholism or adultery) that many of us may recall from old *L.A. Law* episodes. You do not have to find fault or place blame on your spouse's personal conduct in order to get a divorce.

Grounds for Divorce

Marriage is a great institution, but I am not ready for an institution.
        —*Mae West*

The legal grounds for divorce in Hawai'i are simply that the marriage is "irretrievably broken." This basically means that you and your spouse are no longer able to make your marriage work.

Many other jurisdictions use similarly ambiguous but statutory-sounding phraseology to describe their grounds for divorce. California uses "irreconcilable differences." Other jurisdictions use "incompatibility" as the grounds.

I have never quite figured out what exactly constitutes an irretrievable breakdown in a marriage, or what the irreconcilable differences are. The bottom line is that when either spouse decides they want a divorce, they can go out and get it. In a no-fault jurisdiction, it takes only one person to initiate and force the issue. There is simply no way that someone who wants to resist it can successfully stop their spouse from divorcing them if they are really intent on doing so.

The "irretrievably broken" language is something that our eminently wise legislators here in Hawai'i came up with. California's politicians apparently preferred "irreconcilable differences." Ultimately, it comes down to one party's judgment call as to when they feel their marriage is truly over.

The status of the states. Nowadays, only a couple of states (South Dakota and Illinois) limit divorce to the traditional fault-based grounds. Of the remaining forty-eight states, nine (Arizona, California, Colorado, Florida, Hawai'i, Kentucky, Minnesota, Oregon, and Wisconsin) have completely abolished fault grounds. The others have added no-fault grounds to their existing divorce statutes.

Some states use a combination of fault and no-fault grounds. Other states require the complete agreement of both spouses on all provisions of the divorce agreement in order to obtain a no-fault divorce.

The fact that almost all states have switched over to the primarily no-fault format represents a big change from the old days of fault-based divorce. As many people will recall, the concept of proving fault (the transgressions of one side or the other during the marriage) used to be one of the key elements of a divorce case. Under the old fault-based system, if one side was at fault, then a lopsided property settlement was oftentimes used to punish the person who was deemed to be the bad guy or bad gal in the marriage. Thus, if a wife ran off with her tennis instructor, she got less alimony than would a wife whose husband left her for his secretary. I often refer to that kind of fault-finding approach as the *People* magazine style of divorce. Frankly, it is still hard for many people to accept the fact that those days are over.

The modern reality, however, is that nowadays the court doesn't even want to hear evidence of who did what to whom. Judges today have so many of these crazy divorce cases to handle (there are about five thousand divorce cases a year being processed in Hawai'i alone) that they have neither the time nor the inclination to try to play Monday morning quarterback and determine who was right or wrong in the marriage. Instead, they just try to move these cases through the mill as briskly as they can and concentrate primarily on the property settlement issues. Most judges flatly refuse to even admit evidence that relates to fault.

Can't we find some fault somewhere? The one big exception is in custody cases. If custody is the key issue, and if mom did something really stupid (for example, she not only ran off with the tennis instructor, but also partook of sex and/or drugs with him while her three-year-old daughter was asleep in the adjoining room), then that kind of behavior relates to the issue of overall lack of good judgment in parenting. That sort of off-the-charts "Bozo no-no" type of behavior can (and should!) come back to haunt/hurt her custody case on an almost fault-like kind of basis. You had better believe the judge will want to hear all the evidence in these sorts of cases.

Separation

The difference between divorce and a legal separation is that the legal separation gives a husband time to hide his money.
    —*Johnny Carson*

Many of my clients tend to instinctively head toward a legal separation in the common situation where they have begun to experience some level of marital disharmony but aren't quite ready for a full divorce. This is an ambivalent period of mixed emotions and half in/half out feelings. The legal grounds for separations are similarly nonspecific—requiring only that the marriage be "temporarily disrupted." What you essentially have is a temporary break, or hiatus, in the marital relationship. The court will approve a statutory legal separation period (two years in Hawai'i) based upon documents that outline a separation agreement. This situation can in turn sit in limbo for a couple of years. At the end of this time, however, you must then generally go ahead and finalize things one way or the other.

Is a "trial separation" a fresh start or the beginning of the end? A surprisingly high percentage of clients come into my office initially thinking they want a separation instead of a divorce. Perhaps they haven't quite got the heart to go ahead with a full divorce, or maybe they think they should stop short of finalizing the divorce for religious reasons, or "for the kids." Unfortunately, however, it has been my experience that these sorts of reasons do not really prove to be viable rationales for foregoing divorce and relying instead on the separation scenario.

The sad statistical reality is that, for most people, timid efforts at trial separations generally backfire and instead become only a prelude to divorce. A more workable approach is for couples to separate if, and only if, they really believe they can actually (and actively) save their marriage. In fact, my personal view is that a separation is worth doing if, but only if, during that period the couple is indeed actively working on a specific and viable plan for the reconciliation of the marriage.

A real reconciliation is certainly a meritorious goal and worth any price. Anything short of that, however (i.e., simply not having the stomach to go ahead with a full divorce and instead wimping out by seeking only a separation—even though in your heart you know that the marriage really is hopeless), may well do more harm than good. Interspousal friction may continue needlessly during the separation period—with each still trying to run or influence the other's life. Furthermore, the overall emotional recovery can be delayed through a refusal to grapple with the real issues of getting on with one's own new life instead of continuously rehashing the old one.

Some practical problems with separations. People somehow expect separations to be financially more economical, but they generally are not. In fact, separations typically result in much higher total legal expenses. After first paying one set of attorneys' fees for the separation, you then have to cough up another full set of legal fees to get divorced a couple of years later. Also remember that even any short-term move away from the marital residence, or other separation from your children during this period, can severely prejudice your later case for child custody. Furthermore, lengthy separations give whichever party is in primary control of the financial holdings a long window of opportunity to shift or hide assets. Finally, you must remember that your assets and debts will usually remain commingled and at risk during any separation period since courts are still generally in the habit of considering all assets accumulated throughout the entire duration of the marriage as being on the block and divisible as of the actual date of divorce. Thus, prolonged separations can be financially devastating for the wealthier or higher-earning party.

If, but only if, a separation is accompanied by a serious commitment to marriage counseling, getting a better sense of (and respect for) each other's separate selves, and actively working toward a reconciliation, then it is probably worth a shot. Do not enter into a protracted separation period, however, simply because you don't think you have the heart to finalize the divorce or because you can't afford it financially—or for any of those generally lame reasons. And for God's sake, don't lose physical track of your spouse during this period or it will be much more expensive later to implement the service of process that is a prerequisite to divorce. Finally, remember that statistically speaking, the likelihood of trial separations ultimately working out in such a way as to "save the marriage" is relatively small.

Annulment

Bigamy: the only crime on the books where two rites make a wrong.
    —Bob Hope

People have many of the same misconceptions regarding annulments as they do about separations. Many folks tend to think annulments are somehow tied in with the fact that the marriage has only been of a limited duration. People calling my office for annulments seem to think that there ought to be some type of an initial "get out of jail free" grace period, i.e., that if it has been only a three- or four-month marriage, it can't really be all that serious, thus one should be entitled to simply back out.

The legal reality, however, is that once you're married—you're married. Annulments have absolutely nothing to do with the length of time that the marriage lasted. Instead, there are a limited number of very rare conditions that one would have to prove in order to qualify for an annulment rather than a divorce.

Fraud is one viable ground for obtaining an annulment. This would have to include an original intent by one party to deceive the other on an issue that was integral to the basic foundation of the marriage itself. Other statutory grounds that might qualify for an annulment are if either party had a "loathsome disease" that they failed to disclose, or if one spouse was underage, or perhaps a bigamy or incest situation. In these cases, you may be able to get the marriage annulled, rather than having to go through a divorce.

As you can imagine, however, the situations listed above are relatively rare. Courts are very strict about granting annulments, and they are difficult to obtain. An annulment also generally costs more to process than does a simple divorce. Remember, annulments have nothing to do with the fact that you just realized early on in the marriage that it was not going to work out. It is also crucial to understand that in both annulment and legal separation cases, the Family Court can order support, but cannot divide property.

Residency

Marriage is like paying an endless visit in your worst clothes.
    —*J. B. Priestley*

In order to obtain a divorce in any given state, you must be a resident of that state or physically present there for a specific period of time. The essential requirement is that for a state court to have proper jurisdiction to grant you a divorce as one of its residents, you must have lived in that state for a specific statutory period. In Hawai'i, California, and many other jurisdictions, this statutory residency period is six months. Other, more user-friendly jurisdictions, such as Nevada, will grant divorces following reduced residency periods as short as six weeks.

Residency rules. A tricky issue arises as to just what constitutes legal residency. This can hinge on several different factors. Actual physical presence within the state during every single day throughout the last six months is definitely not required. What is required is that the state has been your domicile (i.e., the primary place that you called home) for the last six months.

Some of these criteria are a bit slippery. Because your domicile means the place that you "intend" to be your permanent home, temporary absences do not invalidate your domicile and/or your right to file a legal action in that state. But, you certainly cannot just breeze into some new state one day and expect to get divorced the next. Some factors that indicate the extent of your connections with a given state are where you file state tax returns, vote, obtain a driver's license, own property, or have a bank account. The more of these sorts of connections you can demonstrate with a given state, the more likely the state will qualify as your home state for legal domicile and residency purposes and thereby enable you to utilize its court system.

A somewhat shorter period of residency is often required for a separation. In Hawai'i, for example, the residency period to qualify for a separation is only three months.

Jurisdiction

When I can no longer bear to think of the victims of broken homes, I begin to think of victims of intact ones.
    —Anonymous

The issue of which state takes jurisdiction over a given case can become crucial. In today's highly mobile society, the situation often arises in which someone not only leaves their spouse, but they also leave their job, their home, the state, etc., and head directly into some entirely new life. In this situation, a divorce action might be appropriately filed in either, or both, the old and new states. If the husband moves to a new state and has been there six months, and the wife remains in the old state during those six months, then either of them can legitimately file in their home jurisdiction. Either of those two states would be a legally viable forum for the granting of the divorce.

Getting the jump on home state jurisdiction. This choice-of-jurisdictions issue can become a crucial strategic choice in a divorce case. When I teach classes on divorce law, I often use the example of having the "home court advantage" in a sporting event. Although it may be a tacky analogy to compare a divorce case to a basketball game, the home court advantage that accompanies having the action filed in your jurisdiction can indeed become crucial.

The bottom line is that getting the initial jump on the case by having your home state assume jurisdiction can obviously create a logistical power imbalance in your favor for the processing of the entire divorce case (i.e., you are still in town to conveniently run the case, whereas your spouse would have to travel back to hire an attorney, attend court hearings, etc.). The moral of the story is simple (especially in situations where your spouse is leaving the state): don't let the issue of a pending separation/divorce simply drift for very long without perhaps seizing the opportunity to be the first to file and serve an actual case in your home state. Otherwise, you run the risk of getting slapped with an action from another state by your now-relocated spouse. Remember, different states have entirely different laws regarding property division, custody and child and/or spousal support issues. You need to research both states' rules and precedents in order to determine which will be more favorable to your specific situation. Many clients will try to maneuver the filing/jurisdiction issue toward a particularly favorable state.

Another issue arises if you live in one state but your spouse has not been domiciled there. That may result in serious problems—especially if your child is with your spouse, or if your property is located out of state. In such cases, your home state court can grant you a divorce, but it may not have the personal jurisdiction over your spouse that is needed to make other orders that your spouse will have to obey. Issues relating to alimony or division of property may have to be resolved later in the state where your spouse is domiciled or where the property is located. The disposition of each case depends on its particular circumstances; jurisdictional issues can become very complex if your spouse never lived in your same state or has now moved away to another state.

International and intra-national jurisdictions and laws. Before I depart from this crucial issue of jurisdiction, let me briefly mention the crossover issues that may arise when international and interstate divorce laws can come into play. Divorce laws can vary wildly: from those in countries like the Philippines which still forbid it; to those in Islamic states where (for the husband, at least) a divorce may be obtained in minutes. The rules on the division of property and future financial obligations vary hugely, too. France expects the poorer party (usually the wife) to start fending for herself almost immediately—touché. Conversely, England and some American states insist on lifelong support. Community-property states are often more inclined to award alimony. A few countries, like Austria, still link cash to culpability, most commonly for adultery. Some countries' legal structures look only at the assets built/acquired during the marriage; others count *everything* regardless of when it was acquired. Some U.S. states (like Hawai'i) divide the during-marriage appreciation of either parties' separately held premarital and/or inherited assets . . . other states don't.

Japan offers an appealing quick and inexpensive break, but (for foreigners) little or no enforceable contact with the kids thereafter. Meanwhile, other countries' courts may be prone to side with the mother when it comes to money . . . but then favor the father on child custody. Different U.S. states will often order vastly differing levels of child support. (Hawai'i's is often higher due to our high cost of living.)

England, home to hundreds of thousands of expatriates, has become something of a haven for wives (especially since a judgment was rendered in 2000 that firmly entrenched the principle of "equity" in the division of marital assets). One fifth of all divorce cases registered in London's higher courts now have an international element. English courts are generally viewed as being "wife-friendly" since they seem to be heading toward the principle that the wife's efforts to boost her husband's earning power during the marriage must be compensated—meaning that *future* income, as well as current assets, must be shared.

If England is considered to be pro-wife, then Japan may represent the pro-husband opposite. Japanese wives have historically gotten the notoriously short end of the stick when it comes to property division. It wasn't until 2007 that Japan passed a new law that allows a divorcing Japanese wife to walk away with up to one-half of her husband's retirement pension.

Just for fun, here is a "synthesized strategic tip" for marrying abroad as found in the *Economist* magazine: "A rich man should choose his bride from a country with a stingy divorce law, such as Sweden or France, and marry her there. Second, he should draw up a prenuptial agreement. These are binding in many countries and have begun to count even in England. Third, once divorce looms a wife may want to move to England or America (but should avoid no alimony states such as Florida); for husbands staying in continental Europe is wise."

Some might say that it's how you live that may determine the length and happiness of your marriage; but as the *Economist* article shows, *where* you live is likely to determine how it ends.

Orders for Temporary Relief/Discovery

Marriage is the only war in which you sleep with the enemy.
   —*Anonymous*

Once a marital breakup comes to a head, it often does so in some rather ugly and urgent ways. There are some issues that can get especially nasty. Spouses have been known to snatch kids, physically beat each other, and cut one another off financially. Even if there isn't any physical abuse involved, the emotional and mental abuse can make it intolerable to continue to live under the same roof.

The period surrounding the initiation of the divorce action itself is one of the trickier ones we face as divorce lawyers. Initial or emergency issues requiring expedited temporary relief are handled in Hawai'i by way of motions for pre-decree relief followed by a hearing at which some sort of order for temporary relief is generally issued. Other states have similar procedures; although they may be titled differently, the concept is the same.

The initial documents filed in a divorce case will often focus on these temporary relief issues. These documents (called "pleadings") have to be very specifically directed toward only the most urgent or emergency issues in the case. At this initial temporary relief hearing stage the court will generally refuse to make final determinations regarding custody, support, or property settlement. All these must wait until the time of the final settlement or trial.

Temporary relief orders—the key issues. What the court will decide at the early stage of a case are those key initial issues that must be immediately resolved in order to avoid all hell breaking loose. For example, somebody must take temporary custody of the kids; or, if the parties are really fighting with one another, one spouse may be allowed sole occupancy of the marital residence and the other party forced to vacate; or perhaps some restraining orders need to be put into place to prevent squandering of financial assets or to restrain the parties from physically coming near one another in order to avoid violence.

Immediate temporary custody, temporary child support, alimony, interim occupancy of the marital residence, visitation schedules, advances on attorneys' fees or other payments—all these issues are available on this temporary relief hearing calendar. Furthermore, they are available fast. Judges will often hear the temporary relief issues on a case within just a few weeks of its initial filing. Meanwhile, the remainder of the property settlement issues won't be resolved until the case gets to trial, a year or so later.

The discovery process—drama and delay. Following the issuance of initial orders for temporary relief, but before your case actually gets to trial, it will often go thorough an exhausting, elongated, exasperating, and expensive process called "discovery." This entails an exchange of information between and about the parties. The production of documents, depositions (under oath before a stenographer), interrogatories, physical or psychological examinations may all be involved. The respective attorneys will demand and exchange information on bank accounts, loan applications, canceled checks, credit cards, business or asset evaluations, house appraisals, wills, deeds, and everything else under the sun. This process has been compared to a giant scavenger hunt wherein everything imaginable about the parties and their assets gets investigated. It is also extremely draining, both emotionally and financially, and tends to inordinately prolong the case. Most clients detest this juncture. I recommend reaching mutually agreed stipulations on as many of these items as possible, and as soon as possible.

Gaining the interim upper hand. Not surprisingly, the manner in which a case gets postured in its early stages becomes crucial in determining the final result. Restraining or protective orders are often the legal remedy sought by those dealing with conflict, threats and/or actual physical abuse between family members. Restraining orders are also used frequently for the primary purpose of trying to gain an early advantage in a custody fight.

A good divorce lawyer will try to set things up at the outset so that their client is the person who gets the house, the kids, the support, etc.—at least temporarily. In fact, it is not at all unusual for whichever side has gotten the upper hand during the temporary orders juncture of the case to then try to stall during the discovery phase in order to preserve their strategic advantage as long as possible. More often than not, the temporary orders that are issued (especially regarding custody) will tend to dictate the final result.

Property Division Guidelines

Never marry for money. Ye'll borrow it cheaper.
  —*Scottish proverb*

Hawai'i and forty-one other states throughout the country have
adopted some form of equitable distribution principles with regard
to property settlements. The remaining eight states (Arizona, California, Idaho, Louisiana, Nevada, New Mexico, Texas, and Washington) apply community property statutes.

Community property basically means that everything that
has been acquired during the marriage belongs to both spouses
equally. Thus, the most hard-line community property states
(California, Louisiana, New Mexico) require by statute that property must be divided in an exact and mandatory half-half fashion. Equitable distribution makes a similar presumption that any
and all property acquired by the spouses during their marriage
is marital property and hence subject to division. The difference
is that the courts in these jurisdictions don't always divide everything exactly evenly. Instead, judges in equitable division jurisdictions are authorized to divide things *un*evenly if necessary in
order to achieve what they view as an equitable result.

Equitable vs. equal. Equity is a slippery concept, but one that
the American judicial system attempts to quantify as a serious
and specific legal doctrine. Perhaps it can be most simply stated
as striving to achieve a general sense of fair play. Thus, if a judge
feels the need to deviate from an exact fifty-fifty split in order to
arrive at a result that is fair and equitable in a particular case, then
that judge has the ability to do so.

It is important to understand that equitable distribution principles still generally start at a basic fifty-fifty analysis for property
distribution, in much the same way that a community property approach does. The key difference is that judges in Hawai'i
and other equitable distribution states are not absolutely bound
to follow an exactly even split the way they would be in community property states. Judges in equitable distribution jurisdictions
have the ability to switch to a 40 percent to husband and 60 percent to wife (or vice versa) distribution of the marital assets, or

even 70 percent to wife and 30 percent to husband, or whatever they feel is appropriate. If the court does deviate from the basic fifty-fifty split, generally the judge will explain why.

Criteria that count. Some of the factors a court might consider in making an equitable distribution of a couple's assets include: (1) the length of the marriage; (2) the respective conditions in which each side will be left following the divorce; (3) the nature of the various property items (inherited, separate, or premarital property may be treated differently than that accumulated during marriage and will often be returned to the spouse who was the original owner); (4) the responsibilities each party had during the marriage (including their respective economic and non-economic contributions); (5) whether there are children and who they will be living with; (6) the respective health and education levels of both parties; (7) dissipation of any assets during the marriage; and (8) the relative abilities and earning potentials of the parties.

Specific Property Settlement Items

You don't know a woman until you've met her in court.
  —*Norman Mailer*

The key property settlement items that crop up in divorce cases are exactly the ones you would expect: the house, retirement plans, cars, bank accounts, etc. Virtually everything that has been earned or acquired during the marriage is on the block and divisible. This means *everything*.

It doesn't matter that the Porsche has been acquired by a fiendishly clever husband who has been squirreling away part of his paycheck each month into a separate account titled in his sole name, and that he bought that Porsche with a check from this account, and that he is thus hoping he will be able to keep both the car and the bank account separate in the divorce. It just won't happen. Anything that's been earned by *either* party during the course of the marriage, regardless of whose name is on the title, is generally subject to division in divorce.

Classifications and Allocations of Marital Property

Marriages may be made in heaven, but a lot of the details have to be worked out here on earth.
   —*Anonymous*

Premarital property is generally classified as separate property. When you bring it into the marriage, it generally remains separate property so long as you have continued to handle it in a segregated fashion. For example, say you've got $100,000 that you bring into the marriage and you stash it into a bank account separately titled in your name. That account will generally remain your separate property. However, if you used the money to buy a house, and then put both spouses' names on the deed, this may serve to "transmute" that house into marital property that may now be at least partly divisible between both the husband and wife, regardless of who paid for it originally. If, however, you were smart enough, or conniving enough, or cynical enough, to have worried about the viability of your marriage from day one, and if you kept everything in separate accounts, and kept the house separately titled, then that initial $100,000 principal balance usually remains the property of the original owner.

Who keeps what? Now what happens when the house or the bank account rises in value to $200,000? The $100,000 "appreciation portion" of even separately held property will often be divisible to at least some extent in many jurisdictions. This is certainly true in Hawai'i (where such appreciation will, in fact, generally be divided in half) and it is often true in other "equitable distribution" states as well.

Inherited property received during the marriage is generally treated similarly to property that was separately held at the outset of the marriage. Again, the principal balance of inherited property will go back to whomever inherited it, whereas the appreciation value may be divisible.

How Marital Property Is Divided

I don't think I will get married again. I'll just find a woman I don't like and give her a house.
   —*Lewis Grizzard*

You and your spouse can decide how to divide your marital property and belongings. Theoretically, at least in an uncontested divorce, you can divide the property any way you like—even if the division is not equal. The court generally prefers equitable settlements, however, so you must be prepared to explain to the court's satisfaction any major inequities in the settlement.

If you and your spouse cannot agree, then the divorce generally turns contested and the court must decide how to divide your assets. Unless there are unusual circumstances, your belongings generally will be divided evenly. However, the court may not split the ownership of each individual item of your belongings between you and your spouse; instead, it may give each of you things of equal value. For example, if your spouse gets the furniture and appliances, you may get the family car, or something else of equivalent value.

You should be aware of the fact that once the court approves the property settlement to which you and your spouse have agreed, you usually cannot make changes unless both spouses agree in writing and the court approves.

Real Property

I am a marvelous housekeeper. Every time I leave a man, I keep his house.
   —Zsa Zsa Gabor

Often your house will be the most valuable single item of marital property you and your spouse own. In my hometown, Honolulu, all of one's other possessions added together seldom equal the value of their house. I suspect this has become true in many other parts of the country, as well.

Moving on from the marital residence. If you and your spouse own a jointly titled home or other real property, or if it has been paid for (or improved) with funds earned during the marriage, then the marital estate probably has an interest in it. You must now decide how to divide it. Some of the likely alternatives are: (1) sell the home and split the proceeds; (2) have one spouse transfer it outright to the other; or (3) have one spouse transfer it to the other in return for something else (such as a cash buyout, or the waiver of an interest in a pension fund or some other property item, or for a promissory note and mortgage for some amount to be paid in the future).

The timelines for these buyouts or tradeoffs can be structured around some specific date, or conditioned upon some specified event occurring (such as once the kids are grown, or when the remaining spouse finally moves out or sells the house).

When thinking about what to do with your family home or other real property, you will want to know just how much of it you actually own. This amount is called your equity. Your equity in any property is the difference between what you can sell it for in the current market, less the mortgage amount(s) still due on it, and less the costs of selling it. You can find out the current market value of your property by consulting a professional real-estate appraiser. This will cost some money, so call around for prices. You could also call a few local real-estate agents and ask for comparables of local property prices.

Once you have figured the market value, deduct the amounts you owe on it and perhaps the commission for the real-estate agents (about 3 to 6 percent). There will also be some miscellaneous sale-related expenses. The amount left over is your equity. Assuming the house was acquired during the marriage and held by both spouses jointly, then the entire amount is probably marital property, and each spouse is probably entitled to half.

Doing the deed. It is crucial to remember that any divorce decree or other written property settlement agreement you make with your spouse to have one of you take ownership of your real property must then be followed up with an actual transfer of legal title from one to the other. To transfer real property from joint ownership by both spouses into sole ownership by one spouse, you need to draw up a deed from one spouse to the other. Have that deed signed before a notary public and recorded at the local bureau of conveyances or county recorder. Similarly, if a debtor's note is to be taken back, then it must also be properly prepared, signed, and generally recorded together along with a mortgage. There will be a small fee for recordation and maybe a transfer tax.

Note that the effectuation of the actual recorded transfer of real property is not an automatic part of most divorce proceedings.

Your divorce lawyer may or may not handle this deed transfer as part of your divorce. If not, you should seek appropriate assistance from a real-estate attorney in the preparation of these deed, or assignment of lease, and/or mortgage documents.

If you and your spouse cannot agree on what to do with your home, the court will obligingly make the decision for you. In these situations, the court will most likely rule that the house should be sold and the net profit divided appropriately between you and your spouse. If the house was true joint property, then an equal division of the net sale proceeds will generally occur. It should be pointed out that this mandatory sell-and-split result is a vastly different one from the old days when I first began handling divorce cases. It is also vastly different from the expectations of many of my clients.

A few years back, the typical result in any case where a house was involved was that if there were kids in the family, and if the wife was getting custody (another given in the old days), then the wife would get temporary occupancy of the house until the youngest kid turned eighteen. The basic theory was that the judges would retain the house for the custodial parent and the kids to live in so as to minimize the inevitable disruption to the children that accompanies a divorce. This result used to be virtually the standard gospel when I first started practicing thirty years ago. Of course, houses were worth a lot less back then.

A fire sale of the marital residence. Nowadays, given the rapid escalation in the values of real property over the years, things have changed dramatically. Courts now feel that it is rather unfair to the "out" spouse (whichever spouse had to vacate the house) to leave him cooling his heels in a series of rented residences for the next fifteen years (while he waits for his three-year-old to turn eighteen), until he can finally get the equity back out of his own house via a forced sale. Most modern courts won't take the "delayed sale" approach these days—a house is simply too big a piece of the parties' financial pie to leave on the back burner for up to eighteen years. Instead, the courts in Hawai'i and most other jurisdictions will now order the rapid and mandatory sale of the marital residence and the splitting of the proceeds.

Of course, if the spouses can mutually agree between themselves to some other negotiated approach whereby one buys the other out, or some third party buys out one of the spouses, or they refinance and someone else comes on title, etc., then the court will certainly approve it. The judge is obviously not going to make you sell your house if both spouses desire to do otherwise.

In situations where the parties cannot agree, however (i.e., they *both* want the house, they each want to buy the other out, or there is a dispute over the valuations or terms of a buyout), then the court will generally say, "Put the house up for sale on the open market and let the market decide." The house then gets sold to a third party, and the parties split the proceeds. The split will usually be fifty-fifty, although the court can use its equitable distribution powers to restructure the percentage shares of the split.

Coping with kick-out orders. An order forcing one spouse to vacate the residence may be granted on the court's temporary relief calendar if, but perhaps only if, actual physical violence (or the likelihood of same if both parties were to remain in the house together) can be demonstrated. A kick-out order is also more likely if the house is so small that the couple can't possibly continue to both live there and have any distance between themselves. In these situations, somebody may indeed get thrown out of the house.

Because it's so expensive to force the "out" spouse to rent a new place (especially while still bearing some responsibility for payment of the main house mortgage), and because it's such a severe economic hit for someone to be forcibly removed from their own house, and because it so badly prejudices a custody case to have to be the one who leaves the home while your spouse stays there with the kids—for all these reasons, the court may be very reluctant to make anyone move out. Instead, we often see strange sorts of resolutions where the court will say, "Well, why don't you two nice folks just both stay in the house, move into separate bedrooms at opposite ends of the home, and unless there is actual physical violence or really extreme emotional abuse, we will just leave you both in there for the time being." This bizarre and uncomfortable situation can then remain in effect until the court gets around to deciding a final resolution of your case a year or more later. In the meantime, pay your psychiatrist regularly!

Pensions and Retirement Plans

Marriage is a triumph of habit over hate.
—*Oscar Levant*

If either spouse was a participant in any kind of pension or retirement plan during the marriage, then some part of that plan is marital property. Unfortunately, it can often prove to be extremely complicated and expensive to get at it. In any event, a marital interest in any kind of pension plan must be dealt with as part of the dissolution. This can be handled either via a waiver of that retirement interest, or by way of a percentage computation of each spouse's fractional share therein.

The marital property interest portion of a pension plan is equal to the number of years during the marriage when the employee-spouse was a member of that plan, divided by the total number of years of employed service at the time of retirement. On dissolution, each spouse is entitled to one-half of this marital property interest portion of the plan.

Take, for example, the case of a military wife who was married for ten years during the time her army officer husband was heading toward his full vested retirement after twenty years of service. Thus, this wife has been married to her husband during one-half (i.e., 10/20) of the total time that he was actually accruing retirement. As such, she gets half of the retirement that was incurred during their marriage, i.e., one-quarter of his total retirement. She usually receives it when he retires—at the same time and in the same manner as he does.

Because of the extreme complexity that can be involved in identifying, valuing (an actuary may be required), dividing, and/or paying out pension or retirement interests, they are sometimes waived as part of an overall settlement that offsets the retirement rights against cash or some other asset or property interest. For instance, the army officer in the above example might say, "Okay, dear, you take the whole house instead of just half, but I'll keep my retirement."

Hey, I thought that was my pension! Many of my clients are shocked to find that the retirement they have been earning all along is going to be a divisible marital asset at the time of the divorce. Men in particular tend to take this issue rather personally. They say, "Wait a second, that was my job all along! Why should I have to give up half my retirement?" The divorce lawyer has the unpleasant task of explaining that retirement is indeed divisible on basically the same half-half basis as any other asset.

The theoretical justification behind retirement benefits being divisible is that if these amounts weren't being regularly deducted out of the employee's check for deposit into a retirement account, they would otherwise be a part of the regular paycheck, brought home and deposited into the parties' joint bank account. Thus this money would still be around, at least theoretically, to be divisible at the time of divorce. Personally, I have yet to see this explanation prove particularly comforting to many of my clients who are furious at having their military or other retirement funds be divisible. The fact remains, however, that virtually all states now regularly divide retirement benefits at divorce.

Retirement rights aren't just a guy thing. In this context, it is important to note that both government social security and private pension systems historically have benefited male workers. For example, retired women workers receive only about 76¢ for every dollar that men receive in social security. Likewise, in the private business sector, men generally have the larger and better-funded pension interests. Thus it becomes particularly important for women to make sure they get their fair share. Useful reading on this subject includes "Your Pension Rights at Divorce, What Women Should Know" (available from the Pension Rights Center, 918 16th Street, NW, Washington, DC 20006), and also a free guide published by the American Association of Retired Persons (AARP) titled "A Woman's Guide to Pension Rights" (available from Pension Benefit Guaranty Corporation, 1200 K Street, NW, Washington, DC 20005; telephone 202/326-4000).

Bank and Other Accounts

Marriage is a bribe to make a housekeeper think she's a householder.
  —*Thornton Wilder*

As discussed previously, one can generally anticipate a basically half-half division of all bank, stock, and other accounts that were accrued during the marriage. Furthermore, this remains true regardless of whether the accounts are titled in joint or separate names. Since these are often the couple's most liquid assets, they are often ideal for offsetting other marital property interests.

Debts

Love is an ocean of emotions entirely surrounded by expenses.
  —*Lord Dewar*

If there are bills owed by you and your spouse that were accumulated during your marriage, then they will have to be valued and divided along with the rest of the marital property. The division will usually be half-half. Some modifications may be made for post-separation debts incurred by one party, or for what I call the "drugs, sex, and rock 'n' roll" exception, i.e., where one party totally squanders marital funds on purely hedonistic pursuits. The husband who takes his new girlfriend to Las Vegas, for example, and buys her champagne and diamonds—all on his family's Visa card—may well expect to get those debts allocated solely to him. Normal cost-of-living expenditures, however, still get divided half-half, even if one spends more than the other.

Court orders and/or agreements between the spouses regarding who is to pay what bills do not in any way affect the people you owe. If you owed a legal credit card debt to Visa (either jointly or separately) before the divorce, and if your spouse either agrees, or is ordered, to pay that particular Visa bill, but then doesn't actually follow through to pay it, then *you* still owe Visa the money. In this sort of situation, Visa or other creditors can come after you to repossess the asset and obtain judgments or garnishments against your wages. Your delinquent spouse may well be subject to the same remedies and may also be in contempt of court (for all the good that does you—an ex-spouse in this situation will often follow up by declaring their own personal bankruptcy), but it is *your* credit that gets trashed in the process.

Again, the general rule is that any and all debts incurred during the marriage, regardless of whose name they are incurred in, will be divided half-half. Furthermore, unless the situation is so extreme as to trigger the "drugs, sex, and rock 'n' roll" exception, this general rule will usually be applied to include even the questionable debts run up by the one party who was the big spender and who always tended to buy more than did the other during the marriage.

Clients are reminded that it is not only the divorce court that will hold them responsible for joint debts—so will the banks. Any joint charge cards that you've got—a joint Visa or MasterCard—can turn into real problems in this situation. Don't kid yourself by thinking it's just going to be enough to call your friendly banker and say, "Oh, I'm getting divorced, please don't let my wife charge any more, and please remove me from all further liability on our joint Visa card." Au contraire! The banker loves having two signatories and two people to hold fully and jointly liable for the entire amount of all joint debts incurred. So your buddy banker will likely respond by saying, "Not so fast, bucko, it took two of you to open this account, it's going to take two of you to close it!" Of course, your wife happens to be in Rio at that very moment, literally burning the digits right off the face of your joint Visa card (with the kind assistance of her new boyfriend). Oddly enough, she may not be around to help you close down the account. This can become a real problem. About all you can do is to scramble to get your charge accounts canceled.

I have had clients who, at the first sign of a split, grab their wife's purse, or their husband's wallet. The next thing they do is cut up the credit cards. In some situations this may prove to have been a very prescient move. I've had other clients call Visa and report all their cards lost or stolen.

All this sounds somewhat hostile, and I don't generally preach hostility, but you must be very careful about this joint debt issue, since bills can rapidly spiral out of control.

Final Settlement Payments

It's possible to love a human being if you don't know them too well.
—*Charles Bukowski*

In some situations, it can become quite cumbersome to actually physically divide each individual asset in the fifty-fifty fashion. (After all, who wants half an '89 Subaru?) Instead, practical attorneys and their clients will prepare a general overall balance sheet on which all the assets and debts being assumed by each party are totaled up. Then the party who keeps more of the assets is required to make some kind of final settlement or equalization payment to the one who takes less. In this manner you even out any inequality in the overall settlement. Final settlement or equalization payments are a way of buying your soon-to-be ex-spouse out of the house, out of your retirement plan, or out of any other specific asset that one party wants to retain. This is often more practical than having to sell or literally split up those exact assets (or their sale proceeds) half-half.

Splitting the (spread)sheets. Obviously, joint bank accounts, joint stock accounts, etc., are fairly simple to divide. You just go to the bank or brokerage and start up two separate accounts, each consisting of half the original account value. But retirement plans, '52 Chevys, houses, business interests, yachts, jewelry or antiques are a bit more difficult to physically divide. They may have to be sold (often at reduced values) and their proceeds split. The best approach to dividing assets of this type is often to place an individual value on each item being retained by each party, total them all up, and then have whoever is keeping more "stuff" make an offsetting cash final settlement payment for one-half of the amount by which the total amount of the assets being taken by that spouse exceeds the value of those assets being retained by the other.

Attorneys' Fees

Marriage has teeth, and him bite very hot.
—*Jamaican proverb*

Finally we come to my personal favorite item of divorce settlements —attorneys' fees. Just kidding—Not! The main misconception that people often have on this issue is that the person who "done wrong" is somehow magically going to be held responsible for the payment of all attorneys' fees for both sides (including having to reimburse the more innocent spouse for theirs). Unfortunately, this is not the way it generally works. As a starting point, it is assumed that each party is to pay for their own attorney's fees.

My office must get two or three calls a day from prospective clients who say, "Well, I don't have any money, but I want to hire you and I want you to get your fees from my husband." Unfortunately, I would be even skinnier and more poorly dressed than I already am if I were to run my law firm based on that approach. One would go broke as a divorce lawyer waiting for the other side to be so thrilled about the divorce that they'd rush to pay your fees.

The basic approach nowadays is that everybody pays their own attorney's fees up front. Occasionally, the judge will invoke the equitable distribution concept to even things out with an award of attorney's fees—but this almost always comes (if at all) at the very end of the case. This situation presents a very serious practical problem for the person (usually the wife) who cannot afford to put up enough money in advance to get decent legal representation.

How can I hire an attorney when my husband has all the money? A wife in this situation has got a real practical problem on her hands. She may eventually be entitled to get money out of her husband for her property settlement and/or attorney's fees—but the key word here is *eventually*. Meanwhile, very few attorneys, and even fewer of the good ones, are going to start work for a client based on the hope that they might ultimately get paid. Oftentimes this turns into an outright sexist power imbalance situation because the guys have frequently been the ones in control of the finances during the marriage.

If the husband moves quickly, he can shut down any joint accounts and literally leave his wife penniless—unless she happens to have her own separate accounts. Then a vicious circle sets in if the wife doesn't have any money to retain an attorney. Without an attorney, she isn't likely to be able to even file for any temporary support, so she readily becomes even more broke. Nor will any decent lawyer start work for somebody who can't pay at least some kind of initial retainer. My law firm's policy is to substantially reduce the level of required retainer for female clients in this kind of situation, but we can't drop it to zero. A wife in this situation has got to come up with some money, somehow, and she's got to do it now. Anytime a wife knows beforehand that she is headed for divorce, she is well advised to start squirreling away some money in advance for attorney's fees.

Taxes

What is the difference between a taxidermist and a tax collector? The taxidermist takes only your skin.
  —*Mark Twain*

Marriage, home ownership, and parenthood all result in significant tax consequences. Divorce has its own important tax consequences, some of which have changed with the passage of the Taxpayer Relief Act of 1997.

How will a divorce settlement be taxed? Generally, a cash settlement representing a division of marital property is not a taxable event. This is also true for an award of actual property, such as a house, a car, or a retirement account. The theory is that this is not income to the spouse who receives it, but is property that has already been acquired by the spouses through their incomes and has already been taxed. Therefore, transfers of property between spouses incident to divorce are not taxable. To be on the safe side, these transfers should take place no later than one year following the divorce.

Of course, if you change the character of the property during or after the divorce, the tax man will be waiting to collect. There's the rub.

For example, if a divorcing spouse decides to divide a tax-free retirement account by withdrawing a portion and giving it to the other, that withdrawal is a taxable event. A better approach might be for one spouse to keep the entire account and trade off some other item of property to the other spouse. If it is necessary to divide the retirement account, it should be separated into two individual tax-free retirement accounts via a rollover procedure, rather than having either party take an early withdrawal.

As if the divorce itself isn't taxing enough. What happens when a spouse sells an asset that has appreciated over time? Suppose John and Mary bought two hundred shares of Microsoft Corporation when they got married some twenty years ago. In those pre-Windows days, it cost them only $10,000. Today, it's worth as much as the $200,000 condo they just bought. When they divorce, they agree that John gets the condo and Mary gets the stock. This is a nontaxable event and it appears to be an equal split, but it's not really a fair trade. Eventually, Mary will sell the stock and then she will have to pay capital gains on its entire appreciation ($190,000).

The rule is simple: the person who receives an asset will be responsible for the tax on the appreciation when that asset is sold. No "step up" in basis for capital gains purposes occurs as part of the divorce. Thus, even if you are dividing up assets of equivalent present value, you may be smart to take the one with the higher original cost basis and/or the lower appreciation. Fortunately, the Bush administration's 2003 tax reforms have lessened the sting a little. The new law lowers the top capital gains rate to 15 percent.

Often divorcing couples sell the former marital residence. When this occurs, there are special rules for treatment of capital gains. Current tax law provides that, regardless of your age, if you have owned and used the home as a principal residence for at least two of the five years before the sale, you can exclude up to $250,000 of gain ($500,000 for joint filers). This exclusion can generally be used only once every two years. In the John and Mary example above, John could live in the condo and eventually sell it for up to $250,000 over the original price without incurring any capital gains tax.

Tax timing. If a divorcing couple sells the residence incident to divorce, they may want to file jointly in order to take advantage of the $500,000 capital gains exclusion. They may also want to file jointly for one more year for other tax benefits. If you are divorced by the end of the calendar year, you are deemed to be single for that entire year for tax purposes. Thus, if you want to file jointly for another year, remember to delay the entry of the divorce decree until after New Year's Day. Of course, you can always file separately, even when married. While you may save taxes by filing jointly, remember that if both you and your spouse sign a joint income tax return, each of you can be held responsible for all the taxes due. Be especially careful regarding this joint tax liability issue if your spouse is running their sole proprietorship business income through your jointly filed personal income tax returns or you could wind up incurring liability for any of his/her business tax deficiencies as well.

Spouses and taxes. John Barrymore once said that you never realize how short a month is until you pay alimony. If you pay alimony, take consolation in the fact that it's generally tax deductible. If you receive alimony, declare it and pay your income tax on it.

Because alimony is tax-deductible, some spouses try to structure the pay off of what is really a property settlement through alimony. A typical scenario involves a high-income/high-tax-bracket spouse who wants to keep most of the tangible assets of the marriage such as a house, cars, works of art, or other valuable objects. Strapped for cash to buy out the ex's interest, this spouse may offer to make payments over time. By characterizing the payments as alimony, this spouse can use pretax dollars to buy out the ex. At first this may seem unfair to the ex, who must pay income tax on this property settlement disguised as alimony. However, if the ex is likely to be in a lower tax bracket, a small adjustment to the amount to be paid or the length of payments may make this arrangement advantageous to both parties.

Kids and taxes. When parents divorce, one usually gets the kids while the other gets a child-support obligation. Which parent gets the dependency exemption? Unless there is language in the divorce decree saying otherwise, the dependency exemption automatically goes to the custodial parent. This can add up because tax law changes in 1997 created a new child tax credit of $400 for each child under age seventeen for whom you can claim a dependency exemption.

If you receive child support, it is nontaxable income. Don't pay taxes on it. If you pay child support, you should know that it is not tax-deductible. Don't try to claim a deduction for it. The philosophical theory behind this rule (as brought to you by those philosophical folks at the IRS) is that you would still have to support your children, regardless of divorce or marriage. Therefore, payment or receipt of child support should have no tax impact at all. Because alimony is tax-deductible and child support is not, some divorce practitioners try to camouflage child support to make it look like alimony, or even a unitary family support payment. Sometimes this works, sometimes it doesn't. Anyone considering this course of action should consult with a certified public accountant and tax counsel and carefully weigh the advantages as well as possible disadvantages if the IRS refuses to allow the deduction.

Finally, if you seek "head of household" status, you must provide more than half the costs of a home for yourself and a child or other dependent.

Divorce can have unforeseen tax implications, and most divorce lawyers are not tax experts. For that reason, anyone considering a divorce settlement, or involved in litigation in the divorce courts, is well advised to consult with a competent tax planner to avoid unpleasant surprises.

Alimony

Alimony is like buying oats for a dead horse.
    —*Arthur Baer*

Alimony (or spousal support, as it is often referred to nowadays) is money that one spouse pays to help support the other after a divorce or separation has been filed. This may well be the single most sensitive issue that we handle as divorce lawyers. Both those who are forced to pay alimony, and those who receive less than they feel they deserve, are equally resentful. And because of its nature (generally as an ongoing monthly payment), alimony remains an open wound between spouses for years—and the scab gets torn off monthly.

For our purposes, it should be enough to try to understand the concept of alimony, without all the emotion. Simply put, either the divorcing spouses must agree (or else the court will decide) whether spousal support should be paid, who will pay it, how much it will be, and how long it will last. But the court does not order spousal support in every case. In fact, nowadays alimony is not a part of the majority of divorce settlements.

Often the length of the marriage will be a key factor in determining spousal support. If it was a relatively long marriage, or if one spouse is older and has never worked outside the home, the court may decide that his or her chances of finding a decent job are limited. This spouse might receive spousal support for life or until they remarry. Suppose one spouse is young but has never worked outside the home. The court may say this spouse should receive spousal support for a more limited period of time—perhaps until they either are self-supporting, complete an educational program, or receive training for a job. Now suppose both you and your spouse have decent jobs. In this case, the court may well say that neither of you is entitled to spousal support.

So who gets alimony anyway? Here is a short list of factors to be considered with regard to alimony: (1) each party's earning capacity; (2) the parties' respective ages and physical and mental health; (3) the standard of living during the marriage; (4) the work experience, vocational skills, and educational levels of the dependent spouse; (5) the earning capacity and the ability of the payor spouse to make alimony payments; (6) the length of the marriage; and (7) the needs of both parties.

The court will consider the situation of both spouses in terms of separate and marital property, debts, age, health, and standard of living. It also will consider any special needs each has, whether one has custody of minor children, the amount of money each spouse can be expected to earn, and the length of time it will take an unemployed spouse to train for a job and to find one.

Once spousal support has been ordered, either spouse may go back to court and ask the judge to increase or lower the amount—if there is good reason. This is why I always warn my payor clients that allowing the insertion of an alimony provision in a divorce decree is a bit like leaving the lid ajar on Pandora's box. It is important to remember that federal and state income taxes must be paid by the recipient on any spousal support payments received. Conversely, spousal support payments are tax deductible to the payor. Finally, a custodial parent who receives alimony may get a reduced level of child support.

Whatever happened to alimony for life? Alimony is one of the areas of divorce law that has undergone the most dramatic revision during the last few years. For starters, at least 22 states (including Hawai'i) now routinely refuse to consider marital fault in ordering alimony. Yet, all of us probably knew somebody who got a divorce in the fifties or sixties in which the wife got alimony for life. Nowadays, however, alimony for life is a real rarity. In fact, any alimony at all is fairly rare. In Hawai'i, the courts are reluctant to award alimony—it is ordered in less than 10 percent of all cases.

Hawai'i is at the conservative end of the spectrum. Nationwide, alimony is awarded in approximately 15 percent of all cases. Some jurisdictions—Wisconsin and California—for example, still place a substantial emphasis on alimony. Awards of alimony are more common in a higher percentage of those states' cases and often for a longer duration. California will still award alimony for life to women who are older or have health problems or have been in long-term marriages. Of course, the community property laws in California usually dictate that the maximum property settlement award is one-half.

Alimony vs. property settlement. An interwoven tradeoff between awards of alimony and property settlements is frequently utilized to achieve supposedly comparable overall results in different jurisdictions. The judges under Hawai'i's equitable distribution system, for example, are pretty tight on actual awards of alimony, but will often "equitably" compensate by giving a larger share (perhaps 60 to 70 percent) of the property to the economically disadvantaged spouse. A judge in California, on the other hand, is not allowed to deviate from the community property guidelines, and hence cannot generally award the lower-earning spouse more than 50 percent of the property. Instead, the court may attempt to balance things out with an award of alimony.

"Rehabilitative" alimony? Pursuant to both statute and court precedents in many jurisdictions, alimony is now often awarded with the specific mandate that it be rehabilitative in nature. (Please

note, this is not my wording—it's literally the phrase the judges use. Personally, I feel that the term "rehabilitative" is demeaning.) In order to receive spousal support, the recipient must generally show some kind of transitional plan for how they are going to productively use the money (and the rehabilitation time it buys them) for some sort of self-improvement scenario such as going back to school to get one's nursing or teaching certificate brought up to current standards, or finishing college, or attending graduate school. An alimony recipient generally has to have an actual plan for just what they intend to do with those years during which they are to receive alimony. One must be prepared to demonstrate in a career-counseling context just how much the extra education is going to increase one's earning capacity on the open job market.

Alimony can take the form of either a lump sum or periodic payments. Collectibility can be a real problem, and alimony awards generally should be secured by a life insurance policy on the life of the payor.

Under federal income tax laws, alimony provisions must be in writing and a divorce decree must state that alimony terminates on the payee spouse's death in order for it to be a tax deduction on the payor's gross income and be included instead as taxable income to the recipient. In most states, alimony automatically terminates when the payee spouse remarries. Under unusual circumstances, however, the parties may agree and/or the court may occasionally order, that alimony payments shall continue even after remarriage.

Statistically and realistically speaking, most alimony recipients continue to be women. The stereotype that only women receive alimony is far from true, however. State laws now allow family courts to order either spouse to support the other, regardless of sex.

Many social philosophers have observed that awards of alimony are now much too rare and much too conservative in amounts. This problem seems to stem from the fact that when no-fault divorce emerged, the concept of blame disappeared. Marriage has instead come to be treated as a purely economic partnership. Alimony has been largely eliminated in many jurisdictions. Furthermore, unlike child support, there are no uniform or nationwide standards with regard to spousal support. Instead, it often depends on individual jurisdictions and individual judges. Small wonder that, as I said in beginning this section, alimony is such a sensitive, slippery, and resentment-prone issue.

Custody

There may be some doubt as to who are the best people to have charge of children but there could be no doubt that parents are the worst.
    —*George Bernard Shaw*

Reaching an intelligent resolution of child-custody issues is probably the single most emotionally intense aspect of divorce cases. Ideally, both parents will be able to work out custody arrangements amicably—since no aspect of divorce law is worse than a nasty custody battle and the emotional toll it inevitably takes on the children.

Divorcing spouses can decide with whom the children will live. There are two basic forms of custody—legal and physical. Each of these can in turn be broken down into sole or joint custody. Not surprisingly, if the parties can't reach their own agreement on this issue, the court will enter an order awarding custody.

Custody choices. Physical custody refers to where the child will physically reside—which parent the child will actually live with. Legal custody refers to the decision-making process as to exactly how the child is to be reared. This includes decisions on educational, medical, religious, and other major issues in the child's life, but not day-to-day or routine parental decisions.

The parent who does not have sole physical custody usually has "reasonable" visitation rights. In other words, he or she can see the children during certain scheduled times (often alternating weekends). If the parents cannot agree, the court will set up a visitation schedule.

Sole Custody

The most socially subversive institution of our time is the one-parent family.
    —*Paul Johnson*

The traditional sole custody order granted both physical and legal custody to one parent, with rights of reasonable visitation to the other. Under that approach, the parent with sole custody has the major responsibility for caring for and raising the child(ren), and that parent has the primary say on all matters concerning their upbringing. This is clean, clear, and definite, and judges are accustomed to seeing it. If this is what you want, you should have little trouble obtaining court approval for such a request. However, there has been a growing trend for parents to request joint custody as a means of encouraging the maximum involvement of both parents, and many states' laws have recently changed in an effort to deal with this trend.

The old-school thinking in support of sole physical custody awards was that it is the physical dislocation, the general discombobulating of the child's previously secure environment, that hurts them the worst. Thus, the remedy that seemed to be needed was to maintain as much continuity as possible in the child's surroundings both during the divorce itself and also during the period following the divorce. The belief was that in this way kids would be more able to maintain higher security and self-esteem by having a safe environment and not having to move out of their home.

That is why courts used to grant sole custody to one parent (usually mom) and then let mom stay in the house with the kids. These stability factors were deemed to be the most important aspects in minimizing the emotional damage that kids suffer from their parents' divorce.

Joint custody, on the other hand, means that both parents are involved in making decisions about the children, such as what school the children will attend, what sort of religious affiliation they should have, and where they should reside. Separate provisions can also be individually made for legal and for physical custody, and each of these custody configurations can in turn be handled on either a sole or joint basis. For example, custody provisions that grant joint legal custody while awarding one parent primary physical custody have become increasingly common.

Although judges will now routinely approve joint legal custody agreements, before they will approve a joint physical custody arrangement they may want you to describe very specifically your precise plan for implementing it. Your plan should include a description of how you intend to physically allocate the child(ren)'s time, residence, and actual living situation to approximately one-half for each parent.

Court-ordered custody. If you and your spouse cannot agree on custody, the court makes the decision. Contrary to a widely held (but fallacious) belief, the court does not automatically give child custody to the mother. Instead, the court must decide which parent will serve the best interests of the children. "What is in the child's best interest?" is the question asked by the law, judges, and most parents. This is also the question you and your spouse should ask.

Changing custody. If you later decide the custody arrangements you agreed to are not in the best interests of your children, you can ask the court to make changes. All orders concerning child custody, visitation, and support are subject to modification based upon a "change in circumstances." Hearings may be held and the court may, or may not, approve your request. This request can be initiated by either party at any time while the child is still a minor.

Joint Custody

The two things children wear out are clothes and parents.
—*Anonymous*

Since the 1980s, joint custody has become increasingly popular, with both parents jointly deciding on major issues regarding their children. This can entail either joint legal or joint physical custody—or both the elements of custody can be structured jointly. As noted earlier, differentiating between joint and sole or legal and physical custody can be a slippery concept.

Joint Legal Custody

The value of marriage is not that adults produce children, but that children produce adults.
—*Peter De Vries*

Basically I tell clients that legal custody pertains to the major/macro/life-affecting issues in the life of the child. This often translates into a requirement that both parents must sign documents on behalf of their child for certain key items. Under joint legal custody, these crucial issues are to be decided jointly rather than solely or unilaterally by the parent who has physical custody.

Examples of joint legal custodial issues include choices regarding such decisions as religious upbringing (will the child be raised as a Catholic, a Buddhist, or a Druid?); the choice of attending private versus public school; choices surrounding any kind of elective surgery; when to get a driver's license; parental access to the child's medical or educational records; enlistment in the armed forces while still a minor; and marriage while still a minor. These typify major decisions that parents must make for (and often legally sign on behalf of) their children. Under joint legal custody, these sorts of decisions must be made jointly.

Joint custody's trendiness. Joint custody (especially joint legal custody) has become a progressive and popular trend nowadays. In California, there is now a presumption in favor of joint legal custody, and the courts there will often force the issue. This trend comes as a result of recent studies that seem to indicate that the most wrenching aspect of a divorce for kids is to be totally estranged from either parent.

This new-wave approach (which initially came out of California's touchy-feely brand of child psychology) now argues that kids are much more resilient than had been previously thought, and that they can bounce back and forth between parents much more readily than had been imagined. Indeed, what really constitutes the biggest emotional hit that kids take from divorce is to be estranged, cut off, and emotionally isolated from *either* parent. Under this view, the worst thing that one can do is to place a child of divorce under the auspices of just one parent and to keep the other one away and altogether estranged. In those situations the child winds up having to internalize feelings of estrangement, oftentimes wondering what it was that he or she did that drove daddy away.

The more contemporary and progressive approach is now to maintain a great deal of interaction between kids and both parents. Having joint custody whereby both parents feel that they are actively involved in their kid's existence is one way of doing just that.

Joint Physical Custody

Heredity is what sets the parents of a teenager wondering about each other.
—*Laurence J. Peter*

Most joint physical custody approaches contemplate literally dividing the time the child physically spends with each parent in some sort of roughly half-half configuration. It does not have to consist of half of each individual week. It can be set up as one week on/one week off, or six months/six months, or perhaps alternating years. Any of these approaches can be difficult to implement, but if done right can be extremely rewarding.

Joint physical custody requires maximum communication between the parents and brings several mature parenting skills into play. Two former spouses who still argue every time they see one another are obviously going to have a problem with joint physical custody. Likewise, some couples' logistical situations present nearly insurmountable problems. For example, if two parents now reside in different states, they obviously will have a problem implementing joint physical custody.

In my own family, my wife and her ex-husband shared joint physical custody of their son. Thus, I know from personal experience, having raised this wild and crazy teenage stepson, that it becomes very tricky logistically to choreograph the transitions back and forth between one week with one parent and the next week with the other. It is not impossible to pull this off, however, and many people feel that it is worth the extra effort (and the economic cost) that often accompanies this joint approach to custody.

Some financial fallout factors. Joint physical custody also has the side effect of substantially reducing the monthly child-support amount (often cutting it in half), since each party is now caring for the child half of the time. Also, the total cost involved in raising children under a physical joint custody format almost inevitably increases because duplicate homes have to be equipped with essentially duplicate rooms and accouterments for the children.

Joint physical custody is sometimes referred to as "yuppie Custody" because parents are often only able to make it work if they can afford it. A divorce I handled for a big-shot partner in a major accounting firm provides a good example. His approach to the custody issue was to buy his ex-wife a second house right around the corner from the former marital residence (which he retained). Then his kids could just peddle their bikes back and forth between the two houses. This worked out great since the kids could remain in the same school district, maintain their same friends, etc. So long as we can all afford to buy second homes right around the block—no problem.

Joint physical custody can be a workable approach to accommodating people with unorthodox work schedules—such as folks who work night shifts or have extensive out-of-town travel schedules. One party can handle the parenting while the other is out of town, and the other can parent for a block of time upon their return. Likewise, the ability to flip-flop nighttime and daytime schedules can add some flexibility.

Joint physical custody arrangements can actually allow each parent a bit more free time to live his or her own life. Over the years I have fought to the death to win sole custody for many of my clients—only to have several of them come back a few years later and say: "I don't know why I fought so hard for sole custody. Perhaps I should have agreed to joint custody in the first place. After all, my ex is basically a good dad and he should be doing his fair share to raise our son. Furthermore, I certainly could use a few weeks off."

Joint physical custody is particularly difficult as regards very young infants since all parenting and scheduling decisions must be coordinated. Younger kids probably also need the added stability of having one main place to call home. Many experts recommend against joint physical custody for kids younger than four or five years of age.

For somewhat older children, however, joint physical custody may be just the thing for a fast-changing modern world. After all, kids do seem to learn to adjust well to change and fluidity under joint custody formats, and those may be the same sorts of adaptive skills that will be required for the rapidly changing world in which we all now live.

For children ages six to ten who are in elementary school, joint physical custody seems to be a particularly workable approach. Kids at this age seem to be just malleable enough to make it work, and many of them seem to prefer it. Joint physical custody may also work out well for teens, many of whom can handle their own transportation logistics between households. Figuring out just how flexible any given child seems to be is the key to determining how workable joint custody will be for that child.

Joint custody seems to have a particularly beneficial impact insofar as getting fathers to feel more involved with their kids and the parenting process. The joint custody movement has really sprung up and expanded nationwide over only about the last couple of decades. It is now either accepted as an option, or specifically encouraged, in over thirty states. Since it is a relatively new phenomenon, follow-up studies are still being conducted so as to gauge just how well it works for kids over the long term.

Joint physical custody is often extremely difficult to implement and obviously requires maximum ongoing and mature communication and cooperation between the divorcing parents even during the years following their divorces. Joint physical custody probably won't work for parents who can't solve financial or scheduling issues, or who cannot communicate effectively with one another. When handled correctly, however, I've seen joint physical custody produce some remarkably successful results.

Sole vs. joint custody: advantages and disadvantages. Here is a recap of some of the pro arguments for joint custody: (1) Increased flexibility for parents to rearrange custody and parenting issues themselves, without always having to return to court. (2) A more equal sharing of the emotional, logistical, and financial burdens of child-rearing. (3) Minimizes the problem of a child's divided loyalties between the parents. (4) A viable option if, but only if, the parents still have an amicable relationship, communicate well (and often) with one another, and live near each other. (5) Works well for older children (between six to eighteen years) who are easy-going and malleable enough to go with the flow as they move from one parent to the other.

Joint custody can also have its disadvantages: (1) Frequent back-and-forth movement between parents may be quite stressful for some kids. (2) It limits the geographic mobility of the parents since they must generally continue to reside near one another. (3) It may unrealistically raise the kids' hopes that their parents will one day get back together. (4) It increases the number of issues and incidents for parents who are not on friendly terms to disagree about—since all decisions must be made jointly. (5) It may increase the likelihood of frequent returns to court if no agreements can be reached by joint decision makers. (6) Kids who require more stability/security in their lives, or who have difficulty with frequent changes or with adjusting to new situations, may not do well with joint custody. (7) It is particularly tough on younger kids (approximately aged one to six).

Visitation

Whenever I date a guy, I think, is this the man I want my children to spend their weekends with?
    —*Rita Radner*

Parents may amicably negotiate whatever visitation rights they want, and the court will generally approve them. This is often preferable to leaving it to the court to otherwise impose its "standard" visitation schedule. It is certainly better than having no specific or written visitation schedule at all and instead using only some haphazard approach to visitation that you make up as you go along.

When visitation rights are considered, they should be structured with the ages of the children in mind. For instance, the noncustodial parent might spend shorter installments of time with younger children, although the meetings might occur more frequently. With older children (primarily because their time is taken up more with school and extracurricular activities), visitation might consist of two weekends each month in addition to several school vacations.

It's also a good idea for the custodial spouse to encourage the child to maintain telephone and written communication with the noncustodial parent. Remember, if both parents are flexible, visitation need not necessarily be limited to that schedule agreed upon in the divorce decree.

The court's guidelines. If the parties can't agree on their own visitation schedule, the court will step in (as it often does) and impose one. Visitation periods allocated for the noncustodial parent under current court guidelines in most jurisdictions will consist of every other weekend (either Friday night through Sunday night or Saturday morning through Monday morning). In addition, the noncustodial parent usually gets one day during the week in which they are not getting weekend visitation. The basic noncustodial visitation schedule normally comes out to be a couple of weekends per month, plus a few other miscellaneous days thrown in each month, and then half of all major holidays and the summer vacations.

Parents aren't the only ones who can obtain visitation rights. Divorcing stepparents can retain visitation rights with their stepkids if they get appropriate provisions written into their divorce decrees. Furthermore, about forty-seven states now have laws that can allow grandparent visitation after the parents divorce, separate, or die. Following the recent U.S. Supreme Court ruling in the case of *Troxel vs. Granville,* however, grandparents seeking such visitation must realize that *they* may now have the much heavier burden of proving that such visits are in the grandchildren's best interests and/or that the grandkids would be harmed if they didn't get to see their grandparents. Since that is a difficult burden of proof to establish, grandparents who desire assured visits with their grandkids should make a point of getting provisions establishing those visits included in their kid's original divorce decrees.

Contested Custody

Children must be considered in a divorce—considered valuable pawns in the nasty legal and financial contest that is about to ensue.
    —P. J. O'Rourke

Contested custody cases are the most intense and emotionally draining matters that we as divorce lawyers have to handle. Recent national studies indicate that 90 percent of all child-custody arrangements are arrived at via a settlement negotiated between the parties themselves. If, however, the spouses are unable to reach their own stipulated agreement allocating custodial rights, then the court will (once again) step in and make that decision for them. The court will always base its decision on what it deems to be the "best interests of the child." In order to reach a fair decision, the court will often appoint a social worker, psychologist, investigator, or even a separate attorney to serve as guardian *ad litem* on behalf of the child. They will in turn examine the situation and report the findings back to the court. In many states, the court will also require the parents to attend some sort of conciliation or mediation session, and/or parenting educational classes. Judges may also ask for a custody evaluation, including on-site visits to each parent's home. Finally, a custody hearing will be held that could include reports from the various expert witnesses as well as testimony from each of the parents.

Factors that historically influenced custody determinations. In the old days, custody generally would be awarded somewhat automatically to moms. In fact, a legal principle called "the tender years doctrine" generally prevailed. This held that, especially for very young children, the primary bonding was presumed to be between young kids and their mothers. While it was recognized that this might be somewhat less true for older children, custody of young children was almost always granted to mothers.

Nowadays, custody has by statute become gender neutral. This means that, at least theoretically, dads now have every bit as much chance as moms of getting custody. In fact, the same national studies appear to indicate that in those 10 percent of cases where custody is actually disputed in court, fathers have an excellent chance of being awarded custody. This can also make for more custody battles since parents now technically start out dead even in a custody battle. In a contested custody trial, the judge, the social workers, and the child psychologists will all try to make a determination as to what will be in the best interest of the child, and one parent will be granted custody. The court will rarely force a joint physical custody result in a contested trial (although it will almost always approve that result when reached via a stipulated agreement). Oftentimes both parties can make an excellent claim to being good parents, and it's a very tough judgment call as to which one is truly the better parent.

A laundry list of custody criteria. Here is a listing of some of the key factors that courts may use in deciding custody: (1) a prefer-ence by the court for the existing primary caretaker (sometimes referred to as maintaining the *status quo*); (2) the amount of time each parent has available to spend with the child; (3) the lengths of time the child has previously spent with each parent; (4) the extent of the child's integration into a family or extended family unit; (5) preference for keeping siblings together; (6) each parent's ability to meet the child's health needs; (7) each parent's ability to meet the child's educational needs; (8) overall stability of environ-ment; (9) financial resources of each parent; (10) failure to have paid support; (11) any history of interference with visitation ver-sus a willingness to permit liberal visitation; (12) any history of one parent undermining the other; (13) frequent changes of resi-dence; (14) pending move out of state; (15) abduction of the child; (16) abuse or neglect of spouse or child (any evidence of these issues is an Achilles' heel that will, in and of itself, basically sink an abusive parent's chance of getting custody); (17) sexual abuse; (18) alcohol and drug problems; (19) use of tobacco; (20) mental disability; (21) physical disability; (22) age of parent; (23) age of child; (24) perjury; (25) nonmarital sexual relationships/cohabi-tation; (26) child's relationships with stepparents/stepsiblings; (27) available help from grandparents or other extended family; (28) the child's own preference (especially important for older children, i.e., approximately twelve years or older); (29) conti-nuity of childcare; (30) psychological or psychiatric evaluations; (31) any special needs of the child and each parent's qualifica-tions to fill them; and (32) any out-of-court agreements between the parties themselves.

Let me elaborate a bit on the above list of issues that can be crucial in custody cases by breaking it into three basic overall categories:

- Childcare history: who has been doing the primary parent-ing, who has spent the most time being involved with the kids? It helps to literally check off on a calendar through-out the year the days of each parent's respective involve-ment. Make notations as to who has been attending the PTA meetings, who takes the kids to church or to the pediatrician, who coaches the Little League team, etc.

- Personal history of each parent: evidence may be introduced as to each parent's mental health, morality, intelligence, education, career, religion, criminal record, history of violence or substance abuse, etc.
- Child-rearing attitudes: which parent has the highest working knowledge of child-development principles, stability of residence, etc. One absolutely critical key issue that becomes incredibly important in contested custody cases is the court's effort to maintain the *existing status quo*. This singularly vital status quo issue is a lot more crucial than many clients initially recognize.

All too frequently I will get a call from a woman who says: "Things got absolutely horrible with my husband about six months ago. We were fighting all the time and I wanted to keep things mellow in front of the kids. So I left the house in order to calm things down, and I moved in with my parents. My husband wouldn't let me take the kids with me. I was afraid he was going to hit me. I'd been reading the paper about all this spousal violence. I didn't want to be another statistic. But now I want to go back and try to get custody of my kids."

My reply to this poor woman is: "Oh God, I wish you had called me six months ago. You certainly should have talked to a lawyer before you ever moved out." Now the status quo may be perceived to have shifted such that the kids may at least appear to have become more closely bonded with dad in the interim. After all, dad and the kids are all still in the same house, but now mom has absented herself from the household to at least some degree. The prejudicial aftereffects of these initial separation periods may seem a bit unjust, but the determinative importance of maintaining the status quo cannot be stressed strongly enough.

Changed circumstances can change custody. Unlike the property division aspects of divorce cases, which are pretty much fixed in granite at the time of the divorce itself, any issues relating to kids (such as custody, child support, the children's education or medical needs, etc.) are always subject to the ongoing jurisdiction of the court. As such, they are subject to being reviewed again and reopened. Thus, clients must understand that custody is not a permanently done deal at the time they get the divorce. Instead, the noncustodial parent can always come back into court during the following years and seek revisions based upon a showing of what is known as "changed circumstances." Some examples of what the court might find to be sufficiently changed circumstances are: one parent moving to a new home or new state; remarriage; one parent losing their job or getting arrested for drugs or a DUI; the kids have gotten older and now want to go live with the other parent; mom links up with a new boyfriend who sells drugs; one parent suddenly gets flaky—or finally gets squared away. In these sorts of situations where new circumstances have arisen, you can go back into court and ask for a revision of custody.

Custody evaluations and social studies. As part of any custody analysis, the family court judge will generally try to have either a private social worker, a psychologist, or the social services branch of the local family court system conduct a custodial evaluation or "social study." The social study essentially consists of trained psychologists, attorneys, guardians, or social workers going out to make home-site visits and to interview parents, doctors, teachers and others in order to try to determine firsthand such issues as the extent of each spouse's particular parenting skills, whose house seems to be the best set up for the kids, etc.

These nice folks will physically visit both homes and observe such nuts-and-bolts factors as whose house has separate rooms for the individual children (as opposed to three kids living on futons in the living room); which parent appears to have the best rapport with the kids; whose home has the most toys for the kids or the most nutritional food in the fridge; or who has the best and most helpful extended family support network of grandparents, aunties, etc. The social workers will generally also talk with the kids to subtly try to ascertain their own sentiments/ preferences. (As noted earlier, the children's own preferences as to custodial arrangements often become more of a potentially determinative factor the older they are—starting approximately at ages twelve or thirteen and increasing as they get older.) These are exactly the kinds of issues on which custody cases turn. The social worker will then make extensive reports back to the court on these various criteria.

Frankly, most judges don't like being put in the position of having to rule on something as earthshaking as a custody determination based strictly upon a short courtroom hearing. Instead, at the initial stages of the divorce proceeding, the judge will strive to put some kind of status quo arrangement in place that leaves each party "as is" as much as possible. Perhaps the judge will simply stick with the existing situation and just leave the kids where they are, or perhaps temporary joint custody will be awarded, with half time to each parent.

Then the judge often will defer the case until a custody evaluation has been conducted and the social worker/evaluator reports back. The judge will place heavy reliance (not one hundred percent, but a substantial degree of reliance) on what the experts have to say. The parties usually realize this, and they will often settle the case themselves based upon their receipt of the "handwriting on the wall" as contained in the analysis/recommendation of the custody evaluation.

Conversely, the parties can choose to take the case all the way to trial. They will each then attempt to bring a bunch of child psychologists, their neighbors, or other various character witnesses into court for a full (and very expensive) trial. The neighbors may say, "Yeah, I thought he was a good dad." The shrinks may say, "She did well on the Minnesota Multiphasic Exam," and so forth. Generally, judges won't allow the kids to testify or come into the courtroom, but they may try to divine out their desires in some more subtle fashion. Then the judge rules, often (although not always) following along the lines of the social worker's initial report, but at least everyone gets their day in court. Custody rulings are notoriously tough to appeal. A judge's custody decision will not be set aside unless a manifest abuse of the Family Court's wide discretion in these matters can be shown.

Contested custody cases generally cost a minimum $10,000 in attorneys' fees. They are really messy, emotionally draining, and very tough on the kids. Finally, the parties are rarely speaking to each other by the time it is over.

Interstate Custody

One father is more than a hundred schoolmasters.
    —*George Herbert*

The Uniform Child Custody Jurisdiction and Enforcement Act and the Parental Kidnapping Prevention Act are the governing statutes for custody disputes when parents live in two different states. They basically say that the initial custody determination should be made in the child's "home state," which is defined as being wherever the child has most recently resided with a parent for a continuous period of six months. This, in turn, triggers some major strategic moves and "who files when and where" choices. The state where the initial custody determination has been made retains continuing exclusive jurisdiction to modify custody (and visitation) so long as one parent continues to reside there. If neither parent continues to reside there, the proper forum is usually the child's new "home state."

Child Support

Money isn't everything—but it sure keeps you in touch with your children.
    —*Anonymous*

Three decades ago, when I first started handling divorce cases, child support used to be a negotiated item, just like any other aspect of the property settlement. The parties would agree on whatever child-support figure they wanted, and that would be how much would be paid. If they couldn't reach an agreement, the court would order its own amount. Other than that, however, the court would generally approve whatever figure the parties themselves agreed upon.

Meet the mandatory child-support guidelines. Things have changed. Now, in almost every state, the family court simply sets the appropriate amount of child support owed based upon a complicated and mandatory formula called the child-support guidelines, which focus upon the monthly earnings of each parent (usually the *gross* earnings per month) and upon the needs of the child. The parties are no longer free to decide levels of child support on their own.

Instead, the court must approve all amounts to be paid and will not generally allow child support to be lower than the amount mandated by the child-support guidelines.

Usually, child-support payments are made until the child turns eighteen. However, in Hawai'i and many other states, payments can and will be extended through age twenty-three for a child who is still in college (or undertaking similar schooling) on a full-time basis. At any time, either spouse may ask the court to modify the amount of the payments. Unlike spousal support, child support money received is not taxable to the recipient custodial spouse. Neither can the payor spouse deduct it from his or her their taxable income.

Wage assignments for child-support collection. The mechanics of child-support collection have toughened up, too. Most family court judges nationwide now require all child-support payments to be deducted directly from the paying spouse's paycheck and sent to the state or regional child-support enforcement agency, which in turn disburses the funds to the custodial recipient. These payments are made via an assignment of the wages of the payor spouse, which will generally be processed and forwarded to the custodial payee spouse in all cases involving minor children. If a payor spouse fails to pay, the recipient spouse may ask a judge to charge them with contempt of court.

This is all part of a definite nationwide trend to put maximum teeth into the collection of past-due child-support payments. Collections and enforcement procedures can include tax liens, blocked driver's or professional licenses, tax refund intercepts, pulled passports and frozen bank accounts.

The government began this crackdown in response to statistics showing that single moms tend to become extremely economically disadvantaged following divorce. That early evidence indicated that roughly half the dads in the country were not paying their child support. It was pretty obvious to those of us in the family law trenches just how inequitable and alarming the whole situation had become.

Reaganomics and child-support collection. When Ronald Reagan came into the White House, his Reaganomic budget cutters began taking a hard look at the issue of just who wound up paying the bills for these moms when dad didn't pay his child support. To no one's surprise, they found that it was our government, its welfare department, and in short—the taxpayers, who were in fact paying for all of these nonsupported families. So President Ron and his boys got quite hard line on the child support issue. In the mid-1980s they got nationwide legislation passed that required the enactment of mandatory child-support guidelines (including, but not limited to, its calculation, assessment, collection, and enforcement) in every state of the country.

We still have a lot further to go. A report issued by the U.S. Commission on Interstate Child Support compared America's state-based system of collecting child support to a "cumbersome, slow moving dinosaur" and made the following findings: (1) today, millions of children in the United States fail to receive the financial support they are owed; (2) one in four American children grows up in a single-parent household; (3) children whose parents live in different states suffer the most; (4) each year the system fails to collect about one-third of the approximately $15 billion ordered or promised for some eleven million children.

The bottom line result of all this is that noncustodial parents now generally have to pay a significantly higher level of child support based on the computerized guideline formula. In Hawai'i and many other states, this formula centers on the gross incomes (not the net) of the two parties, the number of kids to be supported, who is assuming the medical and childcare costs, whether any alimony is being paid, and a number of other factors. Much to the dismay of payor spouses, the child-support guidelines do not focus very extensively upon the other preexisting debt or payment obligations of the payor. The rationale is that the needs of the children come first.

One unsettling trend that I have observed in this custody/child-support context is that because higher child-support awards are becoming common, and since the level of child support owed to a sole physical custodial parent is often much higher (frequently double!) than the amounts awarded in joint physical custody cases, some spouses seek sole custody strictly to gain that extra money in child support. The flip side is that some less-than-committed parents may seek joint custody strictly to lower their child-support obligations. The result can be that we divorce lawyers are witnessing an overall increase in custody battles that seem to be more concerned with the high amounts of child-support money at stake than they are with the actual custody.

The bottom line on child support. The situation has now evolved to where most noncustodial parents throughout the country pay their child support by way of a wage assignment. Payments are no longer either voluntary or direct to the custodial spouse. Furthermore, the amounts of child support generated under these guidelines are generally substantially higher than the figures that were ordered or settled upon previously (although many would argue that they are still not nearly as high as the true cost of raising kids).

Medical Insurance

Divorce is the psychological equivalent of a triple coronary bypass.
    —Mary Kay Blakely

Maintaining medical insurance after divorce has traditionally been an area where an unemployed spouse often gets the short end of the stick. This problem stems from the fact that, once you are divorced, you are no longer your spouse's legal dependent. Hence, you are no longer eligible to participate under their medical insurance coverage.

The result has been extremely unfair, and enough societal pressure was finally brought that Congress enacted a law called COBRA (Consolidated Omnibus Budget Reconciliation Act of 1996), which attempts to at least partially deal with this problem. The law now requires most private employers of more than twenty people to maintain former spouses on the company's group health insurance policy for a period of up to three years following the divorce. The recipient spouse will generally have to be responsible for making the monthly payments themselves, but at least the coverage is available to them.

This represents a substantial improvement over the previous rule that the dependent spouse had to be cut off from the employed spouse's group health plan at the time of the divorce.

Under the old rule, even if a nice guy ex-husband had wanted to continue carrying his ex-wife on his medical insurance, his employer and the insurance companies wouldn't let him.

It should also be noted that many federal and state governmental agencies, including the military, are exempt from having to provide COBRA coverage (although the military offers a COBRA-like program called "CHCBP"). Most of the bigger private companies, however, now do have an obligation to continue to provide the option for ongoing health insurance coverage for their employees' ex-spouses for at least the first three years following the divorce.

Finally, remember that medical debts are the leading cause of personal bankruptcy in the U.S. I was totally shocked the first time I heard a cynical veteran divorce lawyer counsel her client, "Either keep your spouse healthy . . . or you may not want to keep your spouse at all!" What a "sick" thought!

Issues in Military Divorces

Nobody will ever win the battle of the sexes. There's too much fraternizing with the enemy.
    —Henry Kissinger

As referenced earlier, military retirement pay and benefits are marital property, and both are generally subject to adjudication in state courts. Spouses of marriages that last through ten years or more of military service can also gain substantial advantages in the pay out and enforcement mechanisms of pension awards. Former spouses of marriages that lasted through at least twenty years of active military service are generally entitled to continuing commissary, medical, and PX benefits. Thus, military dependent spouses shouldn't be too hasty with processing their divorce if they are approaching a ten- or twenty-year mark.

Resumption of Maiden Name

It takes two good women to make a good husband and the first one is his mother.
    —Tom Mullin

Divorce is one occasion where a woman can, for free, take back her maiden name. Ordinarily, if you want to get your name changed you must file a special petition through the appropriate governmental agency and pay a few hundred dollars in legal and filing fees.

However, the inclusion in a divorce decree of a provision returning the wife to her maiden (or former married) name has the legal (and free) effect of a name change.

Premarital Agreements

Keep your eyes wide open before marriage, half shut afterwards.
—*Benjamin Franklin*

Premarital agreements (also known as prenuptial or antenuptial agreements) are contracts entered into prospectively by two spouses before they get married, which essentially dictate, in advance, what the terms of the property settlement will be in the event of a divorce. In the old days, these documents were often viewed as not even being enforceable. In fact, there was a serious concern, from a public policy standpoint, that premarital agreements might tend to encourage people to divorce.

Prenuptials: are they morally and socially acceptable? For many years, even suggesting a prenuptial agreement was considered the ultimate in gauche premarital bad taste—not to mention the tacky public relations problem it posed for the wealthier spouse who wanted such an agreement to try and impose it on their poor, disadvantaged spouse. Furthermore, from a legal enforceability standpoint, these agreements were often viewed as not being worth the paper they were written on. All that has now changed.

Hawai'i, California, and many other progressive states (in fact, at last count, more than one-half of all states) have now passed statutes such as the Uniform Premarital Agreement Act, which essentially represent a total about-face on this issue. The statutes in these states now clearly mandate that properly handled premarital agreements will indeed be binding documents. It appears that the public policy concerns about inadvertently encouraging divorce came head to head with our society's spiraling divorce rate and its attendant effect of jamming up family court calendars around the country.

Eventually a decision was made by legislators in several states that it would be easier to streamline the processing of divorces based upon pre-agreed contracts than it was to keep chasing them all through the increasingly cluttered, and expensive, contested divorce case calendars. Now many jurisdictions do allow premarital agreements to be enforced if and when the marriage turns into a divorce. The courts in these states will follow the terms of the premarital agreement if it was properly drafted and executed.

Are prenuptials legally enforceable? The key criteria for a valid and enforceable premarital agreement are: (1) it must be entered into freely—without coercion, fraud, or duress; (2) both parties must have the opportunity to consult with independent legal counsel before signing the agreement; and (3) there must be a full disclosure of all the assets of both parties. Failure to disclose all assets can be viewed as fraud and may be sufficient to invalidate the entire agreement. Furthermore, many courts have refused to recognize premarital agreements that they find to be unconscionable, not voluntary, or so one-sided as to be blatantly unfair to the other spouse. The bottom line, however, is that in many jurisdictions properly handled premarital agreements *will* be binding and enforceable.

Prenuptial agreements are rapidly increasing in popularity. As a twice-divorced physician client of mine quipped during the signing formalities for the premarital agreement that accompanied his third marriage, "Marriage is the most important contract you will ever make. People should be fully advised and understand in advance just what they are getting into." He advocates a mandatory premarital briefing by divorce lawyers comparable to the physician's doctrine requiring informed consent whereby any and all medical operations are preceded by an exhaustive explanation by the doctor regarding alternative options and possible consequences.

So what do I put in my prenuptial? The Uniform Marital Property Act that was approved by the National Conference of Commissioners on Uniform State Laws states that the premarital agreement may contain the following:

- A specific advance determination of the respective rights and obligations of each of the parties in and to any of the property of either or both of them whenever and wherever acquired or located.
- An agreed upon format for the disposition of property upon separation, divorce, death, or the occurrence (or nonoccurrence) of any other event.
- The modification or elimination of spousal support.
- The making of a will, trust, or any other arrangement to carry out the provisions of the agreement.
- The ownership rights in, and disposition of, the death benefit from a life insurance policy.
- Any other matter, including personal rights and obligations, that is not in violation of public policy or a statute imposing a criminal penalty.
- NOTE: The custodial rights of the parents and the right of their child to support may not be adversely affected by a premarital agreement (i.e., attempts to predetermine child custody awards in antenuptial agreements are *not* binding).

Just who wants a premarital agreement anyway? In my firm, we are finding prenuptials to be a part of many second marriages. One would think that it would be the cynical yuppies who would be asking for them, but ironically it's oftentimes the sixty or seventy year olds. I would estimate that as many as one-third of all my premarital clients are older folks in their sixties and seventies. Many of them are embarking on their second (or third, or fourth) marriages and want to protect their assets. They are determined to pass them down to their own kids by their former marriage, rather than have them wind up going to their new spouse's children. These divorce veterans often have some rather extensive extended families (including multiple stepchildren), and they want to make sure that their goodies go to their own kids rather than to the new spouse or the new spouse's children.

Prenuptials are also popular among people who have been divorced a time or two and have been through the wars with the divorce lawyers and their attendant fees. Frankly, they don't want to see us ever again.

I can envision the pre-wedding checklist for the brides and grooms of the future: (1) tailor—ushers' tuxedos; (2) florist—three dozen table centerpieces; (3) caterer—dinner for 200; (4) attorney—one premarital agreement!

Spouse Abuse and Domestic Violence

Never go to bed mad. Stay up and fight.
      —*Phyllis Diller*

Spouse abuse is probably the single most incendiary issue at the forefront of family law today. The statistics on domestic violence are glaring and appalling—and much higher than anybody ever thought they were just a few short years ago. A seemingly incontrovertible body of evidence has now emerged to indicate that physical violence plays a part in a far higher percentage of spousal disputes and marital breakups than even many experts had previously believed.

This issue has probably been there all along, but apparently in the past couples often kept it buried as an unmentionable part of their relationships. Women in particular were notoriously reluctant to report domestic violence. Now, if anything, the pendulum has swung the other way. Women are encouraged to report the very first signs of violence. Furthermore, myriad new government agencies, women's support groups, and community crisis centers are now available to turn to.

Shocking statistics on spouse abuse. The sheer numbers are staggering. Somewhere between three to four million women each year are the victims of domestic violence right in their own homes. Physicians now warn that domestic violence poses the largest single threat of injury to adult women in this country (i.e., more than cancer, heart disease, etc.). One-third of all female murder victims are killed by their boyfriends or husbands. During the 1990s, somewhere in the range of twenty to thirty thousand domestic violence crimes against women were reported to the police each week. Not surprisingly, this tragic state of affairs passes straight on down to the kids—children in homes with spousal violence are up to fifteen times more likely to be abused or neglected than are kids in peaceful homes.

Horrors on the home front. Domestic violence is the leading source of injury for women between the ages of fifteen and forty-four. One-third of all women who arrive at doctors' offices or hospitals seeking emergency treatment, and up to one-quarter of all those seeking prenatal care, are victims of domestic violence. While all fifty states require doctors to report instances of child abuse, there hasn't in the past been any real requirement for reporting battered spouses. Doctors are reluctant to wade into the domestic thicket.

Many people don't realize just how rapidly a spousal violence situation can arise, flare up, and become physically dangerous. An incident can literally progress (or should I say *re*gress) from mere name calling to homicide—all within a few short minutes. The following list of safety-first tips for abused women was prepared by the Domestic Violence Legal Hotline in Honolulu. I like their practical focus on the basic nuts-and-bolts steps to take when an incident occurs. Most important is to protect yourself and your children from immediate danger. That way, you can escape harm, and you can strengthen your legal claims against the abuser. Here are some of their pointers:

- Decide *now* where you'll go and how you'll get there the next time he becomes violent. Do this, even if you don't really think there will be a next time.
- Leave some money, an extra set of car keys, and extra clothing hidden *outside* your house or at a neighbor's or friend's house.
- Keep copies of important documents (birth certificates, medical records, financial records, marriage license, etc.) hidden near an exit or at a neighbor's or friend's house.
- Tell someone you can trust about the violence; try to develop friendships with neighbors. Ask them to call the police if they hear suspicious noises coming from your house.

- Develop a code word with your children, neighbors, and friends that lets them know that you need to get out *now.*
- Let your children's teachers and school principals know enough about your situation to respond supportively in a crisis situation. Ask them not to release the children to their father should you report to them that you are about to leave home.
- Try to avoid arguments in the bathroom, the garage, in the kitchen, near weapons, or near any other place where there are sharp or heavy objects.
- Do not try to fight back if he seems to be building up, especially if he is drunk or on drugs. Instead, get out of the house immediately.
- If he seems to be building up and you can't leave safely, keep your back toward open space, not a corner.
- If you do leave, *always* bring your children with you.
- Call the police at 911 to report any incident of violence.
- Always remember: YOU DON'T DESERVE TO BE HIT.

The cops and the courts respond. Faced with this spouse abuse spiral, government and law enforcement agencies have now done a total turn-around in their response to spousal violence complaints. Only a few short years ago, the average cop's predictable response to a domestic quarrel was to go out to the parties' residence and tell the squabbling couple, "Now please, both of you, just calm down." Then he would get back into his squad car and drive away.

Now, if the responding officers see any evidence of physical violence, they must make a mandatory arrest. Furthermore, this remains true even if things have calmed down a bit and the wife tries to retract her initial story.

The legal situation nowadays is that an abuser will likely be going to jail. Increasingly, prosecuting attorneys are not allowed to settle or dismiss any of these domestic abuse charges, nor to make plea bargains. Governmental policy now dictates that abuse cases go all the way to trial. Mandatory jail sentences then follow any convictions.

Paternity

A father is a banker provided by nature.
    —*French proverb*

In Hawai'i, about one-third of all children are born out of wedlock. In fact, there has been a significant increase in the rate at which kids are being born to unwed parents even while birth rates overall are declining. Issues relating to custody and child support for these kids are processed through the family court system on its rapidly expanding paternity calendar.

Are you my daddy? Gone are the days when a guy can simply go out, spawn a kid out of wedlock, and then disappear. Any unwed mother who applies for welfare nowadays will be compelled to name the alleged natural father as a prerequisite to getting her welfare payments. If she's not sure who the real dad is, then she will be expected to make her best educated guess (perhaps even naming several different potential candidates).

Claiming responsibility for kids. If necessary, the city or state attorney will summon each and every one of the possible fathers for genetic DNA tests that can establish who the true father is with virtual certainty. Next, an order will be filed to have the proven father pay child support. Conversely, once he has been legally established to be the natural father, this new dad can demand to have visitation rights with his child or even seek to take primary custody.

Common-Law Marriage/Palimony

We want a playmate we can own.
    —*Jules Feiffer*

Over the last few decades, we have witnessed a vast increase in the number of couples who deliberately choose to simply live together without getting married. The obvious question: does living together confer any quasi-marital rights? In Hawai'i, which does not recognize common-law marriages, the answer is still no. Thirteen other states, however, do recognize common-law marriages. In these states, one automatically becomes legally married following an established statutory period of living together (usually approximately seven years).

The other way in which a couple that was just living together could suddenly find themselves turned into surrogate spouses is through the concept of palimony. Almost everyone has heard about the famous Lee Marvin palimony case which came out of California in 1976. In that case, Marvin's longtime girlfriend sought financial support even though they had never married.

Many prospective clients seem to have the impression (perhaps derived from news headlines surrounding the Marvin or other celebrity palimony cases) that if you simply cohabit with someone, you are automatically close to having a common-law marriage or perhaps have some other grounds for demanding palimony. In reality, however, the situation is not quite that simple. Instead, what would probably be required to make for any chance of a viable palimony case would be for a couple to demonstrate a long-term relationship (a virtual domestic partnership) that included continuous cohabitation, commingling of assets, and the representation to the outside world that they were husband and wife. Absent that, just living together probably won't cut it (unless, of course, you have the (mis)fortune to live in one of the thirteen common-law marriage states).

Palimony is an unsettled area of the law, and courts nationwide are divided all across the board on how they deal with this relatively new hot potato issue of quasi-family law. Rulings in these cases seem to hinge largely on the specific facts of the individual case. For our purposes, it is sufficient to say that large palimony awards have generally proven to be far less easy to obtain than the sensational Marvin trial would suggest.

CHAPTER 7

Case Histories, Anecdotes, and War Stories

You never can tell about a marriage from the outside. . . . Some couples hold hands because they're afraid that if they let go they'd kill each other.
—*Anonymous*

We have all heard them, the truly horrible stories of just how nasty—how literally insane—divorcing couples can get on their way out of the marriage. Divorce is a time when people's emotions go into overdrive. We're talking high drama here. When divorce madness grabs hold of some folks, they go to great lengths to apply the old "Don't get mad, get even!" adage entirely too literally. Many spurned spouses, in particular, often refuse to just go away quietly.

This does, of course, make for great theater. Think of the hate-filled duel played out between Michael Douglas and Kathleen Turner in *The War of the Roses*. Then came *The First Wives' Club*, which succeeded in spawning not just its own cult following, but also a whole series of seemingly scholarly sociological articles and analyses. My own favorite scene in that movie is Ivana Trump's cameo appearance, in which she sagely counsels, "Don't get mad. Get everything."

Documenting the divorce wars. One of the best compilations of the venom and vitriol of divorce case histories is *Divorces from Hell* by North Carolina divorce lawyer Jacqueline Stanley. It features 140 stories of the weirdest and worst divorce battles in history, including the one about the wife who mailed her ex-husband a poisonous snake; the wife who actually petitioned the court to award her her husband's toupee (apparently figuring that without it he'd be less attractive to other women); and the husband who held a fire sale of the family home one day while his wife was at work.

I can personally relate to this last one, since I once had a client whose wife actually did try to burn down the family home rather than give it up. In my own practice I have witnessed myriad examples of otherwise very nice people turning into monsters during their divorces. There's an old saying among attorneys: "Criminal lawyers represent some truly horrible people who, when in court, are on their very best behavior. Divorce lawyers represent ordinarily very nice people who happen to be acting their absolute worst during the divorce."

One of my clients took a butcher knife into her husband's clothes closet and slashed several dozen of his expensive Italian silk suits into ribbons. I've seen several cases where one spouse sells every personal effect the other once owned at a spontaneous garage sale, or where one spouse's entire wardrobe winds up being tossed into a dumpster, or out a second-floor window and left to lie in the rain.

Frayed nerves and fisticuffs. Frankly, frayed nerves are so common among dissolving couples that virtually every horrible behavior imaginable can, and does, occur during their divorce. This behavior often stems from a sense of hurt and helplessness.

People feel they have no other way to strike back. I've actually seen people physically attack the lawyers and even the judges.

When people fail to control their rage, rash acts often are performed in the heat of an emotional outburst—anything from dumping a prized CD collection into the Goodwill bin, to driving the family car over a cliff. I had one client whose husband sold their $80,000 yacht to a complete stranger at the boat harbor for $10,000 rather than see his wife (or himself for that matter) get a fair $40,000 share. A favorite horror story among matrimonial attorneys is the one about the Seattle contractor who bulldozed the expensive ranch house he'd just built rather than let his wife get it in court.

We divorce lawyers tend to collect and compile these classic stories of entirely too true life dramas. They are popular at cocktail receptions during Family Law Bar conventions. "They are too crazy to make up," says David Mattenson, a Chicago attorney. When one of his clients found out his wife was having an affair, "he waited until she was working and sprayed her wedding dress red."

Chicago divorce attorney David Levy recollects another case. "The wife insisted on half the house. The husband showed up with a chain saw and said, 'Okay, you want to split everything equally. I'll show you equal.' And he sawed the kitchen cabinets in half." Pennsylvania attorney Lynne Gold-Bikin recalls a battle over access to a safe deposit box. "When the wife got a court order to open it, there was a pile of manure waiting."

Occasionally, a stressed-out spouse will get so out of control that the judge has to lock them up for contempt. Some clients simply collapse, either physically or emotionally (or both!), right there in the courtroom. I've seen several clients get physically sick during trials, and I was once in a hotly contested court hearing where the opposing party suddenly turned blue and passed out.

"Until death do us part" can take on a chilling new twist. A recent rash of divorced men have made good on this vow—setting their sights not only on former spouses, but also on judges and lawyers. In one nine-month period, seven different men, all distraught over their respective divorce proceedings, opened fire in various courthouses across the country. The casualty toll from these incidents alone totaled two lawyers, three ex-wives, and two relatives killed, and an additional three judges, three lawyers, three sheriff's deputies, and two court personnel wounded.

Reports from the Front

They dream in courtship, but in wedlock wake.
    —*Alexander Pope*

The following case histories recount actual true-life legal cases that I or the other attorneys in my law firm have handled. Each case has been selected because it points up key legal and emotional issues that can arise along the thorny pathway of divorce. Each real case study is followed by a moral of the story (i.e., lessons learned) that summarizes an important aspect of divorce law.

If the stories seem too wild to be true, remember these are real cases taken from my office files (although I have, of course, changed the parties' names to ensure confidentiality).

A Murderous Divorce

The call came early one morning from the Alabama Sheriff's Department. A homicide investigator wanted to know the details surrounding a divorce the previous year of our client Beverly from her husband, Mark, a U.S. Army captain. I had no trouble recollecting the case, since it had monopolized my attention for the better part of the preceding year.

Beverly was an extremely sweet Midwestern girl who had married Mark eleven years previously. At the time, he was a dashing young second lieutenant on his way up. Little did Beverly know then that someday she would be the one who got dashed.

They weren't very far into the marriage before Mark began to "scream, shout, and then slug" every time some trigger incident, real or imagined, happened to set him off. Often these episodes had little or nothing to do with anything Beverly had actually done. Perhaps Mark had had a bad day at work, or perhaps he saw her talking to another army wife at the commissary whom he considered to be a bad influence. The cause was far less predictable than the result—which inevitably seemed to be Beverly getting slapped or beaten.

At first Beverly was flabbergasted by these outbursts, but after a couple more episodes, she eventually sought counseling. There she learned the ironic lesson that it is often those members of society who are empowered with the primary responsibilities for keeping the peace and protecting law and order (i.e., policemen, military servicemen, etc.) who are the most likely to abuse the power that is entrusted to them. These pillars of society then embark on a control-freak or power-trip style of behavior that often manifests itself in physical violence.

Still, Beverly loved Mark and tried to hang in. The birth of a young son seemed to settle things down for a while, but then further episodes of imagined jealousy led to incidents of terroristic threatening and severe beatings by Mark. To make matters worse, Beverly did indeed eventually embark on an affair. Perhaps she figured, "Why not, if he is going to accuse me of it anyway, I might as well do it!" or perhaps she just needed someone a bit more understanding to talk to.

Eventually things progressed to the point where Mark and Beverly divorced. They stayed separated for a year and a half. Then, in a change of heart that may seem insane to the rest of us, Beverly (who apparently continued to feel some kind of compulsive misguided love for her dominating ex-spouse) relented, and they wound up getting remarried. Not surprisingly, the remarriage proved to be no better. In fact, this time around things escalated to the point where, instead of simply beating Beverly with his bare hands, Mark began to threaten her with the firearms that (courtesy of the U.S. Army) he so conveniently had available.

It was at this juncture, in a desperate effort to escape from her second marriage to Mark, that Beverly retained our firm. The legal case turned into an absolute nightmare. We obtained numerous restraining orders that Mark consistently defied. We had him thrown out of the house and restrained by court order from coming within a thousand feet of Beverly. Nonetheless, Beverly would return home to find Mark sitting naked in her bedroom, with a gun, demanding sex. (Another problem that often afflicts people who are accustomed to giving orders is that they have a hard time seriously believing that they themselves ever actually have to follow orders—even court orders.) We contacted Mark's superior officers, who placed him on probationary status within his army unit. He even wound up spending time in the army brig for the repeated incidents of threats and violence that had occurred on base.

Nothing was easy in this case. Mark waged a no-holds-barred custody battle for his young son (although, by all accounts, he had never been the primary parent involved in actually raising the boy during the marriage). He seemed to enjoy this absurd custody fight, as representing one last effort to assert control or domination over Beverly. Not surprisingly, Mark retained the most combative attorney he could find—and a spiraling amount of astronomical attorneys' fees began circling the drain.

Finally, after a year of hotly contested litigation, we succeeded in getting Beverly full custody of her son, and a second divorce from Mark. We even obtained ongoing post-divorce restraining orders. We thought we had done our job as good little divorce lawyers, and we moved on to our next case.

Six months later came the call from the Alabama sheriff. Mark had apparently written Beverly a series of letters promising he had changed and desperately begging for a reconciliation. Beverly relented and went to visit Mark for the weekend at his new post in Alabama. According to the sheriff, the couple was last seen having an argument at a shopping mall near the post.

When Beverly failed to return to her job in Virginia the following week, she was reported missing. The investigating officers speculated that Mark had killed Beverly on the way back to the base from the mall and had disposed of her body somewhere along a country road. The sheriff's report was later amended to "missing and presumed dead," and the purpose of the Alabama homicide detective's call was to gather background information to assist in preparing murder charges against Mark.

Lessons learned:

The cycle of violence in spouse abuse is shocking and alarming. Perhaps most frightening are the statistics indicating that once this cycle of abuse has started, it will in all likelihood continue indefinitely until treated through active participation in anger management therapy (i.e., once an abuser, always an abuser).

Here in America, about two million women are physically abused by their spouses or mates each year. As we saw in Beverly's sad case, this is not an area where a leopard is likely to change his spots. Even though the major episodes of violence may frequently be followed by periods of remorse, where the abuser acts repentant and promises "it will never happen again"—in reality it does happen again.

Abusers are much like alcoholics. Unless the abuser admits to himself and others that he really does have a problem, and actively seeks professional treatment, recurrence appears almost inevitable. In this case, Mark's repeated promises to change succeeded in buying him more time—including several reconciliations and even a remarriage. But, as we so tragically saw in Beverly's case, one last reconciliation followed by one last incident of abuse may truly be the *last* incident.

—Contributed by attorney Brad Coates, founder of Coates & Frey

The Forged P-Note

I was approaching the end of a short but extremely hostile trial. From start to finish, both sides swore the other was lying.

One of the debts to be apportioned by the parties, a sizable promissory note, was adamantly declared by Denise, my client, to be a forgery. She swore that she had never agreed to sign a promissory note for that amount—especially not one payable to husband Henry's girlfriend!

The judge had noted more than once on the record during Henry's testimony that he appeared to be lying (or if not outright lying, then at least avoiding answering by claiming loss of memory).

When the judge's decision was recited for the record, the first issue he noted was to deny my client's claim for alimony. This evoked a restrained cry from Denise, and she became very agitated. The next item the judge commented on was the promissory note. Much to our dismay, he found it to be a valid debt of the parties. This was simply too much for Denise! She screamed, broke into tears, swore at the judge, disparaged the system, and stormed out of the courtroom.

When the dust settled (unfortunately with my client no longer present), the judge then proceeded to recite the rest of his ruling, which included making Henry responsible for the entire promissory note as well as all other debts, and giving Denise the vast majority of the assets. The judge further explained that alimony would have been taxable income to the wife, and that Denise would probably have had a difficult time getting a guy like Henry to cough up the court-ordered alimony payments in any event. Instead, the judge ruled as he did because he felt that an immediate unequal division of the property would best compensate Denise. Unfortunately, she hadn't stuck around to hear about it.

> *Lessons learned:*
>
> This case was a classic example of Hawai'i's "equitable distribution" principles in action. It also exemplified the predictable phenomenon that although clients can understandably tend to get really sick and tired of the legal system, sometimes the best judges are crazy . . . like a fox.
>
> —*Contributed by attorney Jack Durham, former associate,*
>   *Coates & Frey*

Drunk Dialing Costs Custody

A seemingly run-of-the mill custody motion came before the court. On its face it seemed like the ordinary "dad never cared all that much about the child before, but now hates mom enough to try to reverse custody"–type case. The same matter had come before the court year after year. Finally, the judge was resolved to end the dispute once and for all, and ordered a trial on Dad Bob's motion. Mom Nancy seemed unconcerned. She had beaten him in court before, she was a good mother, and she felt sure she would beat him again. Certainly the judge would not reverse custody of daughter Nadine, who had lived with her mother (often out of state) ever since her birth. An additional factor was the fact that once before father had even agreed to allow this very same daughter Nadine to be adopted by another man. To an attorney, this seemed a slam-dunk case on behalf of the mom.

During Papa Bob's initial case in chief, he presented no real "smoking guns" to fire at Nancy. Instead, Bob's testimony was the normal, vanilla-type, weekender-dad–style stuff. On cross-examination, Bob was torn up one side and down the other. He admitted to alcohol problems in the past and to having voluntarily acquiesced to Nancy's relocation with Nadine to another state. He even admitted to his initial consensual involvement in the nearly completed adoption proceedings. At this point in the trial, things were certainly not going well for Bob. It looked like smooth sailing for Nancy and for the case in general.

During Mama Nancy's responsive case in chief, things got worse for Bob. Nancy described how Bob had been disinterested in the past, had been abusive with both her and Nadine over the phone, and had failed to exercise even the limited visitation that the prior court orders had afforded him. Mother further detailed how excited Nadine had been about the prospect of being adopted by her new stepfather, only to be crushed when Bob had pulled the plug on the adoption at the last minute.

Then came the bombshell. Bob's attorney led Nancy down a path of testimony describing how she had earlier stated that she had never done anything to block Bob's access to daughter Nadine. Nancy denied cutting off phone calls or ever trying to keep Bob away from Nadine. She further denied failing to inform Bob when she and Nadine had moved from town to town. Nancy also denied any alcohol use of her own.

Bob's counsel, on rebuttal, then pulled out an audiotape of a phone conversation between Nancy and Bob. Nancy's counsel strongly objected to the admission of the tape and argued evidentiary statutes—but to no avail. Nancy's attorney wanted to strangle her for not having informed him in advance of the taped conversation.

The tape was played. In the course of a one-minute conversation, Nancy was taped stating the lethal words: "as long as I live, I will never allow you to be a part of our daughter's life. I will do whatever it takes to keep you away from her. You will never see her again." These dramatic statements were enhanced by the fact that Nancy's statement was obviously made in a drunken slur. Clearly mom was "bombed" and took the opportunity to let dad have it over the phone. Bad call. Dad also happened to be a cop, and was happy to press the "record" button on his answering machine. A one-minute audiotape ruined thirteen years of custody.

Result: Judgment for Bob. Daughter Nadine, who had lived thirteen years solely in Nancy's care, was forcibly turned over to Bob within a week of the court's order. Nadine attempted suicide and was admitted to a psych ward. Nancy has not been heard from since the trial.

Lessons learned:

(1) A lifetime of doing "right" can be ruined by a single moment of weakness during which you do "wrong" (especially if it gets recorded on tape, voicemail, e-mail, video, etc.). (2) Voicemail/e-mail can be very, *very* bad/dangerous—since small snippets of comments/words can be taken out of context. (3) Make sure to tell your attorney if you have any skeletons in your closet that could negatively impact your case. It is best to come totally clean *early* and allow your attorney the opportunity to do damage control/motions to limit evidence, etc., rather than face nasty surprises during trial.

> —*Contributed by associate attorney Christopher D. Thomas,*
> *Coates & Frey*

Divorce and Rape

As a divorce lawyer, I am always cognizant of the possibility that my client may become the victim of the other spouse's temper. One typically dangerous juncture is when a hot-tempered spouse is first served with the initial complaint for divorce. Another danger point is right at the end of a case, following the final trial—particularly if the judge has ruled against the other side.

The courts, as well as numerous public and private agencies, are geared up to provide ready assistance at these junctures—such as obtaining restraining orders, providing temporary shelters in order to avoid explosive confrontations, etc. Usually, however, once the shock of the divorce action is over, and the final decree of divorce has been signed, enough of a catharsis has occurred that the threat then subsides—*usually*.

My client Margaret had described her husband Harold's potential for violence. Accordingly, I had taken extra-careful preventive measures to protect her as we negotiated toward a settlement. Once the settlement was reached and the decree was issued, the results were reasonably fair to both sides. The case was closed . . . or so we thought.

It wasn't until several months later that I learned from my former client just what a terrible time bomb Harold really was. Harold had invited Margaret to come to his apartment a few weeks after the divorce was final, ostensibly to pick up a few of her personal items that were still at the home, which he had retained.

Upon her arrival, and after a drink together to show there were no hard feelings, Harold grabbed Margaret, bound and gagged her, and proceeded to burn her with cigarettes. He then raped her repeatedly (even using various objects such as bottles and a broom handle).

It was not until more than three days later, when Harold went out for more beer, that Margaret managed to get free enough of her gag so that she could scream for the neighbors, who freed her. Harold faced criminal charges, of course. Margaret faced a lifetime of sleepless nights, psychic terror, and insecurity.

Lessons learned:

There is often no end to the vengeance a spurned spouse feels, even *after* divorce.

> —Contributed by attorney Jack Durham, former associate,
> Coates & Frey

Finders Keepers, Losers Weepers

Jesse walked into my office, nervous, unsure, almost too afraid to ask for what she really wanted. She wanted a divorce. "I need to be free," she said. "Even after all this time, after all these years, I'm still terrified of him." The conviction in her voice convinced me. It would have convinced anyone.

Jesse was a pleasant local Hawaiian-Japanese woman, about thirty years old. She was born and raised in the islands. She met Jeff, a dashing young fireman from Chicago. He stole her heart away. She gave up the island life for Jeff, and relocated with him to the "Windy City." Jesse and Jeff had a baby boy. All seemed well. Then, about two years later, the trouble began. It continued for the next seven years.

Jeff injured himself on the job and took early retirement from the fire department. Their son, Michael, was barely one at the time. Jeff became abusive. He frequently hit Jesse. He threatened more than once to kill her—more often than she could remember. Jesse longed to return to Hawai'i. Jeff flatly refused, often in a violent display.

One cold, windy night, Jesse decided she had endured enough pain. She packed while Jeff was out at his favorite watering hole. Unfortunately, he returned home before she could flee. The nightmare began. He grabbed their son and hung him out the window, twelve stories up in 20-degree weather. He threatened to drop him unless she stayed. Jesse agreed. What choice did she have?

Then, without warning, Jeff pulled a revolver and put it against Jesse's temple. "It would be easier to just blow you away," he taunted. "Let's go for a ride," he ordered. Jesse was sure she was going to die. Later, in the middle of a six-lane freeway, Jeff suddenly stopped the car. He ordered mom and child out of the car—right then and there. "Now!" he screamed, with the gun in his lap . . . cocked. Jesse jumped out, her child crying frantically. She ran across five lanes of oncoming traffic. Jeff sped off.

It was five years and many sleepless nights later that Jesse walked into my office. She had not seen her husband since that frightful night. Yes, she had escaped him, but her problems were not yet over. She still had to somehow legally dissolve the marriage. "Where is he now, Jesse?" I asked. "I don't know and I don't care," she replied.

We filed a complaint for divorce and a motion for temporary custody of the minor child. As is required for all pleadings, we then set out to serve Jeff. Given the distance in both time and space, this proved to be an almost impossible task.

Jesse worked with me to locate her husband. What an irony! She had spent so much time trying to rid herself of him. Now, at my insistence, she devoted nearly as much time trying to find him. Her

Chicago friends saw him once in a while, but no one knew where he lived. She spent hundreds of dollars in long-distance phone charges trying to track him down. No luck. I sent certified letters to every address available—they all came back unclaimed. Finally, we were forced to hire expensive process servers and investigators in Chicago to try to locate and serve the elusive fireman. They camped out day and night at every potential address we had. No luck. Jeff was apparently a fairly clever guy. He appeared to have completely vanished.

All the while, the Hawai'i court was getting impatient. Because the documents had not been served within the required timelines, the case stood ready to be automatically dismissed. Needless to say, this was extremely frustrating for Jesse. Here we were spending literally thousands of dollars, trying every reasonable method to find and serve a guy whom she had spent the last five years trying to get away from. Yet, at the same time, the court was saying, "Get it done or your case gets tossed out."

After all other options had failed, we were forced to file a motion for service by publication in the newspapers. This is the last-ditch method when all other service alternatives have failed. It is also extremely expensive, both in terms of the additional document preparation, as well as the costs of the publication itself. My client was furious, frustrated, and almost broke. Yet, she knew it was the only way.

Eventually, almost two years and several thousands of dollars after our initial filing for divorce, and fully seven years after she had fled Chicago in the middle of the night, child in arms, Jesse was granted a divorce. She was free, free at last—but the price of her freedom wasn't cheap, much less "free."

Lessons learned:

Lengthy separations can be extremely dangerous. If you lose track of your spouse, it will become very costly to obtain a divorce. The courts require that proper notice be given to defendants in all legal proceedings. Thus, service of process must be accomplished, either personally, by certified mail, or by publication. The latter is extremely expensive, but many times it is the only alternative when a spouse vanishes into thin air.

So, once you are sure that you want a divorce, it is generally smart to move ahead fairly rapidly on the legal aspects of finalizing one. Don't just leave things in limbo after you have separated physically, even though you may feel temporarily relieved to just be rid of the Bozo. Keep track of your spouse's whereabouts. The greater the distance, in time and place, the more likely the separated couple will lose contact. Then a divorce may still be available, but often at a dramatically higher cost.

> —Contributed by P. Gregory Frey, Managing Attorney,
>   Coates & Frey

Drugs, Dishonesty, and Divorce

At first glance, Terri appeared to be a solid, respectable woman. It had been several years since I had last seen her, and in that time she had matured to be an extremely attractive and successful working mother and wife. When we first knew one another, she had been working with me in another law office. She was a young secretary, and I was a struggling college student busily learning the law ropes. Now she had come to my new office wanting help with her divorce. "It will be messy," she told me nervously.

"I'm afraid my husband will seek custody of the children," Terri said. I pushed her for reasons, or at least theories. "I have no idea," she cried. She went on to deny any problems or skeletons in her closet. I pushed again. She stood firm. Yet, for some reason, I wondered if Terri was being honest with me, or perhaps more important, with herself.

"You can lie to your spouse, your employer, even your hairdresser," I told her (as I do all my clients) when preparing for a child-custody battle, "but don't ever lie to your lawyer." I went on to explain that so long as I knew the full story, I could always help. At the very least, I could try to minimize the potential pitfalls, run interference, handle damage control, etc., provided the client is honest with me. I explained that I couldn't do this, however, if she lied. In that case, I'd be blind-sided at trial. But once again, Terri assured me that nothing was amiss. "I'm a great mom," she repeated.

We commenced the hearing on the issue of temporary custody. Terri's husband alleged drug use. He said that Terri "was always too high on crystal methamphetamine to care for the kids." He also testified that Terri "had exhausted the family's finances on drugs." He turned to the judge and blurted out, "Although my wife is killing herself, I don't want her to kill our family too!"

I huddled with my client and pressed her again about the drug issue. She fidgeted. She squirmed. She refused to look me in the eye. She lamely reaffirmed, "I swear, I have never tried drugs." I nervously replied, "Well, let's try to convince the court of that and get you your kids."

The opposing counsel's cross-examination of Terri began. It was stressful. It was the old and all too common "he lied about this versus she lied about that," back-and-forth scenario. The more heated the questioning became, the more agitated Terri's physical appearance and movements were. She shifted, she fidgeted, she sweated. Her voice trembled at first and then its volume increased. She began to literally shout back her answers very defensively at the opposing counsel.

It was becoming obvious to me that my client had been less than truthful. In fact, she seemed to be all too graphically in the throes of drug-related, paranoid outbursts. She was out of control on the very day that she was trying to convince the court of her even-tempered, maternal qualities. The judge seemed to sense the same thing and immediately ordered Terri to undergo a drug test. Not surprisingly, she flunked.

I understand that the children are now doing well with their father. Custody was his for the asking. He asked. He got it.

Lessons learned:

Drugs can kill. Deceit may not kill outright, but it certainly wounds very badly in the context of a courtroom.

Thousands of couples divorce because one partner (or both) is addicted to drugs. Family courts can offer assistance through a myriad of referral or court-ordered services and treatment centers. However, the addicted person must be able to be honest with themselves and others. It is essential to be able to care for yourself before you attempt to care for others, especially young, dependent children.

Be completely honest with your lawyer, if not yourself. Your lawyer can help you, but only if you are willing to honestly assess your situation. In Terri's case, had I known the full story up front, I might have been able to settle the case with some sort of joint custody compromise arrangement—rather than taking it to trial and pushing for full custody.

Judges will routinely order drug tests of either/both spouse(s) if so requested in the context of a contested custody case. If either side tests positive for drugs, he/she will likely lose custody.

By the time we hit trial, things had gone too far for a joint custody settlement to still be viable. Terri had insisted on going to a full trial to get full custody. Somebody got full custody all right, her husband.

—*Contributed by attorney Sheila S. H. Sue-Noguchi, former associate, Coates & Frey*

A Care Home Gets Carelessly Conveyed

Mila and Reuben married in 1974. They had met in the Philippines a few years earlier, and after Reuben immigrated to Hawai'i and obtained United States citizenship, he sent for Mila. Shortly after Mila arrived, the parties combined their limited savings and purchased a small home.

For the next six years, Mila worked as a private-duty nurse, and Reuben began his own business as a building contractor and real-estate investor. Mila dreamed of opening and managing a care home.

Between 1974 and 1980, the value of Mila and Reuben's home appreciated considerably. In 1980 they decided to sell their home to fulfill Mila's dream and bought a vacant lot for the purpose of building a care home on it. Using their combined income, they applied for a construction mortgage, and Reuben constructed an eight-bedroom home on the property. Meanwhile, he and Mila lived in a rented house nearby.

Unfortunately, shortly after the care home was completed, Reuben began to run into some fairly serious legal difficulties. Various persons with whom he had been doing business had either commenced litigation or were threatening to do so. In fact, as part of one of his deals, Mila had at Reuben's request cosigned a promissory note to a mortgage company.

Reuben suggested that he and Mila transfer title of the care home to Reuben's parents, in order to avoid losing it to his creditors. At that point, Reuben's father was a sugar plantation worker and Reuben's mother was earning income by selling flowers and meat on the plantation.

Mila agreed with Reuben's plan, and, in 1981, Reuben and Mila conveyed full title of the care home to Reuben's parents. The home remained in the name of Reuben's parents until 1995. Between 1981 and 1995, Reuben and Mila treated the care home just like it was theirs. Reuben and Mila refinanced the care home on several occasions by cosigning mortgages with Reuben's parents, and, on each such occasion, Mila was reassured that, one day, Reuben's parents would reconvey title back to them. In several of these refinancings, Reuben and Mila borrowed substantial amounts of additional cash as part of the re-fi of their prior mortgages. Each time they used all of the extra cash themselves and gave none of it to Reuben's parents. Throughout the period of time from 1980 to 1995, Reuben and Mila made all of the mortgage payments and real-property tax payments on the care home, and Mila worked there seven days per week caring for her patients.

In 1995 Reuben and Mila decided to get a divorce. At that time Mila requested that Reuben's parents reconvey title of the care home back to Reuben and Mila so the home could be properly dealt with in the divorce case.

Reuben's parents refused. They claimed they had actually contributed various installment payments totaling $110,000 in cash toward the purchase of the vacant land and the construction of the care home. Mila denied this completely; she had no knowledge whatsoever of any cash ever coming from Reuben's parents.

Mila tried to convince the divorce judge to join Reuben's parents as parties in the divorce case. The divorce judge declined to do this, however, and instead ordered that such a dispute would have to be tried in a jury trial in civil circuit court, not in family court.

There were relatively few other assets left for the divorce court to divide. Thus, the divorce case itself proceeded surprisingly smoothly. The real battle occurred in a separate, and expensive, civil trial in circuit court.

Mila had to wait two years for the circuit court to schedule a trial. She was on pins and needles during this entire time. If Mila lost this trial, she would essentially lose everything she had. Fortunately, Mila won the circuit court trial, but getting to that point took another two years following her divorce and cost her $40,000 more in additional legal fees.

Lessons learned:

Think very carefully before you ever convey away title of any marital assets simply to avoid a creditor's claim. This advice is especially important if there is no adequate consideration to support the actual conveyance, and applies even if the "buyer" makes a promise to reconvey back to you. Not only can the "buyer" suddenly have a memory lapse and claim that he really does own the property, but creditors also have the right to challenge the conveyance. In this sort of case, the court does have the power to overturn and disregard the conveyance, but this is a very risky and unpredictable scenario.

> —Contributed by attorney Paul A. Tomar, former associate,
> Coates & Frey

The Man Who Was Almost a Bigamist

Marco came to see me with a simple case. He and his ex had divorced several years earlier in Texas. She got custody of the two kids, he got visitation. Things had worked out reasonably well in the six years since the divorce. Marco paid his child support, saw his kids in the summers, and got along well with his former wife. Marco had moved to Hawai'i, remarried, and had a third child with his new wife.

Meanwhile, Marco's ex decided to undertake a lengthy religious mission. She asked Marco to have the kids live with him for a year or two while she was out of the country. Marco was elated. He came to see me to find out what ought to be done to make it all legal.

Of course, Marco could have simply let his ex drop the kids off with him on her way to the far end of the world. He was smart enough to realize, however, that various problems would ensue unless he got the custody portions of his former Texas divorce agreement legally amended here in Hawai'i. If Marco tried to register the children in the local public schools, for example, the authorities would want proof that he was the custodial parent. Child support would have remained another problem. Marco didn't want or need any money from his ex. The problem was that the divorce decree required that Marco pay child support to her. Until a new court order suspended his child support, that obligation would keep accruing each month, and his ex could technically still enforce it regardless of the fact that the kids no longer even lived with her. What Marco needed was a court order transferring custody to him and suspending his child support. If his ex would cooperate, we could draft a simple agreement to submit to the court for approval. If not, we would file a motion to force resolution of these issues.

"Can a Hawai'i court modify a prior state's divorce decree?" Marco asked. This question can frequently get quite complicated, but in Marco's case the answer was yes. All we had to do was register Marco's Texas divorce decree with the Hawai'i family court. That's when the trouble started.

"Bring me a certified copy of your Texas decree when you come in," I had instructed, and Marco assured me that he would. What he actually brought me, however, was a little different. It was a divorce decree all right, but it wasn't signed by Marco, it wasn't signed by his ex, it wasn't signed by a judge, and it bore no markings indicating that it had ever been filed in court. Upon closer questioning, I learned that Marco had never actually been to court himself. Instead, all the paperwork had been handled by his ex-wife's attorney. "Marco, are you sure you're really divorced?" I asked. "I think so," was his not-too-convincing reply.

There was an easy way to find out. I wrote to the clerk of the Texas court, cited the docket or case number and title of the case, and asked for an official copy of the decree. A week or so later came a disappointing reply, "Our records indicate this case was dismissed for lack of prosecution." In other words, somebody had dropped the ball and the case had never actually been completed.

I called Marco at home. His new wife answered the phone. Of course, I didn't tell her that her husband was a bigamist and her child was illegitimate. I just asked to talk to Marco.

Marco was shocked when he heard the news. "I'll kill that sonofabitch!" he said, referring to his ex-wife's attorney. I told him to save his bullets until we were absolutely sure that he was still married to wife number one. After all, I had only checked under the case number Marco had given me; perhaps there was a new case, with a new number, which had been completed.

It was a long three weeks for Marco while we waited for a reply from Texas. Finally, good news arrived. The ex-wife's lawyer had indeed let the first case slip by, but had evidently caught her mistake and re-filed and processed all the paperwork under a new case number. We got a copy of the Texas decree, registered it, and went about finishing up the case.

Lessons learned:

Make sure you're really divorced, especially before you remarry. Don't just assume that your soon-to-be ex's lawyer will take care of everything. Get a certified copy of the divorce decree and keep it with your other important papers. Make sure it has a court filing stamp indicating when it was filed, a judge's signature, and a seal, or other markings from the clerk of the court attesting that it is a true copy of the original. If you don't get this from the lawyer handling the divorce, you can get it yourself from the clerk of the court. And don't wait until you're about to walk down the aisle with spouse number two—get proof of your divorce at the time the court grants it.

     —*Contributed by attorney Thomas D. Farrell, former associate,*
       Coates & Frey

Pandora's Box

John and Sue Schmidt were involved in a big-money divorce with lots of assets. Sue ran a pawnshop business and regularly dealt with large amounts of cash. Historically, she kept a safe deposit box that often contained tens of thousands of dollars in cash. John, of course, knew this.

As part of the divorce proceedings, the parties exchanged financial statements. During the case's first few hearings, however, the wife's financial statements failed to disclose even the existence of a safe deposit box.

We started our basic discovery by filing a set of interrogatories. These were simple questions covering many subjects, one of which was the existence of a safe deposit box. When Sue answered the interrogatories, she stated she did not have a safe deposit box. She indicated that she had previously had one but that it had been closed for more than a year. John knew this was false.

We subpoenaed records from various banks in town. One of them disclosed the existence of a safe deposit box. In fact, the safe deposit box had been closed within two days of Sue's giving us her interrogatories stating that she had no such box. We further found out from the bank records that while our interrogatory questions had been pending to her, she had made three trips to the safe deposit box.

When I took her deposition, it became apparent to me that she had not realized that in the records produced by the bank her visits to the safe deposit box, and the actual closure of the box, had all been documented. So at various times during the deposition, and in a variety of different ways, I asked her whether she had a safe deposit box or whether she had visited a safe deposit box at any time within the last few months. Always, the answer was no. When I got the deposition transcript, I counted up nine separate occasions in which she testified falsely about the safe deposit box. I did not, however, confront her about the bank's records during her deposition.

Instead, I waited until trial to trap her on this issue. We began with questions about her interrogatory answers, and I danced around the issue of the safe deposit box and the cash income generated by her business. She reconfirmed on the stand the information she had provided in her interrogatory answers. She repeatedly stated that she did not have a safe deposit box and had not visited one. She even feigned mock offense at the questions. She doggedly confirmed all the testimony in her deposition. Then I showed her the records of the bank.

It was clear that the last several minutes of her testimony were all false. She tried to say that the signatures on these documents, where she had signed to be admitted in and out of the room with the safe deposit box, were not hers. The problem with that explanation, however, was that the bank officer certified on the last page of the documents that he had seen her driver's license at the time she closed the box. Next, she tried to say that the box had been empty when she visited it. I think the whole courtroom wondered why she made three trips to an empty safe deposit box.

The court called a recess. Then the judge proceeded to rule against Sue Schmidt on a wide range of issues that extended far beyond the contents of the safe deposit box. As my client and I walked down the hallway, I overheard Sue's attorney telling her that there was no way he could have saved her after her testimony.

Lessons learned:

The point is credibility. Any party heading into court must realize that they are obligated to tell the truth. Not only is it illegal to testify falsely under oath, it is often just plain stupid. Frankly, in any case that involves more than just the parties themselves as witnesses (and certainly whenever there are extensive documents involved), the chances are pretty good that you will be caught in your lie.

Moreover, being caught in a lie about one issue can lead to an adverse ruling, not only on that issue, but also on others. In this case, the judge gave John Schmidt a favorable ruling not only on the safe deposit box issue, but also on several others. Basically, the judge discounted Sue's testimony in general and gave John a favorable ruling on several ancillary issues as well.

It simply doesn't pay to be greedy or dishonest in court.

—*Contributed by attorney Paul W. Soenksen, Senior Counsel, Coates & Frey*

Separation ≠ Divorce . . . Otherwise It's 'Til Death Do Us Part

Alvin was a career firefighter who was looking forward to his upcoming retirement. He had a full government pension, had been adding to his IRA annually, and had purchased a couple of houses that had appreciated over the years. However, he had scarcely completed filling out his retirement forms when his wife took ill, and soon thereafter passed away.

His adult children were rather surprised when he remarried Andrea less than a year after their mother's death, but they understood he was missing companionship. This second marriage soon clearly proved to be a mistake, however. Alvin and Andrea separated rapidly, and Andrea moved out of state . . . out of sight, out of mind.

Years passed and Alvin eventually embarked on a solid and satisfying "live in" relationship during his retirement years. He did not think much about his second wife Andrea until she filed for divorce some years later. It was then Alvin discovered that in the eyes of the law, he and Andrea still were in an economic marital partnership, regardless of the fact that they had kept separate accounts and lived apart for years.

The parties began negotiating an out-of-court divorce settlement, including appraisals, etc., in order to determine the values of both Alvin's and Andrea's assets . . . all in order to eventually arrive at an appropriate property settlement. During this process, however, Alvin suffered a heart attack and died. His death automatically terminated the divorce proceedings.

Alvin's children were relieved to find out that he had long ago amended his will, leaving nothing to Andrea—but that turned out to be of little help. Under Hawai'i law, a surviving spouse is automatically entitled to a percentage of the deceased spouse's assets regardless of any "disinherit" provision contained in the will. As Alvin's second (and still legally married) wife, Andrea insisted that she get her full legally entitled share of Alvin's probate estate as his "surviving spouse." The executor of the estate had to sell one of Alvin's houses, and liquidate a significant part of Alvin's IRA in order to raise the necessary money to pay her off.

Lessons learned:

There may be emotional, moral, and/or religious reasons for avoiding divorce, but the law does not take morality, religion, or emotions into consideration. In the eyes of the law, marriage is a form of economic partnership which can only be terminated when the parties follow the formalities required to obtain a full and final divorce.

Even a long-term or permanent physical separation (including one that may have entailed an informal or de facto division of all major assets), will not be recognized by the law in the event that one of the spouses dies without having completed an actual divorce. *Bottom Line*: Divorce ain't over until the (fat?) judge sings.

> —Contributed by attorney R. Barrie Michelsen, associate,
> Coates & Frey

Divorce and Bankruptcy

Joanne got divorced and her husband Steve was awarded the BMW on which both parties had signed the loan note. Steve moved to a new town, acquired a new wife, car, and house. Then, he promptly filed for bankruptcy, reaffirming his debts on the new house and new car, but disallowing the debt on the now-repossessed BMW. Steve was discharged on the BMW debt by the Bankruptcy Court. The finance company then pursued Joanne on the deficiency and she came to me for advice on what to do. I had to tell her that her choices were limited to either paying off the debt herself and thereby keeping her credit good, or else following Steve into Bankruptcy Court in order to discharge the debt, but thereby ruining her own credit for a long time.

Lessons learned:

The provisions contained in a divorce decree are not binding upon your creditors. If the debt has your name on it, you may be smart to take it and try to even out the property division by taking other "offset" assets. Otherwise, you had better be prepared to pay it later if the ex-spouse defaults on payments or files for bankruptcy.

> —Contributed by attorney John D. Hughes, associate,
> Coates & Frey

Not Everything Is As It Seems

"You have got to be kidding." That is all I could think of to say after Jonathan, a young married father of two, told his shocking, almost unbelievable story.

"I'm as serious as a heart attack," said Jonathan, his eyes staring directly at me with no emotion at all. I'll never forget that moment or the case. Ever.

Jonathan thought he had it all. Two fantastic young children, both under four years of age, and a beautiful wife. This "glass house" came crashing down the day he was served with "paternity papers" from "Grandpa Joe," his children's maternal grandfather. Jonathan didn't know Joe nor did his children, for that matter. In fact, Grandpa Joe was in state prison at the time, serving a long-term sentence for murder, convicted of killing his wife (Jonathan's wife's stepmother) years earlier. Shockingly, Jonathan's wife (Joe's natural daughter) had apparently helped try to initially conceal the killing, and was only spared a prison sentence herself because she ultimately did testify against her own father at trial. Jonathan had been utterly convinced that his wife had no "relationship" whatsoever with her father. He was so very wrong.

Grandpa Joe then petitioned the Court to be legally declared the children's natural father. He alleged an ongoing sexual relationship with his own daughter that had produced his two grandchildren! The allegations absolutely destroyed Jonathan, who had all along believed himself to be his darling children's father. Jonathan was convinced in his own heart and mind that Grandpa Joe was lying. He simply had to be!

The sheriff brought Grandpa Joe into the courtroom, in shackles, transported directly from the state prison. Grandpa Joe proudly declared himself both Father and Grandfather and calmly told the Court that he was entitled to be legally declared the children's father. He also demanded weekly visits with them at the prison visitor's center. As if this wasn't alarming enough, Jonathan's wife admitted to an amazed Court that she had regularly engaged in sexual relations with her father. She said she simply didn't know if Jonathan was the children's natural father or not. You could have heard a pin drop in the courtroom as these unbelievable revelations were made . . . except, that is, for Jonathan's loud sobs and hysterical cries. In the end, the Court ordered Jonathan to take the children to the hospital for blood tests, a necessary step to establish paternity. Jonathan said, "No." The Court said, "Yes, and do it right now."

As Jonathan left the Courthouse, he looked back at me, tears in his eyes, saying, "I love these kids, and I'll never let either of them be hurt." He certainly meant it. As a father myself, I knew he did.

I never saw Jonathan again. No one has. He took the children and fled the state with Federal authorities in hot pursuit. The idea of being forced to turn the children over to their incarcerated and incestuous grandfather was apparently too much.

Lessons learned:

Stay and fight if you believe you are right. The Family Court can award physical custody of the children to *any person* who ensures that the children's best interests are served, not just necessarily to a natural parent. I had still strongly felt that we could have won that case for Jonathan . . . but, it's hard to try a case after your client has disappeared.

> —*Contributed by P. Gregory Frey, Managing Attorney,*
> *Coates & Frey*

CHAPTER 8

Life after Divorce

"I WANT TO DIVORCE MY FAMILY"

The happiest time in any man's life is just after the first divorce.
—*John Kenneth Galbraith*

Studies indicate that it takes women an average of three to three and one-half years, and men two to two and one-half years, following separation to re-establish a basic sense of order in their lives. In my personal experience, I have watched some clients manage to successfully regroup in about half that time. However, a minimum of at least one year seems to be required before even the strongest people can successfully stage a rebound.

Most of the clients I encounter during the years following their divorce tell me they felt their divorce "had to happen" and that it was indeed "for the best." One particular group that consistently seems to come away feeling very positive about their divorce experience is men in their mid-thirties to mid-forties age range. These guys are often well established in terms of their careers, their finances, and the self-esteem. Young women whose divorces occur between their mid-twenties and mid-thirties are another group who seem to fare fairly well. Guys and gals at these stages also seem particularly prone to having successful second marriages.

Staying single. Those folks, however (both men and women), who stay single following their initial divorce (i.e., either never remarry, or do remarry but then redivorce) tend to be far less happy about their lives over time. Again, things may be a bit easier for a man in this situation. The fact that at least his job, his social and financial status, and contacts within his workplace remain relatively consistent following a divorce enables him to keep a major part of his life fairly stable.

This sort of stability, however, is a luxury that is generally not afforded most women (especially older women) in the period following their divorce. Instead, women often face more forced flux in their lives following divorce. This can be scary, but it can also serve as a major catalyst for change in their lives. Many of my female clients have changed so dramatically in their post-divorce years that they are completely different people—and most of them say that they feel very positive about these changes.

The age factor. In general, men seem to be somewhat better able to insulate themselves from the cataclysmic changes that follow divorce than do women. Not all men emerge smelling rosy, however. Unlike the successful middle-aged men who can readily and happily remarry, older men who are in their late forties or fifties at the time of the divorce, and who fail to remarry thereafter, often paint a fairly miserable picture of unshakable isolation and unhappiness. Meanwhile, although the statistical odds are rather bleak for older women to remarry, they do at least seem to have more of an inclination and opportunity to rebuild their networks and social circles in order to ease their sense of isolation. These are the women who pursue hobbies, take classes, join religious, political, environmental, or other organizations or clubs (something which women have often been more accustomed to doing all throughout their lives), and who thus manage to structure a level of self-satisfaction in their post-divorce existence.

The Single Parent

Even a family tree has to have some sap.
—*Los Angeles Times Syndicate*

The economics of single parenting are brutal. I have seen many of my single custodial parents literally hit the wall as their income begins to hopelessly lag behind their expenses and their rapidly increasing responsibilities.

Problems for single parents. Single parents are inevitably stretched pretty thin financially following their divorce. This leaves them with less money available to cover any sudden emergencies that may occur. They often don't have the same extended familial, monetary, or logistical support system to help deal with a sudden sickness or crisis. They simply don't have the same resources available to help solve the inevitable problems that arise.

Single-parent families are particularly vulnerable, since they continually seem to experience more emergencies than do intact families. Arrangements for the children's care, feeding, transportation, etc., tend to break down as children enter new developmental stages and as the adults themselves enter new relationships. Single parents also have a harder time making even their subsequent relationships work. Not surprisingly (especially given the difficulties inherent in stepparenting), second marriages that include children from a first marriage are themselves far more prone to divorce. As we saw earlier, adolescence is a particularly difficult period, and second marriages that include the responsibility for stepparenting an adolescent child can be hugely difficult.

Uncommon closeness. Predictably, a single parent's relationship with their child is likely to be far more intensely interdependent, and far more expansive, than would be the case in a two-parent family. Essentially, the single parent often shoulders both the maternal and paternal roles in child rearing. Of course, the child of a single parent often has to return the favor by being a friend, confidant, and possibly even wage earner for their now-single mom or dad who may still be on emotional and financial thin ice.

New Romances and New Relationships

Many a man owes his success to his first wife and his second wife to his success.
  —Jim Backus

Today we seem to be witnessing the emergence of a widespread restructuring of the very nature of relationships in the postmarital arena. I refer to the increasingly high incidence of formerly married folks who now make a deliberate choice to simply live together in some sort of semipermanent cohabitation relationship, rather than risk running the gauntlet of formal remarriage.

The Continuing Cohabitation Option

Love at first sight is easy to understand; it's when two people have been looking at each other for a lifetime that it becomes a miracle.
  —Sam Levinson

Cohabitation outside of marriage is increasing dramatically throughout American society in general—and the figures seem to be particularly high for veterans of the divorce wars. I would estimate that perhaps 25 percent or more of my formerly married clients have now deliberately chosen the increasingly popular continuing cohabitation option.

I am not talking here about folks who just live together for a spell prior to their next remarriage. I am talking about people who make a deliberate choice to never remarry and to instead permanently cohabit. The reasons for this vary: the man may not want to take a second bath, financially speaking; the woman may not want to have her alimony terminate upon remarriage, etc.—but for whatever reason, permanent cohabitation in lieu of remarriage is definitely a discernible trend. Many of my former clients admit quite candidly that after having gone through one expensive and emotionally draining divorce, they would never be willing to risk another one. Still fuming about their alimony or property settlement payments, they claim they will never marry again. These veterans of divorce often enter into their subsequent relationships insisting that cohabitation, rather than remarriage, be the preferred format for the new relationship.

Facing Your Family

A family is but too often a commonwealth of malignancy.
    —Alexander Pope

An obvious aspect of the period following divorce is the restructuring and redefining of one's relationships with former family and friends. (Were the Joneses really his friends or hers?) Not so obvious is the need for the divorcing parties to renegotiate their relationships with their own parents. My own divorce is a good example. My parents thought I was crazy to have let my picture-perfect first wife get away. Their initial reaction to my divorce was extremely negative, and there was no question in my mind that they actually came away thinking less of me as a person. It took years before we got things back on an even keel—largely as a result of my finally finding a second spouse who passed muster.

What are my parents doing in the middle of my divorce? One should never underestimate the role that the divorcing couple's parents can play throughout the divorce process. For starters, they represent at least some form of continuity for the grandchildren. A child's faith gets shaken by watching their parents' relationship dissolve. Their ability to move up a generation and watch at least their grandparents' marriage stay stable represents some sense of a lasting, dependable, traditional, and intact relationship. This helps to reduce the child's otherwise understandable temptation to think that all relationships are undependable and disposable. In this context, it may be smart for divorcing couples to encourage the maximum possible amount of grandparent visitation. In fact, it is often smart, and surprisingly easy, to insert specific provisions granting grandparent visitation into your actual divorce decree.

Refinding Your Friends

Bigamy is having one husband too many. Monogamy is the same.
         —*Erica Jong*

Perhaps the most cogent observation I have ever read on the tricky issue of friendship fallout following divorce was made by Abigail Tafford in her classic treatise on the trauma of divorce, *Crazy Time: Surviving Divorce*:

> You really get two divorces—a private and a public one. In your private divorce, you face your ex-spouse, your past and your self. In your public divorce, you confront the community you live in—the network of friends, family and acquaintances that you built up as a married couple. The courtroom becomes a prime setting for a convergence in the twin elements of the public and the private divorce. One surprising element occurs when people suddenly start telling you things that they have never shared with you before. Not so surprising is the friend who confides "to tell you the truth, I could not figure out why you married him to begin with." More surprising, however, is when that same friend now views you as a convenient receptacle in which to confide their own marital problems, "I've never mentioned it before but to tell you the truth I've been having many of the same problems with Jane that you seem to have at work in your divorce with Mary."
>
> It's easy to forget that your divorce presents a crisis for your friends, too. Not only are they threatened in their own marriages, but they get trapped in the hall of mirrors of your divorce. They see your divorce as reflecting back on their own lives and their own marriage, and it causes them to question the issues underlying their own relationship.

Divorce's domino effect. Needless to say, the "happily married" couples in any given circle of friends start getting a bit nervous when too many of their close cronies start divorcing. The obvious concern is that many of the underlying problems in all the surrounding relationships start looking a bit exposed. I have personally witnessed numerous occasions where the divorce of one couple within any given social circle began a domino effect that toppled half the marriages inside that group within the next couple of years. When I extrapolate a bit on this divorce domino-effect theme, and when I factor in my own personal and professional experiences, I have to come to the regrettable conclusion that the current high incidence of divorce throughout contemporary society may itself have become a self-fulfilling prophecy that can in turn threaten the marriages of the other members of that society.

Remarriage

Remarriage, sir, represents the triumph of hope over experience.
        —*Samuel Johnson*

Statistics show that over 80 percent of divorced men and about 75 percent of divorced women eventually remarry. Most remarriages take place within three years of the divorce. In the California Children of Divorce Project study, 43 percent of the men and 33 percent of the women remarried within five years of the separation date. Californians do everything fast, of course, but nationwide statistics also indicate that over one-half of the women, and about 70 percent of the men, remarry within ten years following their divorce.

Men race down the remarriage route. As a rule, men seem to act more quickly than women in taking the remarriage plunge. Oftentimes men marry women who are far younger, and/or women they had already been actively involved with on a liaison level during their original marriages. As pointed out earlier, men seem (somewhat ironically) to need the nest even more than do women. Hence, guys are far less likely to leave even a bad marriage until they have a secondary substitute relationship already lined up on the side. The fact that men undergo relatively more rapid remarriage rates seems to be a further indicator of this phenomenon.

Many second marriages—while statistically more risky—can indeed result in a relationship that is much more happy and fulfilling than the first. Amazingly enough, some people are actually smart enough to learn from their past mistakes. (Others, of course, seem destined only to repeat them.)

Redivorce rates. It remains a depressing statistical fact that the redivorce rate for people who have been previously divorced and remarried is significantly higher than the divorce rate for people in first marriages. Even more depressing is the fact that with each remarriage, the risk of redivorce increases. According to a recent statistical analysis compiled by professor Mavis Hetherington, in her excellent book *For Better or For Worse—Divorce Reconsidered*, whereas 45 percent of first marriages end in divorce, those odds rise to 65 percent for second marriages and 85 percent for third marriages. Finally, the redivorce rate appears to be slightly higher for men than for women.

Children can be the make-or-break issue for many second (or third) marriages. Remarried couples cite children as the number one source of marital stress and tension. The divorce rate is 50 percent higher in remarriages that include stepchildren than in those without.

A successful remarriage should be built on the foundation of a successful psychological divorce. One problem I have witnessed repeatedly is that many people enter a second marriage before they have had time to truly recover psychologically from the demise of their first. This may unfortunately leave one programmed to repeat the patterns and mistakes of the past. Another trend I have observed over the years is that when my clients do get remarried, they often keep remarrying various versions of their former mates. People tend to bring their same old emotional habits and baggage directly into their new relationships. People marry on the rebound, they marry to save face, to be secure, to ease their pain, or to erase the past. Perhaps most common is a remarriage intended to provide financial security.

Probably none of these somewhat short-sighted "raisons de remarriage," however, is really the right foundation for a successful remarriage. Instead, what seems to distinguish successful remarriages are the basic themes of equality, communication, sharing, and closeness—all combined with a heightened level of respect for each other's individuality. Divorce veterans often learn how to better share the various aspects of their lives with their new mate.

Sex and the second marriage. Physical chemistry, including sexual energy and compatibility, also seem to play a more vital part in remarriages than they do in first marriages. Remarried couples seem to pay more attention to their sex lives. Perhaps having witnessed firsthand how a bad sex life can weaken or destroy a marriage, they take it more seriously the second time around. As clinical psychologist Robert Kirsch says, "I don't think two people can have a good sex life if the marriage is unequal. Sex is the second language of behavior and it's important to pay attention to its message."

Successful second marriages. Many people also seem more willing to work harder on a second marriage. Having failed at marriage once, each partner may now be more mature in resisting the temptation to simply blame the other for any and all failures within the relationship (something they may have done in their first marriage). The partners in a second marriage are older now and have each established their independent past histories. Thus, they are more likely to retain their own separate but equal identities—a factor that is so crucial to a successful marriage. As my favorite divorce-recovery guru Abigail Tafford states:

> People who have been through a divorce have certain advantages in remarriage. You know about suffering and pain. You know how relationships don't work and you understand fatal power plays that overtake many marriages. In many ways, you know more than people who remain in an original marriage. You know all about avoiding conflict and dying slowly in a marriage. You may also know more than people who get divorced but who never make a long-term commitment again. Unlike permanent divorced singles, you learn to apply your divorce experience to your remarriage. In the process you come to grips with the myth of marriage as well as the reality. People who are happily remarried are a special breed. Like a decorated war hero, you have been tested in the wars of both marriage and divorce. You lived through a number of crisis now with your own psyche, your children, the network, your boss, your current spouse, your new mother-in-law. Your sense of self is pretty strong by now or you wouldn't have gotten this far.

Joan Kelly of the California Children of Divorce Project puts it another way: "Divorce has the potential of not only freeing men and women from destructive and unsatisfactory relationships, but of allowing adults to develop and change in gratifying ways in the aftermath of divorce."

Prime times for divorce and remarriage. The average age ranges for divorce are the early to mid-thirties. The precise median ages are thirty-five for divorcing husbands and thirty-three for divorcing wives.

In general, the "prime time" for divorce to occur extends from about age thirty to fifty-five. Not coincidentally, these years constitute perhaps the most exciting and dynamic periods of most people's lives. For many folks in this age group, getting divorced is part of the midlife passage. As Ms. Tafford says, "In many ways divorce is the cultural phenomenon of middle age. With luck and perseverance you can bring to this revolution in your personal life a tremendous amount of energy and talent."

Approximately forty years ago, the median time for those who remarried to do so was somewhere between three to five years after divorce. In those days there was also a period of about two years between initial separation and divorce. Nowadays, of course, everything gets compacted down into ever-shorter time frames. According to the U.S. Census Bureau, approximately 16 percent of all men and women who remarry after divorce do so within the first year.

Remarriage rates. Nearly half of all American weddings nowadays consist of remarriages for one or even both partners. There is no question, however, that rates of remarriage decline with age. Statistically speaking, rates of remarriage tend to be higher for those who have recently divorced and for those who initially married at a younger age. Amazingly enough, an astounding 16 percent of the U.S. population has been married three times.

Interestingly enough, remarriage rates are higher for whites than for other ethnic groups. Remarriage rates are also higher for those who have fewer than two children than for those who have more than two. While on the subject of statistics, let me close this section with one last rather disheartening one that I read recently (although God only knows how they quantified/verified this one): only about 12 percent of all divorces go on to see *both* parties recover from divorce in happy second marriages.

Re-Tying the Knot: Some Pros and Cons

Choose your life's mate carefully. From this one decision will come ninety percent of all your happiness or misery.
　　—*Anonymous*

There was a fascinating 2007 *Time* magazine article that made a rather compelling case for the fact that the American love affair with matrimony is as strong as ever. According to *Time*, "more than 90 percent of all women have eventually married in every generation" ever since as far back as the mid-1880s. For even the more cynical current generation of today's women, it is projected that at least 80 percent will marry. Just look at how much gets spent on weddings . . . more than $50 billion dollars a year.

So on the one hand we still love love and the institution of marriage. On the other hand, however, we face the frequently touted and semi-shocking recent statistic that nowadays most current U.S. households are no longer home to a married couple. This is indeed an accurate demographic statistic—but only barely. Furthermore, it also includes never weds, "later to weds," and some entirely too young widows. However you explain it though, married-couple households today make up only 49.7 percent of America's total.

Americans are also waiting longer than ever to wed. And it's undoubtedly no coincidence that the rise in marrying age almost exactly mirrors the rise in life expectancy. In 1970 the average American woman could expect to live 74.7 years; by 2003 she could expect to make it to 80.1—a 5½-year difference. Similarly, in 1970 the median age at which women first wed was 20.8; in 2003 it was 25.3—a 4½-year difference. Similar trends apply to men. Folks are waiting longer to get married, at least in part, because they are living longer.

So it still appears to be true that Americans continue to love marriage—and the conventional wisdom has always been that the married state is good for you from a mental, physical, psychological and financial standpoint. Lately, however, many have begun to question whether being wed really does make you happier.

Bell DePaulo is a commentator in this field who claims that people who marry, and then divorce, are not as happy as those

who stay single. DePaulo concludes, "It's better to have no relationship than to be in a bad relationship." DePaulo also tries to
further re-analyze a few other claims of the pro-marriage propo-
nents. For example, it's indeed true that currently married people
report a better sex life than single people . . . but men who are
divorced and living with a new girlfriend report even better sex.

So, does being married really make you happier? Here's one good
reason to get married . . . you may live longer. According to a
recent study conducted by two UCLA professors, individuals who *never* marry have the highest risk of early death! Their
data seems to support the hypothesis that the greater level of
social isolation associated with having never married tends to
trigger other negative health consequences. Their statistics also
seem to indicate that those whose spouses had died were almost
40 percent more likely to die sooner than married people still
living with their spouses. Those supposedly apocryphal stories
about spouses who die within days of each other may have a fair
amount of truth to them. After all, there is certainly something
favorable to be said about the institution of marriage, which is
specifically structured to keep a permanent companion and caretaker constantly nearby.

Perennial bachelor types fared even worse than did those who
had been married, but later divorced. Folks who had married
and then divorced were 27 percent more likely to have shorter
lives, but those who had *never* been married were 58 percent more
likely to die a premature death. The "never-married penalty" was
greater for men than women.

Marriage isn't all good news, however, even on the health
front. For one thing, it may apparently make you *fatter*! According to a study done by the School of Public Health at the University of North Carolina, marriage does tend to cause weight gain.
This is especially true for newly married men and women in their
early twenties who gain six to nine pounds more than their single
peers. Overall, married people are more prone to be overweight
or obese. Married men in particular are nearly 20 percent more
likely than unmarried men to be overweight.

Married couples build up more wealth. So we now know how being
married may affect your weight and your life span, but what about

its affect on your pocketbook? A study by Jay Zagorsky, an Ohio State University researcher, shows that a person who marries (and stays married) accumulates nearly twice as much personal wealth as a person who is single or divorced. Furthermore, for those who divorce, it is even more expensive than just giving up half of everything they own. They lose, on average, three-fourths of their net worth. Finally, this downward slide often starts a lot sooner than just the date of divorce. People who divorced started losing net worth four years before their divorces were final.

Conversely, married people tend to accumulate wealth much faster, amassing fully 93 percent more than single or divorced people over a fifteen-year period. Economists Andrew Oswald and David Blanchflower actually tried to put a somewhat precise dollar amount on the value of a happy marriage. They figure a happy marriage is worth about $100,000 a year.

Does being a parent make you happy? Studies report that the standard trajectory of the average marriage goes something like this: married couples start out happy. Then, as time goes by, they begin to feel gradually less fulfilled over the course of their lives together. Married parents in particular tend to become somewhat complacent and accepting of their "married with children" stage of life, but they also tend to become slightly melancholy while their children are growing up. Then, according to many experts, they return to their initial levels of bliss only after their children have grown up and moved away.

As Harvard psychology professor Daniel Gilbert writes in his fascinating book *Stumbling on Happiness*: the "indicators of happiness are actually lowest among those who have children but increase exponentially as the children leave the nest, whereupon we mis-remember what a joy it was to raise them."

Alarmingly, psychologists have found that people are less happy when they are interacting with their children than they are while pursuing other activities such as shopping, eating, exercising, or even watching TV. Apparently, the task of parenting makes most people feel just about as cheerful as doing any other basic household task. Psychologists have studied the impact of many of the variables that can impact couples' lives and they have found time and again that children have only a small impact on people's overall happiness. And as it turns out, it's a small, *negative* impact at that. (Although it is apparently less of a negative for moms than for dads.)

The comforting counterpoint to these disconcerting studies is this: children may not make us all that happy all that often—but when they do, the happiness is both transcendent and amnesic. It seems that children as a whole require so much of their parent's energy and resources that other sources of personal gratification tend to all but fade away. Fortunately, society seems to have ingrained in our psyches the unquestionable (and unquestioning) perceived truism that "our children are our greatest joy." But, this may be something of a self-fulfilling prophecy, since when you invest such a huge part of yourself (both time and money-wise) into one singular source of joy . . . then you tend to rationalize these costs and conclude that our children must be repaying us with happiness—so it is bound to be exceptional.

No matter how you conduct the overall cost/benefit analysis of being a parent, there is no denying that the hard-wired biological drive for motherhood is huge for women. Sixty percent of women in their thirties have responded to surveys by stating that having children was their very top priority in life.

Some premarital agenda items. Whether you decide to re-marry or not hinges on numerous factors, not the least of which are the legal and financial plusses and minuses of entering into an officially sanctioned marriage versus simply "shacking up" and living together out of wedlock. I will list some of the various pros and cons at the end of this section, but law and economics aside, the "verge of re-marriage" juncture should be a logical time to verbalize, hash out, and hopefully reach agreement on, some of the crucial premarital agenda items that you may have naïvely or inadvertently failed to sufficiently discuss with your spouse the first time around.

Listed below are some of those key *Premarital Agenda Items*. (Author's Note: Even though this list may come a bit late for some of my readers, it is also a good list for your "first-timer" friends and relatives as well.) (1) *Kids*: Do you want them or not? Do you have similar child rearing philosophies? Private vs. public school? How will you provide for your children's education? (2) *Wealth Accumulation*: Are you a spender or a saver? What is your basic investment strategy? What type of investments do you tend to favor? Do you believe in insurance? How important is money, career and success to each of you? Do you now own, or plan in the future to own, your own home? Where? How? (3) *Retirement*: What age would you like to retire? What is your plan for your retirement? (4) *Business Planning*: Do you have complementary careers/schedules? Do you plan to work for yourself or others?

To Wed or Not to Wed? The Legal and Economic Issues. Shacking up is no longer just a precursor to wedding bells; it now often becomes a long-term alternative to marriage. Over the past decade, according to the U.S. Census Bureau, the number of unmarried couples living together grew 72 percent to 5.5 million couples. And 1.1 million of those couples are over the age of forty-five.

Obviously, different folks are evaluating various factors and coming to different conclusions with regard to the "To marry or not to marry?" issue. So, now, as promised, here are some of the legal and financial pluses and minuses of both arrangements, as derived from several sources, including *Money* magazine.

If You Get Married, You . . .

+ Are eligible for spousal employee benefits—including health insurance.
+ May qualify for lower car insurance rates.
+ Can file negligence or malpractice suits if your spouse is hurt or disabled.
+ Will not have to pay estate taxes on inheritance from your spouse.
+ May double how much of the profits from the sale of your principal residence are free from capital gains taxes ($500,000 if married vs. $250,000 for a single person).
+ Will probably qualify for your deceased spouse's pension or Social Security benefits.
− May have to pay the high cost of divorce if you break up.
− Will often face a cutoff of any remaining alimony payments still due from the divorce settlement of a prior marriage.
− Will receive a lower social security benefit (in a dual-income marriage).

- – May not be eligible to continue receiving pension or social security benefits of your previous deceased spouse.

If You Live Together, You . . .

- + Can skirt the legal entanglements of divorce (say sayonara to those damn divorce lawyers). (Caveat: be careful of common-law marriage states.)
- + Will continue receiving pension and social security benefits of any deceased previous spouse.
- + Will continue receiving any pending alimony payments stemming from a prior divorce settlement.
- – May not be eligible for spousal employee benefits.
- – Will not be automatically named guardian of your partner's child(ren) if your partner should die.
- – Do not have automatic visitation rights to see your partner in intensive or critical care units of hospitals.
- – Will have to pay estate taxes if the estate you inherit from your deceased partner is worth more than the maximum estate tax free inheritance threshold.

Stepfamilies

Having a family is like having a bowling alley installed in your brain.
  —*Martin Mull*

Perhaps the most difficult familial relationship of all to successfully establish is that between stepparent and child. No matter how hard stepparents try, the simple reality is that kids continue to long for their original nuclear family. They simply do not feel as much an integral part of the "remarried" family. Instead, they almost inevitably tend to feel displaced or estranged from even the most enthusiastic stepparents.

Older boys, particularly those who remain in fairly close contact with their natural fathers, often find it very difficult to develop a truly close attachment with their stepfathers. More often than not, there is at least some level of ongoing friction with children whose mothers remarry. They rarely manage to feel truly welcome in the new family.

The shifting roles of stepparents. In earlier times, stepparenting was often a pretty positive role. Nowadays, however, stepparenting has turned into one of the more difficult familial roles that anyone could ever have to fill. One major difference is that in the old days a stepparent would most often enter onto the scene following the premature death of the natural mother or father. In this context, they became something of an unselfish savior of the family that otherwise might have totally disintegrated. Unfortunately, the role of a modern-day stepparent has changed dramatically and generally for the worse. The primary difference causing this change is that nowadays most people's remarriages follow on the heels of a divorce, rather than death.

Today, instead of being a savior entering onto the scene to keep a family together, the stepparent is more often viewed by the kids as an unnecessary and unwanted intruder—one whose presence would be totally unnecessary if only mom and dad could be back together again. And God forbid if it was the stepparent's entry onto the scene that actually precipitated mom and dad's divorce initially—that poor step-sucker will probably never be accepted.

The thankless position of a stepparent. Children are understandably extremely tentative about accepting a stepparent into their lives. It is virtually impossible for such children to bring themselves to allow stepparents to become full substitutes for their natural parents. This becomes particularly problematic the older the children are at the time their parents remarry. Generally, younger children are more open to accepting stepparents fully into their lives than are older kids, who feel extremely conflicted about this scenario and who are reluctant to develop any real closeness or loyalty to the stepparent.

Older children seem to instinctively sense that accepting a stepparent somehow represents betrayal of their absentee natural parent. This sense of alienation can even be borne out statistically by surveys of children aged nine and ten or above. Such surveys indicate that a surprisingly large majority of these kids actively resent their stepparents. Furthermore, the older the child gets, the more strident this becomes.

Adolescents, in particular, tend to resent their stepparents since they are in a rebellion mode anyway. Any stepfather who comes along and tries to assume the role of substitute dad or disciplinarian in place of the natural father will likely find that he has entered onto the stage of the child's life at exactly the wrong juncture of the ongoing drama that comprises an adolescent child's life.

Stepfathers suck! Stepfathers have an especially tough row to hoe. Perhaps the single most difficult quasi-parental role to fill is that of a stepfather to an adolescent boy. The best the stepdad can do in this situation is to try to be a low-key friend or maybe a mentor to the boy. The worst mistake is to move too readily to shoulder the role of disciplinarian to a child who is by no means willing to accept his authority. This can be compounded when mom, eager to keep the new marriage together, errs on the side of supporting the new husband in any conflict between him and the children. This has the makings of a very frustrating and potentially disastrous combination. About the only hope a stepfather has of putting a remotely positive spin on this situation is if he can somehow manage to develop an avenue of relating to the children that is totally independent from his relationship to their mother, thereby indicating that he really likes the kids on their own merits.

I had the dubious distinction of occupying this role as a stepdad to my wife's son by her first marriage. He lived with me from age eight to eighteen and I can tell you from firsthand experience that this is a rather exhausting exercise in human relations. Although I knocked myself out trying to be the absolute best stepdad I could to that boy, I never for one minute believed that he ever really even remotely appreciated all that I did for him.

Being a stepfather can also, of course, be quite rewarding and work out really well, but that seems to be a decidedly less frequent result. In any event, I certainly wish the very best of luck to any stepdad who finds himself in this position.

A more mellow situation for stepmoms. The situation for stepmothers is generally somewhat less strained. For starters, fewer children wind up living with their dads as custodial parents following a divorce. Most go with their moms. An obvious result of this situation is that fewer kids actually end up physically living full time with a stepmother. This is in contrast with the vast number of kids who live with stepfathers while in the custody of their remarried mothers. Thus, the stepmother often plays a far more tangential, less crucial, and hence less threatening role in the lives and development of the children.

Given the limited parenting role of most stepmothers, it is not surprising that far fewer of them ever grow quite as close to the children as do stepfathers. In general, stepmothers seem to get more of the benefit of the doubt since they are often simply viewed as a reasonably pleasant adjunct to dad and his new life. One problem: a woman's maternal instincts may push her to try to meddle and bond more than she probably should, thereby fostering more resentment. Overall, however, it is probably a less risky, although perhaps less rewarding, role.

In-laws and extended families. A major part of entering into any marriage is getting to know your spouse's family. During the second time around, the task is usually much more complex: stepchildren, ex-in-laws, former spouses, and interim lovers, all get mixed in along with blood parents and siblings. For many people, one of the most difficult and explosive areas in remarriage (and one of the larger causes of redivorce) involves relations with each other's children. It's truly a package deal.

Relations between Former Spouses

Marriage isn't a word—it's a sentence.
　　—*King Vidor*

A number of studies show that no matter how bad the prior relationship was, most people feel a persistent attachment to their former spouse and past marriage. In a well-known study on the newly separated, conducted by Drs. Bloom and Hodges at the University of Colorado, half of those folks who had been separated less than six months reported that they still wanted to spend time with their estranged spouses. Some 45 percent discussed reconciliation at some point during the separation period. Interestingly enough, warm and fuzzy feelings and discussions of getting back together occurred more frequently among spouses without children than among those who were parents.

I still love you, but let's divorce. A significant number of couples do in fact get back together. Some people get divorced and remarry each other five, or even ten, years later. Researchers consistently find that three-fourths of divorcing spouses experience some lingering attachment to their former mates after the separation. In my practice, I have witnessed many cases where ongoing incidents of sexual intercourse between separating spouses continued to occur right up to the eve of, and beyond, the actual divorce itself. (In fact, experts estimate that this "surviving sexuality" occurs between the parties in as many as 30 percent of all divorce cases.)

CHAPTER 9
Conclusions, Predictions, and Prognostications

Marriage may be compared to a cage, the birds without despair to get in, and those within despair to get out.
—*Montaigne*

No-fault divorce may have become increasingly popular as a legal doctrine, but when I listen to my clients talk, it is obvious to me that they are a long way from truly accepting almost any divorce as being "no fault."

Many authorities have now come to question the entire philosophical underpinning of the no-fault divorce movement. No-fault was originally considered to be a breakthrough divorce reform, but it seems to have had many unanticipated and negative effects for society in general, and especially for women. The end result is that, in many respects, divorced women are worse off today than they were in the past.

The origins of no-fault divorce. This was not the original plan. In 1970 the California legislature introduced no-fault divorce during a wave of goodwill. Conservatives and liberals alike hailed the reform as a bulwark to the family and a relief from the adversarial scourge of fault finding into which divorce cases had turned. (This had generally taken the form of a parade of nasty accusations in order to up the ante in a settlement.)

Under no-fault, no one was to be found innocent or guilty of such grounds as cruelty, adultery, or desertion. Irreconcilable differences, even if claimed by only one spouse, was now sufficient cause for divorce.

Sayonara to sexism? In that egalitarian spirit, sexism was to be removed from property settlements and replaced by a gender-neutral distribution of marital assets. Alimony, supposedly obviated by the rise of the "new working woman," was replaced by short-term rehabilitative maintenance (two to four years). In fact, alimony was often dispensed with altogether. Maritally owned property was to be divided fifty-fifty, rather than according to its title. Marriage had finally shaken itself free of its ball and chain, and the sexes were put on equal footing, or so it seemed.

Theory vs. practice. But the theory has fallen short in practice. "Right across the board, women are not doing well," states celebrity divorce lawyer Raoul Felder. He cites the loss of alimony (previously awarded until death or remarriage) as a classic example.

Perhaps the single largest change has been in the custody arena. Nowadays, the judicial trend nationwide is toward joint custody awards. After all, we have entered the age of the diaper-changing father. Says Felder: "Under the old laws you had to show a woman wasn't fit for her to lose her children. Today, children are up for grabs. It opens doors to blackmail and coercion. You can tell a woman there's not the slightest chance she'll lose and she'll say, 'I'll take less money rather than risk it.'"

Reforming the reforms. In response, the earlier idealistic reforms are being rethought. Task force reports around the country have documented the disparity between the spirit of the law and its practice. I fully expect this reevaluation trend to continue. Many sociologists are now calling for a rollback of no-fault divorce laws and even for premarital waiting periods.

Perhaps the strongest recent statement is a recent Louisiana law that creates an optional form of "covenant marriage," entailing a more binding set of vows that can be ended only under extreme circumstances and/or after a mandatory waiting period. After the passage of this new covenant-marriage law, Louisiana couples registering to wed now make an initial choice between a conventional marriage (which can be ended on typical no-fault grounds) or the beefed-up level of commitment contemplated by the new covenant marriage. If they select the covenant-marriage option, they cannot get divorced except in a situation involving domestic violence, or following a two-year separation period that includes mandatory counseling.

Impacts and Aftershocks for the Divorcing Parties

Divorce is the future tense of marriage.
    —*Anonymous*

Let's face it, divorce discombobulates everybody! Comfortable and familiar roles are turned upside down and inside out. New relationships and new family structures emerge. Both adults and children find themselves playing unfamiliar parts on unfamiliar stages. New lifestyles get explored, experimentation abounds. Adults often start acting like children, whereas their children frequently take on adult roles. Life can suddenly turn into a giant game of musical chairs, as both the parents and their kids move into new homes, new schools, new communities, new relationships, new careers, new personal or educational goals, new friends, and new attitudes. Everything is in flux.

Statistically speaking, somewhere between one-half to two-thirds of all divorcing parties claim to be basically content with the quality of their lives in the period following their divorce. Nevertheless, the remaining one-third or so apparently continue to feel an intense sense of bitterness for many years following the divorce.

Confucius say: "Time of change = time of opportunity." There is no question that divorce represents a major turning point for both men and women. It forces them to ask soul-searching personal questions about who they are and want to be, what their values are and ought to be. They spend time pondering how they can lead a more full or enriched life or engage in a more meaningful relationship in the future.

On the positive side, as brutal as divorce can be, there is no question but that it offers people cathartic second chances to start over, to embark on a new beginning, and to literally rebuild their lives. For a divorce lawyer, this can be a tremendously important juncture to perform a constructive service for your clients—to be intimately involved in working to help them try and get on with their lives.

As the lawyer for people in this position, I feel I have the opportunity to do some good for many of my clients if I can successfully assist them through this crucial stage. (Frankly, in our modern over-litigious culture, it's not all that often that a lawyer gets the opportunity to feel that they are really doing much *good* any more.) Divorce can be a springboard for tremendous psychological and personal growth, as well as for some major social and economic changes. I have seen some of my former clients truly soar during this period. Unfortunately, however, many others become truly "sore" as they suffer the personal, psychic, and economic deterioration that can accompany this process.

Men

A man in love is incomplete until he has married—then he's finished.
    —Zsa Zsa Gabor

A few years back I received a letter from Asa Baber, a well-known journalist who wrote the "Men" column for *Playboy* magazine. In his letter, Mr. Baber enclosed a copy of an article he had written about the hazards of being a male in divorce court. In that article he outlined his perception of the typical male's experience of divorce: "If he sued for custody of his children, 96 percent of the time he would lose; he could count on paying his ex-wife's court costs and at least some of her attorney's fees; he'd probably lose his home, as well as his kids, and if debts had to be settled, he'd get the larger share of them; both alimony and child support could cut into his earnings to the point where financial reversals were inevitable."

Mr. Baber then went on to describe some typical aspects of life after divorce for men. Some of the more interesting of his assessments are as follows:

- When a woman refuses to grant her ex-husband visitation rights with their children, only rarely does she suffer any serious sanctions. If in turn, however, he withholds alimony or child-support payments in retaliation, the chances are that he will face prosecution and possibly even jail.
- Men are much more vulnerable than women to mental illness and self-destructive physical diseases following divorce. Dr. Stephen Johnson of the University of Oregon, who is doing research in the area of divorce and mental health, says: "There's no doubt about it, men take divorce much harder than women. Divorced men seem to have higher rates of mental illness and suicide than do divorced women."
- Men are less apt than their ex-wives to seek any kind of professional counseling. According to Dr. Johnson: "it's obvious . . . that women come to get help much more often than men. I'd guess nine women for every man; something like that. Men just can't admit they need help. . . . Men are an unexplored area, really. They don't identify their emotions very well. They usually know when they're angry, but they hardly ever can admit to grief."
- At present there are no national men's rights groups that are anywhere near as strong or as prominent as are comparable women's groups such as the National Organization for Women. There is no coordinated male-oriented divorce reform organization. Instead, all that is really available to men are a number of independent divorce advisory groups that focus on male-type problems. (Nonetheless, Baber advised that every man about to go through a divorce should consider joining such a group.)

The ultimate solution? What Mr. Baber related about divorced men having higher suicide rates than divorced women hardly surprises me. I've read elsewhere that the count of men who commit suicide after an unhappy love affair is actually three times that of women who do so. Frankly, I am not exactly sure what to make of this scary statistic, but I point it out for whatever it's worth.

Women

It is he who has broken the bond of marriage—not I. I only break its bondage.
    —*Oscar Wilde*

As referenced earlier, women today are often worse off following a divorce than they were in the past, although many are finding that they value their new independent lives.

The good news. The National Center for Women and Retirement Research recently produced an interesting study. The findings are published in a book titled *Our Turn: The Good News about Women and Divorce.* Some of its surprisingly positive findings are: (1) 77 percent of the women surveyed said they valued independence and privacy over remarriage; (2) 82 percent said they experienced new independence and strength after divorce; (3) 63 percent said the divorce created a better situation for their children; and (4) 77 percent reported that they had a better relationship with their children after the divorce.

The bad news. The bad news, of course, centers on post-divorce economics: women's incomes generally drop severely and financial devastation often follows. The Policy Center on Aging in the Heller School at Brandeis University produced a study specifically on this topic, "The Economic Status of Divorced Older Women." The trends are sobering.

One key finding of the study was that actual impoverishment is resulting for an unacceptably high proportion of divorced women in their sixties. Too many of these women are being forced into the untenable position of having to live only on social security income. The experts suggested three factors contributing to this: (1) the growth of no-fault divorces, which ignore women's generally tougher economic situations; (2) women's work patterns of tending to transition in and out of the work force, often at low-paying jobs without pensions or adequate health insurance; and (3) women's longer life spans, which put them at risk for outliving their incomes and assets.

Sad realities for older women. Divorce poses some especially serious difficulties for older women. Relatively few of them are financially secure. Many feel depressed and lonely despite their admirable efforts to keep socially busy with friends, groups, and organizations. A sad reality of the situation for these older women is that they have often devoted their entire lives and personal identities to the roles of housewife, mother, charity volunteer, etc. As has been pointed out earlier, they have a far different row to hoe in their post-divorce years than do younger women who divorce in their twenties or thirties.

While the personal and psychological impact of divorce may be tougher on older women, the economic impact can be brutal for any woman. The dire plight of the economic underclass of divorced women, and their undersupported children—the so-called feminization of poverty—has forced our courts and our legislators to take a serious look at the issue of just who suffers the most under the emerging concepts of no-fault divorce statutes.

Working women. One thing is certain. Women are now a critical mass in America's work force. By the year 2000, half of the work force was female, and more than 80 percent of all women age twenty-five to fifty-five were working. Most women with infants (53 percent) now work, up from 38 percent in 1980. Educated women are more likely to work—60 percent of college graduates work versus 32 percent of those without a high school diploma. Yet, despite these overwhelming numbers (which constitute a true social upheaval), America seems to have been very slow to adapt to the change.

Only in relatively few American families has daily responsibility for household maintenance (cooking, cleaning, etc.) and child rearing (diaper changing, car pool driving, etc.) truly become an equally shared project. Instead, as we enter this the twenty-first century, women are now in the uncomfortable position of being expected to participate fully in the workplace while still bearing primary responsibility for running the home and family.

(Although a truly liberated husband may assist some by taking the trash out during the halftime of Monday night football).

In fact, one recent study concluded that married men's average time spent on household tasks has increased only 6 percent in the last twenty years, even as women have flooded the workplace. You should hear the warm and fuzzy sentiments that issue forth from my female clients when I cite them that statistic.

Does divorce make women sick? A "sickening" study recently conducted by the University of Iowa has shown that divorced women are more prone to illness over the long term. It appears that during the years immediately following their divorces, these divorced women initially reported somewhat higher levels of *psychological* distress than did married women, but they did not, at first, report any increase in physical illness. Then, ten years later, those effects on mental health apparently led to adverse effects on physical health as well. At this later stage, the divorced women reported 37 percent more *physical* illness. A connection between the higher number of physical illnesses may well have been triggered by the stresses and attendant difficulties associated with divorce.

The study pointed out that women can certainly get clobbered with a cascading set of problems when they divorce. In many cases they lose financial security and may have to move to a different (and often smaller) place of residence, plus they frequently must manage childcare alone. Having added responsibility for the kids, in turn, often means they lose ground at work, making their job and financial situation even more precarious. It looks like they are trapped in this vicious circle of financial problems and other stressful life events.

More scary statistics for women. Here are some scattered statistics that point up the difficult plight faced by many women: (1) women are out of the labor force for an average of 11.5 years for child rearing, thereby vastly limiting their upward employment mobility and their progress in accumulating a viable pension or retirement portfolio; (2) women now live to an average age of eighty, which is 5.2 years longer than men (guys die, on average, at 74.8 years); (3) 80 percent of all women outlive their husbands; and (4) the average age of widowhood is a seemingly way-too-young fifty-six years.

Author Nancy M. Newman reminds us that some experts have predicted that in the future, the vast majority of poor people will be women and children. There is a sizable list of reasons for this, which include lack of child-support payments, teenage pregnancy, the divorce rate, and the impact of a growing acceptance of single motherhood.

Some Final Miscellaneous Factoids
Re: Marriage and Divorce

Marry someone you love to talk to. As you get older, their conversational skills will be as important as any other.
—*Anonymous*

As anyone who has read this far in this book has already figured out by now, I love statistics. These tiny little snippets can provide some amazing, thought-provoking and occasionally amusing insights. Even when the various statistics are inconsistent, hard to verify, or seem to flat out contradict each other, they are still fascinating and illuminating. So here, taken from various "surveys" are some more items to ponder as we try to divine out the true nature (and future) of marriage and divorce in America.

- According to the U.S. Census Bureau, the divorce rate rose most sharply in the early 1970s. Then it stabilized for a spell . . . but at pretty high rates.
- The U.S. divorce rate has been dropping ever since 1990. But, 21.8 million Americans still wound up getting divorced in 2004.
- There has been more than a 30 percent drop in the marriage rate since 1970.
- Thirty-six percent of women surveyed said they would *not* marry their same husbands again.
- Forty percent of all couples are estimated to be simply co-existing in unhappy marriages.
- Fifty-one percent of all American women were living single as of 2006.
- Middle-age couples (i.e., fifty somethings/Boomers) make love an average of once a week.

- Home builders are predicting that by 2015, 60 percent of all new residences will be designed with two separate master bedroom suites (i.e., separate sleeping quarters for husbands and wives). Query: what does that do for couples' sexuality/ marriages?).
- One-half of all divorces happen by year seven of the marriage. Second unions that end in divorce likewise do so after seven years.
- Fewer than half the couples who first got married in the late 1970s made it to their 25th anniversary.
- Of the women who first got hitched in the late 1980s, only 57 percent reached their 15th anniversary, compared with 79 percent of brides in the late 1950s.
- Marital satisfaction increases with each successive year (once you have made it past the first twenty-five years, that is).
- At any given time, twenty-six million people around the globe are looking for love on the World Wide Web on-line dating sites.
- The average working woman spends 102 minutes per day caring for her family, versus 48 minutes per day for men.
- Eighty percent of Americans were married in 1950, now only 52 percent.
- One in five men with kids is a stay-at-home-dad nowadays.
- As of 2006, America's annual national divorce rate has dropped to 3.6 per 1,000 people, the lowest since 1970 and well off its peak of 5.7 in 1981.
- The number of unmarried couples living together is up tenfold since 1960.
- The U.S. state with the highest divorce rate: Nevada at 6.9 percent. The lowest divorce rate, at 2.1 percent is in the state of Pennsylvania.

Here are some divorce statistics/factoids that are specific to Hawai'i where I practice. Many of them are comparable to similar trends around the country.

- Approximately 5,000 divorces are processed per year in Hawai'i.

- The median age for divorce is Husband = 35, Wife = 33.
- Median number of years of marriage = 6.3 years.
- Children are involved in 52 percent of all marriages.
- 9.6 percent of Hawai'i cases include alimony, 15 percent of nationwide cases include alimony.
- The physical custody of approximately 70 percent of all dependent minor children goes to women.

Divorce in America: Some Future Trends

The world has grown suspicious of anything that looks like a happily married life.
—*Oscar Wilde*

Will the divorce disease restructure America? More than at any previous time in our history, America during the last twenty-five years has witnessed the unfolding of a divorce explosion in which society's pro-marriage constraints (i.e., social pressures forcing people to remain married and ostracizing those who fail to do so) have broken down. Instead, people are now free to divorce at any time their little own self-centered free will desires. Furthermore, they can now do so almost entirely free of any serious negative societal repercussions. For virtually the first time in our nation's history, we are seeing divorced men (such as Ronald Reagan) and "philanderers" (such as Bill Clinton) elected president.

That divorce has now become socially acceptable seems indisputable. And as we explore later in this chapter, the argument can also be made that, for the parties themselves, a divorce may well be "for the best." One area where the negative ramifications seem entirely too clear, however, is the social regression that seems to inevitably accompany the weakening of the traditional American nuclear family structure.

The virtue vacuum. Former U.S. education secretary and all-around "virtuecrat" William J. Bennett has compiled a list of social indicators that he feels point to a stark decline in American cultural values. He reports that the following dire statistical changes have occurred just since 1960: there has been a 560 percent increase in violent crime; illegitimate births are up 400 percent;

divorce rates have quadrupled; the percentage of children living in single-parent homes has tripled; the teenage suicide rate is up 200 percent; and average SAT scores have dropped almost eighty points.

Bennett argues that America's children are now in pretty bad shape. He feels they have been victimized by the cultural trends of easy and acceptable divorce and the rapidly spiraling rates of illegitimate births and the accelerated movement toward single-parent households. Both Mr. Bennett and the Bush administration continually contend that the lack of adequate male role models in modern "single mom" households is a huge problem for our society in general and for its poorer elements in particular.

I read a fascinating article on this topic in *Atlantic* magazine, which seemed to hit the nail right on the head when it concluded: "After decades of public dispute about so-called family diversity, the evidence from social-science research is coming in: The dissolution of two-parent families, though it may benefit the adults involved, is harmful to many children, and dramatically undermines our society."

America is not alone—meet "Flash Divorce" Chinese style. As we bemoan the demise of our traditional American family and social structure due to the dreaded "divorce disease," perhaps we can at least draw some solace from the fact that we Americans are not alone. Let's take a look at China, which seems to be setting the tone for the "fast forwarding" of everything from economic development to social trends. Modernization and materialism seem to be causing rapidly accelerating divorce trends in China. In fact, a look at the recent radical change in China's attitudes toward marriage may be an insightful eye-opener and predictor of marriage's future worldwide.

Divorce in China has gone from being shameful and illegal to becoming a snappy court proceeding. Breaking up is fittingly uncomplicated to do in China nowadays. The forward-thinking unhappy couples in China have taken a progressive route through their legal proceedings with a method known as "Flash Divorce." Even the government has now accepted the trend by simplifying the process. As of 2003, the Chinese government streamlined the divorce process from being a months-long ordeal to a quick spin through the civil affairs bureau which can take as little as fifteen minutes. Overwhelmingly, the Chinese women are the ones who end their marriages—often citing extramarital affairs as the biggest reason for divorce.

Time magazine has been my favorite "weekly read" ever since college and they did one of their typically excellent articles on this Chinese "Flash Divorce" trend entitled, "Breaking Up Is Easy To Do." *Time* pointed out that nationwide in China, the number of divorces skyrocketed 67 percent just between 2000 and 2005. Peering into the future through the looking glass of mass media and the World Wide Web, there is now a ninety thousand member website for divorcees in China. Fourteen million Chinese were registered users on matchmaking websites as of 2006, and that number is expected to triple by 2010. And one of last year's hottest TV series highlighted, you guessed it: *Divorce, Chinese Style*.

The number of divorce attorneys in Chinese cities has quintupled in the past five years and detective agencies specializing in marital investigations are proliferating. Divorce as a business is booming in China.

Some Chinese are so spooked by the prospect of divorce that (like Americans) they too are tending to avoid marriage altogether. In 2006, it was reported that almost half a million fewer couples had married nationwide than had wed just two years earlier.

Upheavals in American Households

We sleep in separate rooms, we have dinner apart, we take separate vacations—we're doing everything we can to keep our marriage together.
—*Rodney Dangerfield*

The composition of the American household is changing dramatically. There is a definite nationwide trend toward a vastly increased number of smaller-sized, and differently configured, households. The size of the average household in America has declined substantially—from 3.7 persons in 1950 to 2.62 by 1990. The increase in single-person households, as well as the general trend toward independent living on the part of young people, explains much of this phenomenon.

The rise of single-parent households. Another key factor contributing to this trend has been the rise in the number of single-parent households. Births out of wedlock have increased dramatically, and many moms are raising their children by themselves. It has been estimated that perhaps as many as 33 percent of all births nationwide occur out of wedlock. Obviously, the increasing frequency of divorce has also created many single-parent and single-person households.

According to a recent University of Chicago study entitled "The Emerging 21st Century American Family," the number of children living with single parents increased from less than 5 percent in 1972 to almost 20 percent in 1998. It is commonplace nowadays for more and more children to live with someone other than both parents. Whereas fully 85 percent of all children under age eighteen lived with both parents in 1970, this percentage had dropped to about 50 percent by 1998.

Some kids aren't even being raised by either parent. According to a recent AARP survey, one out of nine *grand*parents is defined as a primary caregiver for a grandchild.

Is cohabitation cool? It now seems pretty obvious that the growing emergence of cohabitation in lieu of formal marriage has become an ever-increasing phenomenon in American society. According to the Year 2000 U.S. Census, the number of households consisting of unmarried adults and no children had more than doubled since the early 1970s and is now up to approximately 30 percent. People of all ages are adopting the cohabitation mode. While living together seems particularly popular among the young and the divorced, senior citizens also now routinely hold off on a formal marriage in order to preserve their individual estates, social security, or other retirement benefits. Since living together is much more widely accepted nowadays, and is less likely than before to attract societal disapproval, it seems safe to predict that cohabitation will continue to be an increasingly visible part of American society.

Overall, about half of all cohabiting relationships end within five years. But, it is also true that approximately 55 percent of couples who live together first do end up eventually marrying. Oddly enough, however, according to most studies, living together first does not seem to either enhance or detract from a couple's chances of having a satisfying marriage later. Numerous surveys have reported that marital satisfaction was roughly the same for couples who had and had not cohabited prior to marriage.

One well-publicized study conducted by Brigham Young University researcher Jeffrey Larson argued against this, however. He found that couples who live together before marriage have a 50 percent greater chance of divorce than those who don't. He theorized that cohabiters are poor marriage risks to begin with because they are too commitment phobic, too accustomed to demanding personal freedom, and too willing to cut and run when things don't work out.

Is marriage dead? By 1998, only 56 percent of adult Americans were married compared with nearly 75 percent as recently as 1972. Anyone reading all these wild statistics about divorce and our unraveling social structure might well ask, "Is marriage dead?" John Naisbitt, the author of the cult classic book *Megatrends*, doesn't necessarily think so. As he puts it: "We believe that after decades of disruption, the family is moving into a new era of stability. The family is more important than ever. We realize how much we need each other."

It is also interesting to note that the somewhat-trite phrases that characterize the human potential movement (such as "becoming your own person," or "finding yourself") were vastly more trendy during the 1970s and 1980s than they have been during the present decade. Instead, the recent problems of our nation regarding economics, social values, personal and national security in an era of terrorism, etc., seem to have focused people's attention on more immediate concerns, such as keeping their jobs and feeding their families. The probing of one's inner psychic conflicts has been relegated to a slightly lower level on the hierarchy of human needs and values. This may well argue for a return to a strengthened institution of marriage.

In any event, marriages certainly seem to have become more "egalitarian" nowadays. Stacy Rogers is a sociologist at the Pennsylvania State University and the co-author of *Alone Together: How Marriage in America Is Changing*. Rogers' new book compares the attitudes of married couples in 1980 to those in 2000. According to the book, from 1980 to 2000, the main shift was away from bread-winner-homemaker marriages to what the authors call "egalitar-ian marriages." In those marriages, modern husbands and wives may both have their own jobs and incomes, share decision-making power more equally and allocate housekeeping and childcare duties more equitably. This may not be too surprising in view of the fact that over the past two decades, wives' contribution to fam-ily income rose sharply from 21 percent to 32 percent. The Rogers book studied a nationally representative sample of 1,000 couples. They found that, on average, couples in "egalitarian marriages" were happier than couples in traditional marriages.

However you look at it, it is undeniable that the basic structure of American society, and the individual family structures within it, are undergoing seismic changes on a massive scale. Modern-day Americans have an incredible multiplicity of options for pur-suing their personal and professional lives, and this is coupled with unprecedented physical mobility. It may logically follow that new styles of relationships (i.e., still more divorces, followed by multiple remarriages, cohabitations, etc.) may be an inevitable outgrowth of all this.

Societal Impact: The Long-Term Implications of Divorce in America

Immorality: the morality of those who are having a better time.
    —H. L. Mencken

The divorce explosion has dramatically altered the face of our nation today. The nuclear family, as we once knew it, has been uprooted. Faith in relationships has been strained, perhaps irre-vocably. The divorce epidemic has unquestionably fueled the fires of the battle of the sexes, and that battle has now moved into the courtrooms and the political process, where issues such as sexual harassment, domestic violence, and equal pay for equal work are now at the forefront of our legal and social agendas. So just how do the social-gain versus social-cost aspects of divorce shake out? Certainly it can't be great for society to have large numbers of its men and women plagued by marital unhappiness, or its children warped by growing up in friction-filled homes. But is divorce any less harmful, or does it cause as much or more social disruption than it solves?

It may be that divorce (like so many of our other snazzy modern social advances) affords us some immediate, but temporary, present comfort at the price of future upheavals in our society. Perhaps every divorce decree granted today should be accompanied by a surgeon general's warning: "Caution: Every 'easy divorce' granted in over 50 percent of all marriages at the turn of the 21st Century . . . may contribute to the demise of our family/society/nation by the year 2025!"

The inalienable right to divorce. The reality of the situation in America today is that we all tend to take for granted, as some sort of inalienable right, the expectation of a happy marriage. If this fails to transpire, then everyone feels an ancillary right to escape the trap of an unworkable marriage. In today's America, virtually everything is disposable, from razorblades to relationships. This is certainly a far cry from preceding generations, where marriage was embraced as a societal and economic necessity, and where religious and community standards made divorce an anathema.

Divorce can indeed be a positive development for many people. It can represent the conclusion of a difficult or unhappy time in their lives—one they may feel quite relieved to see end. It can bring them to the threshold of a new growth phase of their lives, in which they can successfully structure a more meaningful and more happy relationship for themselves and improve their quality of life in general.

Does divorce = personal growth? One of the most trendy and popular treatises on divorce that appeared back in the 1970s was an excellent book entitled *Creative Divorce: A New Opportunity for Personal Growth*, by the divorce therapist Mel Krantzler. His upbeat and optimistic view was that a series of positive lessons learned through the divorce process could be healthy contributing factors to one's own personal growth—that this could in fact go a long way toward improving the next juncture of that individual's life—not the least of which might be their next marriage.

Krantzler's book was extremely well received, and the very terminology he employed seemed to embody the popular view (one that was widely held a couple of decades ago) that divorce truly presented a creative opportunity for self-improvement. This book remains extremely relevant today. I would recommend reading it in its entirety. However, even a brief scanning of its chapter headings gives a great deal of insight into the main theory it embraces. Chapters such as: "The Promise in the Pain," "Coming to Terms with Your Passed Marriage," "The Healing Process of Mourning," "Avoiding the Nine Emotional Traps of the Past," "Coping with New Reality," "New Ways of Relating to People," "New Commitments"—all these themes point out the possible positive results that can be derived from the admitted pain of the divorce process itself.

Personally, I tend to agree to a large extent with Mr. Krantzler. After all, if one finds oneself getting a divorce anyway, it certainly makes more sense to try to turn the whole thing into a positive experience and an opportunity for personal growth, rather than dwelling on the negative. Krantzler talks pretty convincingly about the fact that a divorce provides its participants with opportunities to rethink their values and their priorities, to exercise new levels of choice and assertiveness, to learn to live alone without having to feel lonely.

A divorce can also be an opportunity for parents to rediscover new relationships with their children and the new levels of understanding and closeness that follow. Perhaps best of all, it can present an opportunity to open oneself up for a new and improved level of intimacy in the form of a new relationship or second (or third, or . . .) marriage.

All of these approaches, which essentially focus on the opportunity for divorce veterans to find previously unsuspected inner resources within themselves, present the divorcing parties as having tremendous opportunities for personal growth and development. For the divorce resisters, these "opportunities" may have been reluctantly born out of necessity—but they are opportunities for (forced?) growth nonetheless. The question, of course, is whether or not the divorcing parties can come to grips with all these issues in time, and to the extent necessary, so that they can indeed turn the whole thing into a positive or creative experience.

Clinical psychologist Dr. Robert Kirsch puts it this way: "Divorce often forces people to grow up. You get over your divorce by confirming the kind of relationship there was in the marriage. You realize there ain't any victims. You recognize your own complicity in the breakup. Then you learn how to carry on a relationship that works. You can't do this intellectually; you learn through experience."

Despite the obvious pain of divorce, it is possible to derive a sense of hope and opportunity in the years following one's divorce. The vast bulk of my former clients have managed to somehow adjust to their divorces and to re-establish themselves in fulfilling new lives. The bad news is that, in my experience, the minimum recovery time for either party (even the initiator) to get over the emotional and logistical upheaval of divorce is at least one year. The good news, however, is that most folks (even the divorce resisters) seem to have gotten pretty much back onto an even keel within two or three years. During this time, most folks come to view their separation and divorce as a traumatic but necessary transition in their lives, during which they were forced to learn a great deal about themselves, their emotions and their needs, in order to survive.

The fault factor. Many social critics today (particularly those who are of a more conservative or moralistic bent) feel strongly that it is terrible public policy to allow no-fault divorces to be so easy to obtain. They further feel that the trend toward equitable property settlements, wherein each party is allocated roughly one-half of the property regardless of who is "at fault," is a mistake that results in a dramatically economically disadvantaged underclass of divorced women and their dependent children. These critics contend that: (1) we should return to the fault system of divorce; (2) divorces should require a lengthier processing time that would make them more difficult to obtain; and (3) divorce settlements ought to be made more punitively expensive financially for those initiators who "caused the divorce."

Slow down, you move too fast. A key argument made by those who seek a more conservative reformation of our divorce system is that the entire process is allowed to progress too fast. They would rather see the whole procedure delayed and made more difficult. The conservative's contention is that the law's tendency to move for a quick resolution in divorce cases penalizes the partner who is unprepared to end the marriage.

"It's generally true that the party who initiates the divorce gets a better deal," says attorney Raoul Felder. "That's because the person who does the leaving is also the one who has done all the legal planning."

A departing husband often has access to more skillful legal representation than does his spouse. "The legal deck is stacked against the woman," says attorney Michael Kennedy. "The man generally has control of the money because he is usually the one earning most of it."

Should society try to rein in the divorce dogs? Those who feel that America is leading the way to oblivion by unleashing the divorce dogs to the degree we have can perhaps derive some support for their views from the writings of anthropologist Margaret Mead, who observed:

> There is not a single society anywhere in the world where people have voluntarily chosen to remain married simply of their own accord. Rather, continuing viability of the marital institution almost inevitably depends upon the extent that the surrounding community or society applies tremendous amounts of pressure on its citizenry to remain married in order that the family structure can continue to remain as a primary solidifying force for that society.

John Naisbitt crystallizes the debate still further when he writes in *Megatrends:*

> For the past two decades, doomsayers and thoughtful observers alike could make a pretty good case that the family was disintegrating and that society was the worse for it. When the family is in trouble, the children suffer most, robbed of love, emotional security, values, role models. Some have offered their ideas. The right argues that the only hope is putting women back in the home where they belong. The left says it is government's responsibility to provide free daycare.

In my opinion, Mary Jean Hall, president of Parent Action, seems to have one of the clearer visions as to just how complex this problem really is. It is not a question conducive to simple (or simplistic) answers. Ms. Hall writes:

> We have to be able to blend the growth of women and the women's movement into a new family movement rather than moving backward in time. We believe parents need options, not ideology. There is no dominant family model so how can one monolithic answer restore the family unit. The traditional family—homemaker, husband as breadwinner and children—now makes up only ten percent of families. The multiple option family comes in all shapes and sizes. Married couples with children, stepfamilies, single parent, lesbian couples, adopted kids, househusbands, you name it. There is no moral or politically correct way for the women in each family to juggle home and family responsibilities. Some are giving up successful careers to care for children. Others start home-based businesses. Most schedule childcare and work full time. Yet, examples like these do not even begin to describe the diverse courses families take.

Ms. Hall's comments kind of remind me of one of my favorite quotes from one of my favorite comedians, Lily Tomlin. As she said, "If love is the answer, could you rephrase the question?" Well, there is no question in my own mind that there are numerous factors at work in our rapidly emerging twenty-first century society which are going to provide all of us as members of that society a multiplicity of options to explore our own personas. We will be living longer and enjoying more leisure time. As a result, we will have more time to take in-depth looks at ourselves and our relationships, and to consider just where we want to be at various junctures of our lives.

Correctional changes. To put it in navigational terms, correctional changes in the course and direction of our lives may well be required as we go. Unquestionably, a divorce constitutes one of the ultimate correctional course changes available to an individual—one that if handled correctly can present an incredible opportunity for personal growth.

Most divorcing parties when interviewed after the divorce say that for them it was well worth it, that the divorce was necessary, and that they are happier and more successful human beings as a result of it. Many of those who are back in love or have remarried say that the divorce was the best and most important change they ever made in their lives.

Many of the folks I have represented over the years felt that they were somehow trapped in a desperate situation during the time when their marriage started to turn bad. They use the phraseology of sickness or disease as the analogy for a condition they had to cure. Interestingly enough, the state of health they strive to regain is generally not perpetual singlehood but a "new and improved" happier marriage. Specifically, they want a restructured marriage that works better for them at a new and different stage of their life.

The more upbeat view, then, is that in this modern context divorce has become not so much the antithesis of marriage, but an essential aspect of a revamped marriage system. I have heard it argued that perhaps serial marriages are the only way an individual can remain happily married nowadays (i.e., by changing partners as his or her needs change over the course of an elongated lifetime). Divorce may even be an essential adaptation that permits the institution of marriage as we know it to survive and to perform the expanded functions we require of it.

If one accepts this view, then it follows that a sensitive and smoothly functioning divorce process (and, I daresay, sensitive divorce practitioners) can perhaps work to the benefit of society as a whole. In this sense the divorce process, while admittedly focusing on the death of love at least in one relationship, can also extend to include the concept of the rebirth of love, perhaps in another context. It may be that the divorce process is a societal adaptation that simply must be made, given the fast-paced, wired, supermobile, ever-changing, and option-overloaded world that faces the modern-day, post-yuppie American.

If indeed a constructively structured and intelligently processed divorce can serve as a mechanism for fine-tuning relationships in our constantly evolving society, then it needs to be handled in as sophisticated and sensitive a fashion as possible. Hence the need not only for Mel Krantzler's term "creative divorce," but also for an extrapolation of that concept to include the style of "creative divorce lawyering" that I have tried to emphasize in this book. I hope you have found it to be useful. Aloha!

Glossary

affidavit   A written statement of facts made under oath and signed before a notary public.

alimony   Payment of spousal support from one party to another; treated as taxable income to the recipient.

alimony *pendente lite*   A temporary order of court that provides support for one spouse while the divorce is in progress.

annulment   The legal ending of an invalid marriage; according to law, neither party was ever married, but all children born of the annulled marriage remain legitimate. Grounds for annulment vary from state to state.

answer   The second pleading in an action for divorce, separation, or annulment, which is served in response to the petition for divorce and which admits or denies the petition's allegations and may also make claims against the other party.

appeal   The process whereby a higher court reviews the proceedings resulting in an order or judgment of a lower court and determines whether there was reversible error.

appearance   A respondent's formal method of telling the court that he or she submits to the court's jurisdiction. Appearance can also refer to a party's physical presence at court.

child support   Support for a child (not taxable to the recipient or deductible to the payer spouse).

community property   Generally, the property acquired during the marriage by the work and efforts of the parties; applies in those states known as community property states.

contested case   Any case in which the court must decide one or more issues on which the parties have not agreed.

custody   The legal right and responsibility awarded by the court for the care, possession, and rearing of a child.

deposition   The testimony of a witness taken out of court, under oath, and in writing.

discovery, or production of documents   Procedures followed by lawyers to determine the nature, scope, and credibility of the opposing party's claim and his or her financial status.

dissolution   The act of terminating a marriage; divorce; does not include annulment.

equitable distribution of property   A system of distributing property in connection with a divorce or dissolution proceeding on the basis of a variety of factors without regard to who holds title.

ex parte   An application for court relief without the presence of the other party. In some states the other party is present but is given short notice of the application.

guardian *ad litem* (GAL)   A lawyer appointed by the court to represent the children.

joint custody   The shared right and responsibility awarded by the court to both parents for possession, care, and rearing of the children.

jurisdiction   The authority of the court to rule on issues relating to the parties, their children, or their property.

legal separation   A judgment of the court or written agreement directing or authorizing the spouses to live separate and apart. A decree of separation does not dissolve the marriage and does not allow the parties to remarry.

marital property   Accumulated income and property acquired by the spouses, subject to certain exclusions in some states.

marital settlement agreement   The parties' settlement reduced to a written document or orally placed on the record in open court; may also be called a property settlement agreement.

motion   A written application to the court for some particular relief, such as temporary support, injunction, or attorney's or expert's fees.

no-fault divorce   A divorce granted without the necessity of proving one of the parties guilty of marital misconduct. Fault is marital misconduct that may be considered for some issues in some states.

petition (complaint)   The first pleading in an action for divorce, separate maintenance, or annulment, setting forth the allegations on which the requested relief is based.

pleading   Formal written application to the court for relief and the written response to it. Pleadings include petitions, answers, counterclaims, replies, and motions.

pro se   A litigant who represents themselves in court rather than being represented by a lawyer (also *pro per*).

subpoena   A document served on a party or witness requiring appearance in court. Failure to comply with a subpoena can result in punishment by the court. A subpoena *duces tecum* is a subpoena requesting documents.

summons   A written notification that legal action has commenced, requiring a response within a specified time period.

temporary or *pendente lite* motions   Applications to the court for interim relief pending the final decree of divorce, separation, or annulment. Typical temporary motions include those for temporary maintenance, child support, attorney's fees, court costs, expert fees, custody, visitation, enforcement or modification of prior temporary orders, or requests for exclusive possession. The court enters a *pendente lite* order after determining a motion. Motions are brought on by the service of a notice of motion or order to show cause, with affidavits.

temporary restraining order (TRO)   An order of the court prohibiting a party from doing something—for example, threatening, harassing, or beating the other spouse and/or the children; selling personal property; taking money out of accounts; denying the other spouse a motor vehicle.

uncontested divorce   A proceeding in which a person sued for divorce does not fight it and instead reaches an agreement with the spouse during the divorce proceedings.

Selected Bibliography

Ahrons, Constance. *Divorced Families*. New York: Norton, 1987.

———. *The Good Divorce: Keeping Your Family Together When Your Marriage Comes Apart*. New York: Basic Books, 1995.

———. "The Binuclear Family." *Alternative Styles*, November 1979, 499–515.

———. "The Continuing Co-Parental Relationship between Divorced Spouses." Paper presented to the Family Law Section of the Hawai'i State Bar, Honolulu, 1991.

Bernard, Janine M., and Harold Hackney. *Untying the Knot: A Guide to Civilized Divorce*. Minneapolis: Winston Press, 1983.

Bohannan, Paul. *Divorce and After*. Garden City, N.Y.: Doubleday, 1970.

Chadwick, Bruce A., and Tim B. Heaton. *Statistical Handbook on the American Family*. Phoenix, Ariz.: Oryx Press, 1992.

Cherlin, Andrew J. *Marriage, Divorce, Remarriage: Social Trends in the United States*. Cambridge and London: Harvard University Press, 1981.

Coates, Jennifer. *Women, Men and Language*, 2nd ed. New York: Longman, 1993.

Diamond, Jared. *The Third Chimpanzee*. New York: HarperCollins, 1992.

Einstein, Elizabeth. *The Stepfamily: Living, Loving, and Learning*. Boston: Shambhala, 1985.

———. "Stepfamily Lives." *Human Behavior*, April 1979, 63–68.

Engle, Margorie, and Diana Gould. *The Divorce Decision Workbook*. New York: McGraw-Hill, 1992.

Fisher, Helen E. *Anatomy of Love: The Natural History of Monogamy, Adultery, and Divorce*. New York: Norton, 1992.

———. *Everything Men Know About Women*. Sydney, Australia: Camel Publishing, 1986.

Fisher, Roger, and William Ury. *Getting to Yes: Negotiating Agreement without Giving In*. New York: Penguin USA, 1981.

Gardner, Richard. *The Parent's Book of Divorce*. Garden City, N.Y.: Doubleday, 1991.

Glick, Paul C. "A Demographer Looks at American Families." *Journal of Marriage and the Family* 37 (February 1975): 15–26.

Goldstein, H. "Reconstituted Families: The Second Marriage and Its Children." *Psychiatric Quarterly* 48 (1974): 433–440.

Goldstein, Joseph, Anna Freud, and Albert Solnit. *Before the Best Interests of the Child*. New York: Free Press, 1980.

Gottman, John. *Why Marriages Succeed or Fail: And How You Can Make Yours Last* (Paperback). New York: Fireside, 1994.

Gottman, John M., Julie Schwartz Gottman, and Joan Declaire. *Ten Lessons to Transform Your Marriage: American's Love Lab Experts Share Their Strategies for Strengthening Your Relationship* (Paperback). New York: Three Rivers Press, Reprint edition, 2007.

Gottman, John, and Nan Silver. *The Seven Principles for Making Marriage Work*. New York: Three Rivers Press, 1999.

Gray, John. *Mars and Venus in the Bedroom*. New York: HarperCollins, 1995.

———. *Men Are from Mars, Women Are from Venus*. New York: HarperCollins, 1993.

———. *Men, Women & Relationships*, 2nd ed. Oregon: Beyond Words, 1993.

Greenfield, Susan. *The Human Brain: A Guided Tour*. New York: Basic Books, 1997.

———. *The Human Mind Explained: An Owner's Guide to the Mysteries of the Mind*. New York: Henry Holt, 1996.

Herman, Peter J. *A Practical Guide to Divorce in Hawaii*. Honolulu: University of Hawai'i Press, 1991.

Hunt, Morton, and Bernice Hunt. *The Divorce Experience: A New Look at the Formerly Married*. New York: McGraw-Hill, 1977.

Kimura, D. "Are Men's and Women's Brains Really Different?" *Canadian Psychology* 28, no. 2 (1987): 133–47.

———. "How Different Are the Male and Female Brains?" *Orbit* 17, no. 3 (October 1986): 13–14.

———. "Male Brain, Female Brain: The Hidden Difference." *Psychology Today* (November 1985): 51–58.

Krantzler, Mel. *Creative Divorce: A New Opportunity for Personal Growth*. New York: M. Evans and Company, 1991.

Levinger, George, and Oliver C. Moles. *Divorce and Separation: Context, Causes, and Consequences.* New York: Basic Books, 1979.

Mayleas, Davidyne. *Rewedded Bliss.* New York: Basic Books, 1977.

Naisbitt, John. *Megatrends: Ten New Directions Transforming Our Lives.* New York: Warner Books, 1982.

Nolan, J. F. "The Impact of Divorce on Children." *Conciliation Courts Review* 15, 2 (December 1977).

Pease, Allan and Barbara. *Memory Language.* Sydney, Australia: Pease Learning Systems, 1993.

———. *Why Men Don't Listen and Women Can't Read Maps: How We're Different and What to Do About it.* New York: Broadway Books, a division of Random House, Inc., 2001.

———. *You Just Don't Understand: Women and Men in Conversation.* New York: William Morrow, 1990.

Ricci, Isolina. *Mom's House, Dad's House: Making Joint Custody Work.* New York: Macmillan, 1981.

———. "Divorce, Remarriage and the Schools." *Stepfamily Bulletin,* September 1980.

Rofes, Eric, ed. *The Kids' Book of Divorce: By, For, and About Kids.* New York: Random House, 1982.

Rogers, Stacy J., Paul R. Amato, Alan Booth, and David R. Johnson. *Alone Together: How Marriage in America Is Changing.* Cambridge: Harvard University Press, 2007.

Sheehy, Gail. *New Passages.* New York: Ballantine Books, 1996.

Stanley, Jacqueline D. *Divorces from Hell.* Clearwater, Fla.: Galt Press, 1995.

Strean, Herbert S. *The Extramarital Affair.* New York: Free Press, 1980.

Tafford, Abigail. *Crazy Time: Surviving Divorce.* New York: Bantam Books, 1982.

Visher, Emily B., and John S. Visher. *Stepfamilies: A Guide to Working with Stepparents and Stepchildren.* New York: Mazel Books, 1979.

Walker, Kenneth N., and Lillian Messinger. "Remarriage after Divorce: Dissolution and Reconstruction of Family Boundaries." *Family Process* 18, 2 (June 1979).

Wallerstein, Judith S., and Sandra Blakeslee. *Second Chances: Men, Women and Children a Decade after Divorce.* New York: Ticknor & Fields, 1989.

Wallerstein, Judith S., and Joan B. Kelley. *Surviving the Breakup.* New York: Basic Books, 1980.

Wear, Bill, Jr. *Recovering from Divorce . . . and the Horse You Rode In On!* Springfield, Mo.: Insight Productions, 1991.

Weitzman, Lenore. *The Divorce Revolution.* New York: Free Press, 1985.

Whiteside, Mary F., and Lynn S. Auerbach. "Can the Daughter of My Father's New Wife Be My Sister?" *Journal of Divorce*, Spring 1978, 271–283.

About the Author

Bradley A. Coates is the founder of Coates and Frey, the largest divorce and family law firm in Hawai'i. He now serves as Of Counsel to the firm. Mr. Coates graduated from the School of Law at the University of California at Los Angeles and is a member of the Hawai'i and California State Bars. He has been a divorce practitioner for over three decades. Mr. Coates is a popular lecturer and newspaper columnist on the topics of divorce, human and romantic relationships, alternative dispute resolution, and family law. He is also the founder and administrator of "Divorce with Decency," a low-cost divorce mediation clinic.

Mr. Coates has been selected as "Best Divorce Lawyer" by the readers of both *Honolulu Weekly* and *Honolulu* magazine. The first edition of *Divorce with Decency: The Complete How-To Handbook and Survivor's Guide to the Legal, Emotional, Economic, and Social Issues* won the Hawai'i Book Publishers' Award of Merit for *Excellence in Guide and Reference Books*. Mr. Coates can be reached at divorce@coatesandfrey.com. The website for this book is http://www.divorcewithdecency.com.

Production Notes for Coates / DIVORCE WITH DECENCY

Cover and Interior designed by Nighthawk Design

Composition by Publishers' Design and Production Services

Text in Palatino and display type in Goudy Old Style

Printed on 60# Starbrite Opaque, 435 ppi